# TESTING YEARS

*Above:* Canberra B Mk8 off Blackpool. *BAe*

*Below:* RPB tests new fin for Mk3 Lightning.   *BAe*

# TESTING
# YEARS

## Roland Beamont

LONDON

IAN ALLAN LTD

XG310

To my colleagues in 87, 79 and 609 Fighter Squadrons and
150 and 122 Tempest Wings, and in Hawker Aircraft Ltd,
and to the great team at the Preston aircraft factories of
English Electric. But most of all to Pat who shared and
endured so much of it.

# Glossary

| | |
|---|---|
| AAL | Above airfield level |
| AMSL | Above mean sea level |
| ASI | Airspeed indicator |
| $C_L$ max | Maximum coefficient of lift |
| CSI | Combined speed indicator |
| Depth Perception | Judgement of height at low level in poor light or visibility |
| DI | Gyro direction indicator |
| g | Measurement of normal acceleration times gravity, eg normal=1g; twice normal gravity=2g; etc |
| IMN | Indicated Mach number |
| Max cold/dry | Maximum power without reheat/afterburner |
| Max $R_H$ | Maximum power with reheat/afterburner |
| MPA | Maximum power altitude |
| $N_V$ | Directional stability derivative |
| ORP | Operational readiness platform |
| PIO | Pilot-induced oscillation |
| q pot | Dynamic pressure level |
| RPM | rev/min |
| $V_{appr}$ | Approach speed |
| $V_{LO}$ | Lift-off speed |
| $V_r$ | Rotation speed |

First published 1980

ISBN 0 7110 1072 2

Design by Anthony Wirkus

© R. P. Beamont 1980

Published by Ian Allan Ltd, Shepperton, Surrey,
and printed by Ian Allan Printing Ltd at their
works at Coombelands in Runnymede, England

# Contents

*Below:* TSR 2 climbing from Boscombe for its first supersonic flight, 22 February 1965, and delivery to Warton. *BAe*

# Introduction

The 40 years from 1939 to 1979 saw many major milestones in aviation from the final replacement of the biplane by the monoplane through the first major war in which air fighting and air attack were to play a dominant and decisive part, to the postwar advent of the gas turbine 'jet' engine leading to the era of practical supersonic flight.

During this fascinating period in which aviation 'grew up' in terms of all-weather operation and of transformation from its role as an instrument of mass warfare to that of the primary method of world-wide travel, the author was privileged to experience flying over 170 different types of aeroplane ranging from the beautiful silver doped fabric and wire biplanes of the 1930s through the classic propeller-driven monoplane fighters of the 1940s to the swept wing jet supersonics of the 1950s and the highly automated Mach 2 fighter and strike aircraft of the 1960s and 1970s, and some of these are discussed in the following chapters with relevant quotations from the author's original test flight reports. The aircraft chosen represent those most interesting to the author for their capability in their design roles or, in some cases, just for the sheer exhilaration of flying them.

These experiences led to a number of conclusions, among them that a prototype 'First Flight' is far removed from the mass media idea of 'the test flight!' and is only the beginning of the third and vital stage of the evolution of a new design which starts with specification and design-study, continues with design and initial build and ground testing through to the flight testing and development programme before being finally cleared for service trials.

In all fields of human endeavour it is human to err and no one designs an aircraft which is right first-time. The final polish has to be done by trial and development and with high performance aircraft this phase can require many years of team-work by highly skilled and dedicated engineers and air-crews before the aeroplane can be said to be safe and efficient for service.

In this experience it has became obvious that while this country has no monopoly in ability to build fine aircraft it has built better than most and in many cases supreme aircraft without superior anywhere, and the Royal Air Force and our airlines and flying schools have demonstrated to the world that we are a race of aviators to be reckoned with as we were seafarers before.

In the short 60 years since practical flying began we have built a great heritage throughout this field of aviation on which new generations must continue to build with pride our part in the great flying world of the future.

The following reminiscences may recall some great events to those who were there, and perhaps be of interest to some of those who are just entering the fascinating and demanding world of the aeroplane. The views and opinions expressed are the author's own and do not necessarily reflect those of any other persons and authorities mentioned in the text.

My thanks are due to Mr Kitchener and Mr Whittaker of British Aerospace for their valuable assistance in sorting out many unique photographs from the Warton archives and to British Aerospace for making them available. I am also indebted to Mr Hine and the Staff of the Imperial War Museum photographic library for their ready help in research, and finally to Chrys Butcher for volunteering so much of her time and enthusiasm to researching and typing.

*Below:* Tornado long range fighter version for UK defence.

# Hawker Hurricane

As the first type that I had any part in testing the Hurricane has a place in this record, but only a small one as my experience was limited to production testing and a few development flights on late modifications.

Posted to Hawkers at Langley in December 1941 for a 'rest period' after a two-year tour of operations including the Battles of France and Britain, I came to the business of test flying confident that I knew all that was necessary about the Hurricane but I soon found out the true position to the contrary.

It is customary today in the jet era to think warmly but a little condescendingly of the Hurricane as a quaint old feature of a bygone battle quite unrelated to today's conditions; yet for all its simplicity and ruggedness the Hurricane had speed, climb, altitude and dive performance well in excess of today's business executive aircraft of equivalent weight and more than ten times the cost, and better control qualities than any of them.

Simplicity was the keynote with welded steel tube construction, fabric-covered where practical, an on/off fuel system, external electrical starting with manual (Kigass pump) priming, and the famous and rugged Rolls Merlin engine that seemed to be able to take all the caning a fighter pilot could give it and survive.

The only advanced 'system' was hydraulic operation of the undercarriage and flaps by Dowty 'Live Line' pump, and in over three years and 700 hours I never had a failure either with the hydraulics or with a Merlin engine. I could not say as much for any other aircraft or engine in my subsequent experience.

At Langley the handling development of the Hurricane had been complete for some time and up to 250 a month were coming off the conveyor belt production line to be tested before delivery to the Service. The schedule of tests was, by today's standards of complexity, simple but adequate to ensure a given performance. After recording full throttle engine figures before and during take-off, a full power climb was made to MPA* with figures taken every five thousand feet and any discrepancies such as drop-off in boost or RPM or over-run in temperatures noted.

If satisfactory, full power performance level was done at MPA and then the aircraft was dived to 400mph indicated at about 10,000ft, checking trim and control forces on the way. On Flight 1 there would generally be quite powerful trim asymmetries needing correction and this would be done by the pilot calling for a number of inches of trimming cord to be fixed to the appropriate aileron or the rudder (sometimes both). If there were no serious snags this retrimming would

normally be carried out without stopping the engine, the airframe fitter standing in gusts of exhaust smoke (and during winter in a bitter wind) while wielding a paint brush to dope on the cord.

Initially a pilot would need two or three tries at estimating the correct adjustment, but with practice it was often possible to clear the trim with only one landing for correction.

Extraordinarily enough in those days of considerable radio unreliability no radio tests were made. Radio was not even fitted at the factory and all flying was carried out without aid from the ground, pilots being required to be entirely self-reliant in working over weather and recovering safely to base in all circumstances.

This did not seriously impede production clearance overall as pilots developed remarkable abilities to find their way home unaided in appalling weather, and 1,000 yards visibility or total overcast with a low base did not stop flying. We knew intimately even the smallest landmark features for miles around, and I remember vividly on one occasion being caught out by a deteriorating frontal system and getting back into Langley in torrential rain under a 400ft base by

*Maximum Power Altitude.

8

*Below left:* Pilots of No 87 Squadron at Lille Seclin, December 1939. Author 4th from right running. *IWM*

*Left:* Trophy from 87's first victory in France, a Heinkel 111 shot down by Flt Lt Voase Jeff. November 1939. *IWM*

*Below:* Sighting the guns. Hurricane of 'A' Flight 87 Squadron at Exeter in Battle of Britain.

following the Thames through Eton to Datchet, turning sharply left at the Stag public house and with undercarriage and flaps set and trimmed for landing, making a final turn at 100ft over the grounded barrage balloon (now the site of the Holiday Inn) which marked the clear path in the invisible balloon barrage and which appeared out of the murk about 500yd ahead confirming that it was in fact grounded and that the final approach to the airfield boundary was clear — to my considerable relief.

Heavy snow or fog stopped the work then as now, but backlogs were soon cleared when the weather improved, sometimes with heavy pressure on the Flight Shed staff and test pilots — on one day in February 1941 for instance my log book records 12 Hurricane production test flights between 9.00am and dark and, after sleeping well that night, a further ten test flights on the following day.

As it had for me in two years of active squadron operations the Hurricane proved sound and reliable on test, and in more than 200 test flights at the factory I had no serious difficulties and only a few of a minor nature such as an undercarriage leg becoming unlocked in a dive causing loss of a fairing and damage to the wheel brake hydraulics. The latter resulted in subsequent complication when I landed without taking proper account in the circumstances of a slight crosswind. This inevitably caused the aircraft to start a weather-cock into wind which without brakes I could not stop or control. Finally switching off the engine, the aircraft and I trundled on in silence and increasing embarrassment in

*Above left:* 87's CO at Exeter, Sqn Ldr 'Johnny' Dewar.

*Top:* Pilots of 'A' Flight 87 Squadron, Summer 1940. Watson, Tait, Gleed, Rayner, Comely.

*Above:* Hurricane with Rotol propeller and Watson. Exeter 1940.

*Above right:* CO and Flight Commanders of 79 Squadron at Fairwood Common 1941. Leading, David Haysom; nearest camera, Beamont; furthest, Trevor Bryant-Fenn. *Air Ministry*

a gentle curve straight into another Hurricane which was off-test and parked on the tarmac ready for delivery; an event which was not popular with the production authorities.

This case of 'two Hurricanes confirmed damaged' rather tended to offset my personal score of enemy aircraft and to tarnish any reputation I might have had as a pilot in the somewhat critical atmosphere of the factory where I was the first active fighter pilot to work with the Company test pilots; and this was a salutary experience.

On another occasion a further error of judgement on my part resulted in one of the shortest landings ever recorded on a Hurricane. With many sorties to be flown in the day it was our practice to take-off and land on the grass airfield in the directions which would result in the shortest practical taxying time. Accordingly on one grey winter day with a strong, cold easterly blowing, I elected to land across the narrow Langley aerodrome from west to east at a point normally considered

too short for a Hurricane, aiming to finish the landing run on the tarmac ready for trim adjustments.

All seemed to be going well as we came over the hedge at about 80mph and flared out for a slow, taildown landing, when suddenly and very smoothly we touched down and almost immediately stopped. From the windsock and nearby chimney smoke I hadn't thought the wind to be all that strong but we were still about 300yd from the tarmac and so I opened the throttle to taxy in. We didn't move!

I slid back the canopy to look back and there was a remarkable sight. Almost as far as the eye could see, barbed wire coils strung from either side of the rudder to the airfield boundary. Our final approach had been a few inches too low and the tail wheel had picked up the top strand of the coiled security wire. The aircraft suffered hardly any damage, but the pilot's dignity rather more.

Flying the Hurricane was a never-failing pleasure. Its steady and predictable characteristics were always enjoyable and had helped me out of considerable difficulties in combat over France and southern England and in the night Blitz of 1941, and now in hourly flights every day with brand new aeroplanes straight off the line and redolent of dope, hydraulic oil, newly stove-enamelled equipment and hot new engine, there was a warm confidence in taking these new examples of a proved and battle-tried design into the air so recently defended by their predecessors, and testing them in preparation for future battles. The only real problem in fact was navigation without aids and we tended to range far and

wide in recovery routes to base after extended flights over the overcast. There was one aid however which, though unpredictable, was very effective.

The Langley factory was protected by its balloon barrage through which a clear 'lane' was provided for test flying take-offs and landings by lowering the balloons along a path approximately 400yd wide. In poor visibility it was standard practice to fly round the outside of the barrage looking for the one on the ground to identify the approach lane and establish that it was in fact 'open'.

The normal operation of this barrage was to fly its balloons at just below the main cloud base so as to deter hostile bombers who had broken through cloud in search of their target. However for some unfathomable reason estimation of the thickness of the cloud seemed to defeat the barrage unit and very often one solitary balloon was to be seen flying just above the cloud sheet. This would undoubtedly have provided an ideal check point for enemy bombing and it certainly functioned as an effective navigation reference and homing aid for the Hawker test pilots, but such was the confident atmosphere following the Battle of Britain that no serious efforts were made by us to correct these balloon errors.

The Hurricane was remarkable in a number of ways in addition to being the highest scorer in the Battle of Britain. Its docile qualities of stability and responsiveness with good damping were superior to those of the Spitfire's rather oversensitiveness in pitch and poor directional damping. Its

thick wing developed a higher $C_L$ max than the Spitfire, and with the same engine it could out-turn it up to 20,000ft.

Its strength was phenomenal and as a 'last ditch' evasive manoeuvre we used to practise a full power break away 'with everything in the bottom left corner of the cockpit'. This produced a remarkable inverted spiral dive with high negative 'g' forces and as the engine cut and the IAS built up around 400mph it felt as if something must give way. But it never did and many aggressive Me 109s were shaken off and probably amazed by this tactic. By contrast the Spitfire with its many and great virtues was not very strong in this sense and many were lost in high speed dives.

Another feature favourable to rough service in the field was the wide track undercarriage which provided easy landing and stability on the ground and allowed flexibility of operation in wet and windy conditions, in contrast to its more sophisticated and elegant sister-ship whose very narrow undercarriage made crosswinds, gusts and mud, snow or slush embarrassing problems.

Experience with 87 Squadron in France and the South of England in 1940 had given us confidence that the Hurricane could hold its own in the daylight operations of the period, but the winter of 1940/41 brought new and varied responsibilities.

Hurricanes were brought in to fill the existing gap in the night defences, and operating in most weathers out of grass airfields from a line of paraffin lamps with groups of flares 1,000 yards off the airfield in line with the runway as lead-in/lead-out lights the pilots managed to cope with remarkable reliability although with little operational success.

The method was to take-off, often on instruments from lift-off even in those far-off days, and climb on course until reaching patrol height (usually 10,000ft). If at that point the ground was clear below the three patrol line flares would be seen at ten-mile intervals, and if they could not be seen the patrol would be flown on times and courses without navigation corrections of any kind except the pilot's guessed allowance for wind on which there would not have been anything but the sketchiest met information before take-off and no confirmation thereafter.

Frequently these patrols were made in conditions of hazy darkness with no outside references except the searchlights, guns and bomb explosions showing enemy activity and with the pilot's visual world restricted for an hour and a half to the dull red glow of the the cockpit lights.

When the patrol time was up it was always something of an act of faith under these conditions to turn away on to the heading for where the base flashing beacon ought to be; and the following period of cautious descent looking firstly for the cloud base in pitch darkness and then for welcoming flashing light which said quite clearly if it appeared, 'you've made it this time', were experiences of an indelible nature.

Sometimes the weather was clear and the patrol line and the airfield area could be seen throughout the patrol which would be relaxed and enjoyable. On other occasions the take-off was made in rain, mist or even snow and from then on the sortie was a trial of the skill and determination of the pilot

which did not relent until he was able to set the safety course finally from the home beacon and with wheels and flaps set, power to trim 95mph and the hood open so that he could peer unobstructed by oil-smeared or scratched Perspex for the faint intermittent glare in the mist ahead which would show where the duty flarepath pilot and probably the Flight Commander would be firing a succession of Very cartridges in the general direction of his engine noise.

Seeing them once and straining not to lose them he would aim directly at the lights, losing height to the safety minimum for the airfield and hoping to see the runway lights in time to correct and perhaps with violent swish-tailing to kill excess speed, touch down with a considerable bounce and even more relief about half way down the flarepath; and then with braking to the limit short of standing the Hurricane on its nose (which happened on occasion) to slither and weave to a thankful standstill in the pitch darkness beyond the last flare.

In all this activity the qualities of the Hurricane were of paramount importance. For long periods on instruments by pilots mostly inexperienced in the art, it was stable and undemanding, and in the business of groping back to a visual landing in all weathers its ability to fly gently and almost by itself with light guidance at low speed was of vital importance and enabled pilots to make often violent S-turns to line up after seeing the flarepath clearly for the first time from only 500 yards or less and far off the centre line.

Similarly once between the flares and more or less lined up, the stability of the aircraft with its elevator precise and effective down to low speed and the wide stable undercarriage, together enabled the pilot when necessary to chop the power and slam the aeroplane down in what in other circumstances would have been regarded as a clueless and even irresponsible manner, and which would have broken any other fighter of the time.

Hurricane night-fighter pilots had no benefit of radar or ILS approaches, but they were able to perform feats of

*Above:* New Hurricane on test at Langley. *British Aerospace*

'visual' flying in conditions which would be regarded as unbelievable and probably irresponsible by today's standards.

In concept these operations were rather more hopeful than practical as the pilots were without exception inexperienced in night-flying, 10hr at night total experience being an exception rather than the rule when we began.

In these circumstances the achievements of the Hurricane squadrons were remarkable, and this winter of groping around in the dark fostered a degree of confidence and self-reliance among the pilots which enabled them by the spring of 1941 to accept as quite normal short notice night cross-countries for reinforcement of other sectors, or night formation aerobatics as a means of sharpening our skills and in the process maintaining the high morale in the squadron.

The spirit in 87 was high indeed in late autumn 1940 with the dawning realisation that the battles we had fought in our Hurricanes in the previous summer over France and Belgium, and over the Channel as the Battle of Britain, had been won. We had no time for the excesses of the news media in their all-too-vivid descriptions of the 'rout of the Hun', and we knew that it had been a close run thing. Then into this atmosphere of mild but justified elation came a thought new to us since the outbreak of war a year before, the emergent possibility that some of us might even survive. But it was going to be a long drawn-out affair and as young fighter pilots we still could not be regarded as a good insurance risk!

So it was against this background of moderate pride in victory, immoderate pride in our squadron and lack of the immediate daily and hourly challenge of combat, that we found ourselves faced at the beginning of the winter of 1940/41 with the different kind of challenge of pitting ourselves against the night weather of the UK winter in the operation of what soon became known as 'Politician Patrols'.

The Hurricane was a strong, stable, forgiving aeroplane and if one had to go flogging round rain-soaked, fog-ridden and snow-swept night skies with no effective navigation aids but a recalcitrant T/R9 radio, it was probably the best aeroplane for the job at the time.

So at the end of that winter when it was apparent that the Hurricane was becoming outclassed in Europe in daylight by the superior performance of the Me 109F and G and the new Fw 190, and with the radar-equipped Beaufighters taking over at night, it was possible to assess its value in those critical first battles. Available in greater numbers than the Spitfire it had been thrown into contact with the enemy at once as the main defence force. With superior aiming stability it was most effective in attack. It could out-manoeuvre all enemy aircraft and also the early marks of Spitfire up to 20,000ft. Above this its advantage was reduced and was reversed by Spitfire and 109 above 25,000ft. It could reach its 'Terminal Velocity' without danger of structural failure and carry out violent manoeuvres in the dive, making it superior to 109 and Spitfire in this respect. It was easier to fly on instruments and far less critical in adverse circumstances than the 109 and Spitfire, both of which had significantly higher accident rates on these counts. It had less performance than 109 and Spitfire but this did not outweigh its other advantages in the first battles.

The Spitfire was perhaps the most elegant fighter of all time, a delight to fly and with all the charisma of a delectable sports car for the young men of the day, but when it came to fighting in all conceivable conditions the Hurricane was in a class of its own in 1940.

# Supermarine Spitfire

As a Hurricane pilot and subsequently moving on to Typhoons and Tempests I did not have benefit of a Spitfire conversion course or any major period of experience on that delightful aeroplane, but I did contrive to fly them on the odd occasion and some of these were odd indeed.

The first occurred at Fairwood Common on the Gower peninsular in South Wales on one wet and windy day in June 1941 where I commanded 'B' Flight in 79 Squadron on cannon-armed Hurricane 2s. We were at 'Readiness' for shipping patrol over the approaches to the Bristol Channel but with no immediate commitment when a visitor from Warmwell came in on a Spitfire 2. Befriending him at lunch I persuaded him of my urgent need to borrow his aeroplane without actually mentioning that I had not flown a Spitfire before. Accordingly a little later in a typical Gower fine drizzle of rain which would today probably not be considered suitable for a first conversion flight, I settled into the surprisingly deep cockpit of the Spitfire while its 'owner' pointed out the taps and said 'Watch out for the swing on take-off and don't land cross-wind'. Then he disappeared off the wing-root and I was alone with my first Spitfire.

After the starkness of the Hurricane the cockpit seemed a little precious with gleaming white plastic throttle and pitch levers and chrome-plated flap control, and although it fitted like a glove at the shoulders the deep well effect down to the rudder pedals gave an impression that one was standing rather than sitting in it. Starting the Merlin was no different from the procedure in the Hurricane. After building up pressure a half stroke on the Kigass pump brought the already warm engine into raucous and smoky life and much of the exhaust from the up-wind side of the aircraft came straight into one's eyes and nose from the exhaust ports immediately in front of and at virtually the same level as the pilot's face. This was shut out by closing the canopy which brought home the surprising fact that overall vision was no better than in the Hurricane despite the one-piece canopy, and that the heavy framed windscreen, vast engine cowling ahead and high rear fuselage cut-off behind made vision seem unfortunately restricted.

Taxying vision was blind ahead and it was necessary to swing the nose continuously from side to side to see the way. This at once drew attention to the differential wheel brakes which proved soft and 'spongey' especially when taxying down the prevalent gusty wind. A tendency to rock away from the wind on the narrow-track undercarriage added to the feeling of insecurity and the Spitfire was certainly less easy to handle on the ground than the Hurricane.

But once lined up for take-off the narrow and almost submerged cockpit behind the enormous nose with its Merlin belching thunderous power, gave an impression of extreme performance which once airborne was matched by the delicacy of handling for which it has always been famous. This was a real thoroughbred and one felt immediate pleasure in flying it into a steep climbing turn away from the airfield.

On changing hands on the stick to select undercarriage UP there had been the characteristic momentary oversensitivity in pitch, but thereafter longitudinal control seemed not unduly sensitive until pulling tight turns at low speed and maximum power where it became clearly essential to watch the stall boundary carefully. The ailerons were pleasantly light at low combat speeds but all controls heavied up considerably above 300mph, and with the prevailing turbulence and in sharp combat manoeuvring directional stability was marginal and seemed likely to interfere with gun-aiming.

Switching on the GM2 gunsight and peering through the persistent rain I picked out our dispersal on the northern edge of Fairwood Common and made some ground attack passes varying the speed from 220 to 320mph, and this confirmed the very limited vision over the long nose and through the restricted windscreen, and also that directional damping was indeed poor and resulted in excessive wander of the gunsight aiming spot around the target in the prevailing rough air.

Aerobatics were delightful and this was clearly a tremendous aircraft for combat manoeuvrability. However I doubted if it could out-turn a Hurricane at low level even though it was certainly distinctly faster. Circuit weather was now 'clamping' but I already felt confident to roll the Spitfire smoothly over the runway in the rain at about 250ft before 'breaking' sharply downwind for landing. Then came a problem. The wheels locked down with reassuring lurches and green lights at about 130mph and then, after adjusting throttle and pitch controls for 120mph, I selected flap down which produced an immediate and powerful roll to starboard which needed almost full port aileron to correct to wings level.

This was embarrassing and UP selection of flap returned the situation to normal — apparently we had a flap system asymmetry, but as the weather was not improving it was necessary to land. The runway was near-flooded and the question was whether to land fast with flap up and nose high on the rather short into-wind runway covered in standing water, or to use what flap was available under severely asymmetric conditions on the longer cross-wind runway with more room to spare.

As I did not know the aircraft and forward vision seemed the most critical problem I decided on using the longer runway with asymmetric flap and brought the Spitfire in on a continuous curve approach to keep the runway in view, arriving over the runway threshold at about 90mph with almost full port aileron to hold the starboard wing up, and then as forward vision was virtually lost over the nose, felt

*Above:* Author at Wisley in 1963, flying the Spitfire V which was later handed over to the RAF Battle of Britain Flight. *Ian Macdonald*

the wheels touch quite gently. There followed a moment of anxiety as the asymmetric flap drag, spongey brakes, cross-wind component and wet runway all added up to a certain amount of swerving and increased pulse rate, and then we were safely down and swinging the nose round about the winding perimeter track back to dispersal with the canopy slid back and the Gower rain streaming resfreshingly into the face.

The starboard flap had failed completely to lower and an interested group at dispersal surveyed the Spitfire as it taxied in with the port flap fully down and the starboard fully up. It had been a fascinating experience and I felt that although it had drawbacks in ground handling, combat vision and directional stability, this Spitfire would certainly be a better bet against Messerschmitts at altitude than our Hurricanes but not I thought at low altitude or in ground attack. I also felt that it was far more limited than a Hurricane for bad weather or night operation.

My second Spitfire flight was in retrospect even odder, although at the time it seemed quite normal.

About one year after the Fairwood episode and while on attachment to Hawkers as a Service test pilot I had begun to feel deprived of contact with my friends in the 'operational' squadrons and so, borrowing a Miles Witney Straight from Philip Lucas, Hawker's Chief Test Pilot, I flew down from Langley on the morning of 16 March 1942 to West Hampnet, the Tangmere satellite airfield where I knew South African Pete Hugo who was commanding No 41 Squadron with Spitfire VBs with clipped wing tips and cropped blower low-level engines, or 'clipped, cropped and clapped' as they were inevitably known.

Hugo, in his usual irrepressible form in the bar even on tomato juice, expounded the virtues of his latest aircraft and

in the process apologised for hurrying me in to lunch because they had got a show on at 2.30pm. I asked where to, and he said, 'Shipping strike to Le Havre/Cherbourg — want to come?' This sounded like fun and I agreed quickly before he could change his mind.

In a short time and with no formality whatsoever I found myself listening to a briefing on this all-low-level sortie to be done with eight aircraft in 'finger four' formation with my aircraft flying No 2 to Hugo in the lead. Then in borrowed helmet, oxygen mask and Mae West, followed a quick briefing on the cockpit in which it was comforting to find that there were few differences in this Mk V from the Spitfire 2.

Hugo said, 'Open out to search formation at my signal and keep radio silence — you know what to do if we meet anything.' My previous experience on Spitfires or lack of it was not questioned and I did not raise the subject, but just had time for a few moments of doubt about my sanity in setting off on an offensive patrol with a unit I had never flown with before on an aircraft type I had never flown operationally and only once before at all and then on a different mark. Then came the start-up signal from Hugo and I became busy with starting, checking the gauges and taxying out at the leader's wing tip.

A few minutes of warming up and then the formation was pounding across the West Hampnet grass and turning away over my family home at Summersdale as I slipped into Hugo's No 2 position. There was barely time to reflect on this strange combination of circumstances when the coast was ahead and we slid out to sea from West Wittering, low under a comforting overcast.

It was at this point that I became actually aware that I would be judged a prize mug if things developed on this trip and I failed to return for any one of a number of reasons which were now beginning to seem not only possible but highly probable.

Enemy interference on the radio began to sound ominous as the sky lightened ahead and then at about mid-Channel the clouds cleared and we broke into brilliant sunshine. There was no longer the low cloud cover prescribed for the mission but Hugo pressed on until the enemy coast appeared ahead and we turned as planned to sweep south-westerly down to the Cherbourg peninsula.

I sat comfortably about four spans away from the leader's tailplane, watching the sky all round and the other Spitfires gently rising and falling in the mild low-altitude turbulence and enjoying this Spitfire V with its sweet-sounding Merlin. I found the restricted vision irksome though and wondered how I would manage with it in a dogfight. But the Me 109s and Fw 190s did not appear nor any shipping and we were soon heading back north with Hugo taking us down from 200ft to wave top height for the fun of it at our cruising 250mph — which I noted was about 70mph slower than the low-level cruise of the Typhoon that I was currently involved in testing.

As the Sussex coast appeared over the horizon I was starting to relax and enjoy myself and could relish the strange experience of crossing in tight formation over my favourite schoolboy sailing haunts of East Beach and Itchenor in Chichester harbour, in an unfamiliar fighter aeroplane on a reprehensibly improperly authorised flight. Hugo led the formation in for an exhilarating 'break' over Summersdale and I once more looked down at my old home while lowering undercarriage and flaps and curving down for a moderately respectable 'stream' formation landing on the rough grass airfield. In a hilarious debriefing outside the dispersal I revealed my somewhat comprehensive lack of experience of Spitfire flying, and Pete Hugo observed that under the tutelage of 41 Squadron they might make a Spitfire pilot of me yet!

Back at the Langley factory later that day news had travelled fast so that I had to admit to having gone on a Spitfire Sweep after lunch, and the unanimous verdict was — 'he must be bloody mad'. Hindsight, mature judgement and the rest of it suggests that they were quite right — but it was good fun at the time and did no one any harm.

It also convinced me that the Spitfires were for Spitfire pilots and that I wanted something faster for my next tour of operations.

16

# Hawker Typhoon

One day in the summer of 1941 as a Flight Commander of No 79 (Hurricane) Squadron, I was turning over the photographs in the latest Intelligence Summaries in my office at Fairwood Common when I came across a new and odd-looking shape.

Described as a new Hawker interceptor prototype, this had none of the aesthetic grace of the Spitfire or of the compact aggressiveness of the Hurricane. With an extraordinary thick and cranked wing, a bulky 'chin' radiator under the nose, a cylindrical rear fuselage terminating in a tall and inartistic tail and a hump-backed look about the cockpit area, it was scarcely an attractive aeroplane; yet the thought of nearly twice as much power as a Hurricane in an aircraft from the same famous stable was intriguing. No more information on this exotic device filtered through to our operational outpost, yet that one blurred photograph was to have a significant influence on my own future.

It was towards the end of that year, following a minor diversion caused by an ill-humoured Station Administrative Officer at Pembrey whose quite accurate report to Headquarters Training Command on my delivery to that Station in my single-seat Hurricane of a WAAF officer for a dance had resulted in my subsequent court martial, that the powers decided that as my first tour of operations had by

then exceeded two years it was time for a change. I was offered the options of Personal Aide to Sir Sholto Douglas then Commander-in-Chief of Fighter Command, or a Special Duties List posting to Hawkers at Langley for production test flying.

The latter was a revelation as it had never occurred to me that I might even begin to qualify for such exotic responsibility, and the thought of that new and immensely powerful Hawker fighter still under test was an added and overriding attraction. I reported to Langley in December 1941, and soon after arriving was taken down to the Experimental Shop past an impressive security check and with experimental test pilots Bill Humble and Ken Seth Smith met Philip Lucas, acting Chief Test Pilot in the absence in USA of George Bulman, in front of the awesome mass of the prototype Typhoon.

In the metal the new fighter gave an immediate impression of ruggedness and its conventional and well-proportioned aerodynamics suggested stable and unembarrassing, if unexciting, handling qualities. But to an operational fighter

*Below:* The prototype Hawker Tornado. Note lack of rear vision.  *BAe*

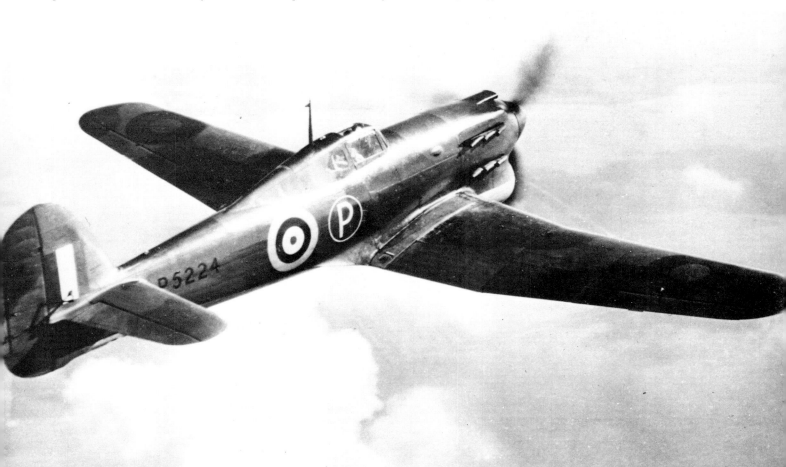

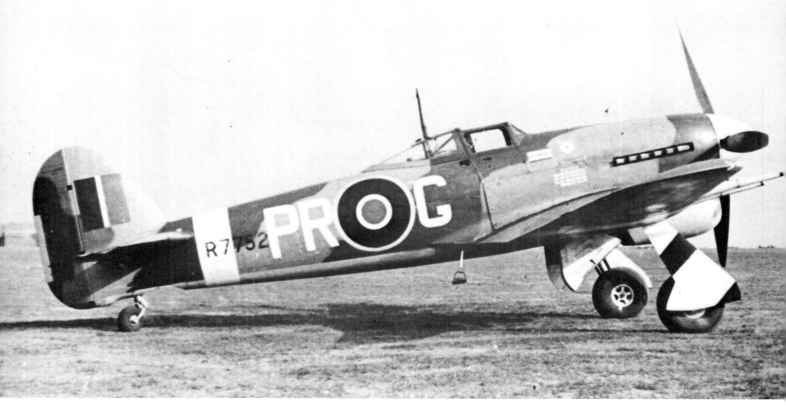

pilot with two campaigns of day-fighting and a winter of night-fighting operations behind him there was one aspect of the design which struck forceably, and when as I climbed out of the cockpit Philip Lucas asked what I thought of it I said 'It'll never make a fighter with that bloody awful vision!'

The resulting silence was noticeable even against the factory background of riveting guns. I was having my first major experience of our well-known national reluctance to hear a spade called a spade, and I was to learn in the years to come that this 'facing facts' syndrome was a prominent feature at some levels in the aviation world and one which the test pilot had to recognise and persevere against if he is to be effective at his job.

This particular silence was based more on puzzlement than bias and I was soon told how the all-metal rear cockpit fairing which allowed no aft vision to speak of had resulted from Air Ministry philosophy that this class of aircraft would be so fast as to virtually preclude fighter versus fighter combat, and that as a bomber destroyer the Typhoon pilot would not need to look back! Although this unsound theory was soon discredited the same story could be repeated in nearly identical words for almost every new British fighter design reaching service since 1950, and three generations of jet fighters have appeared in America repeating the same mistake.

It was not in fact until the cumulative lessons of the air wars in Korea, Vietnam, India and with final effective argument the Middle East June War of 1967, began to take effect at last that the Air Staffs started in the early 1970s to call once again for improved combat vision for new fighter designs. They stressed that once more pilots of fighter and strike aircraft would need the best possible facilities for using their eyeballs outside the cockpit in defence and attack. Those of us who had consistently advocated this policy on cost-effective rather than emotional grounds for more than

twenty years felt no great satisfaction at this revelation, but distinct relief.

The designed vision area of the Typhoon prototype was a disaster, as even forward of the pilot vision sideways and upwards was only obtained through a rough and ready imitation of the front of a popular family car with a 'sunshine' roof with small wind-up windows incorporated incredibly enough in car-type doors with thick metal framework and a small hinged window acting as a lid on top.

The net effect was that in our early Service trials we found the cockpit noisy, draughty and almost blind in some critical directions. At the risk of the fast-waning local popularity I pressed this aspect hard while at Langley and subsequently when on working-up trials with the Series I Typhoon in No 609 (WR) Squadron, and with the eventual support of

*Left:* RPB's Typhoon as CO of 609 (WR) Squadron at Manston in 1942. Squadron Commander's emblem, Squadron badge and score panel on fuselage in front of cockpit. *Ziegler*

*Below left:* The same aircraft showing the car-type cockpit doors. *Ziegler*

*Right:* First Typhoon Sector Commander, John Grandy and Wing Leader, Denis Gillam. Duxford 1942. *Ziegler*

*Below:* Because of its blunt nose and straight taper wings the Typhoon was often mistaken by allied pilots and AA gunners as a FW190, and black and white identity stripes were introduced in 1943. *BAe*

Lucas and the Hawker pilots a drastic modification programme was arrived at to introduce a refined front windscreen and a one-piece blown Perspex canopy which gave the Series II production Typhoon, and its successor the Tempest, all-round and rear vision which was near perfect and certainly as good as that of the German Fw190 whose designers had got this particular message rather earlier.

As a junior production test pilot on Hurricanes no handling work came my way initially on the Typhoon, but by taking on less popular tasks such as ferrying the Vulture-engined 'Tornado' prototype to Hucknall and the Centaurus-engined prototype to Filton, and in long and wearying vibration investigation sorties on R8220, an early production Sabre Typhoon, I began to get a feel for this heavy, rough but impressive aeroplane. It was stable and sure in flight and quite precise; it had good gun-platform stability and, when flown enthusiastically, manoeuvrability that belied its shape. It was also about 80mph faster at low level than anything else in service at that time.

These features coupled with four 20mm cannon armament and docile characteristics for bad-weather flying and particularly for landing, began to suggest that whatever it had been designed for this aeroplane should show distinct advantages in low level combat and in ground attack. So from my restricted though shortly to be improved point of influence, I began a lobby in this area which gained some staunch supporters but came up against much opposition. This culminated in a meeting at the Bentley Priory Headquarters of Fighter Command where I was summoned to give my views on the operational practicability of the Typhoon before the Commander-in-Chief and staff.

I was confident in presenting the case but had not anticipated the strength of the opposition. It soon became clear that a massive lobby of Spitfire protagonists headed by Gordon Findlay, 11 Group Senior Engineering Officer and famous athlete prewar, were resolved on forcing cancellation of the Typhoon and they came very close to doing it. But after this meeting there was apparently no further talk of cancellation; Typhoon production was pressed ahead with the clear-view windscreen and rear-vision canopy and other improvements, and with bomb and rocket armament this type made a significant and at times critical contribution to the battle for Europe in the final phases of World War II.

After completing service trial operations over France and the Low Countries when commanding 609 Squadron in the winter of 1942/43, including the first assessments and operations at night, I experienced some interesting experimental work in the Typhoon programme when back at Langley for a second period — this time experimental flying mainly in the Tempest programme from June 1943 to February 1944.

During 1942 and early 1943 a number of unexplained structural failures had occurred in service and one at the factory in which Ken Seth Smith, a determined and courageous experimental test pilot on the Typhoon, had been

killed as were all but a few of the squadron pilots involved. One exception had a miraculous escape in finding himself outside his disintegrating Typhoon and on his parachute without any particular contribution from himself. A further complication was that his eyeballs were both forced from their sockets by the blast but he was saved from further damage after landing by the extraordinary and providential arrival of a doctor who had seen the parachute from his car, went over at once and inter alia put the eyes back in place.

This pilot was able to fill in some of the missing pieces of the jigsaw in this case, and it seemed that something was happening to make the aircraft pitch violently to the point of structural disintegration. Discovery of some parts of tail units well separated from the main crash sites added to the evidence. Nevertheless after six months and further unexplained crashes the cause had not been found and an emergency programme of tests was in progress at Hawkers when I rejoined them in June 1943.

In what was one of the first scientifically instrumented flight test programmes in this country, rudimentary but

*Below left:* Cockpit of Typhoon series II. *BAe*

*Right:* 609 Squadron Readiness state board at Manston 1942 with RPB. *Ziegler*

*Below:* Typhoon operations from 609 Squadron 1942/43 — a Ju88 under accurate attack in Holland.

*Below centre:* An R type minesweeper off Boulogne on 4 April 1943 (RPB's camera gun). *Ziegler*

*Bottom:* Van Lierde shoots down a Ju52 near Brussels in 1943.

effective strain-gauge pick-ups had been fitted to the rear fuselage transport joint and at other significant points on the tail unit. Measurements had been made by Seth Smith and Humble across the full spectrum of performance and power settings and up to design diving speed in trimmed flight and calm air, and Seth Smith had been killed in this programme when his Typhoon broke up at high speed. All strain gauge readings had been well within acceptable limits and so the programme was now being extended to cover what was described as 'more humorous' conditions. These were to include out-of-trim dives, engine cuts at max power and max IAS, and combinations of these in one 'g' and negative 'g' flight.

This was a fairly extreme example of ad hoc investigation and although we were nominally probing to look for rapidly increasing strain gauge values, there was no mistaking that in the process of trying to establish the exact point which could bring the tail off there could be no assurance that this would not happen before the pilot could do anything about it.

After a few flights in this programme I began to wonder if a return to combat flying might be less strenuous, and I soon encountered a regime which was entirely new to me as it was to most pilots at that time. This was the high speed phenomenon known as 'compressibility' when airflow, accelerated locally over aerofoils, fairings, bumps and uneven surfaces, compressed as it approached the speed of sound and broke from laminar into turbulent flow patterns with results varying from mild vibration to violent buffeting and from changes of trim to violent nose-up or nose-down pitching with associated progressive loss of control effectiveness.

There was a certain mystique about all this — the scientists took the view that transonic aerodynamics were well understood, and pilots the view that whatever the boffins were saying something clearly unpleasant was happening when current fighters were dived to their limits at altitude — and there was a mounting list of unexplained diving incidents involving partial loss of control.

A few pilots had experienced these circumstances under test conditions in recent months including some of the Hawker pilots and also Service test pilots at the Farnborough Aero Flight. There Martindale and Zurakowski were beginning a programme to explore the ultimate dive

*Above right:* With Air Minister Sir Archibald Sinclair and Station Commander Desmond Sheen. Manston 1942. *Ziegler*

*Right:* Author's aircraft at 'Readiness'. Manston 1942. *Ziegler*

*Below:* Hawker test pilots and staff at Langley in 1942. L to R: Lucas, Broad, Humble, Silk, unknown, Pegg, Hymans, RPB, Mallet, Fox, unknown.

*Above:* Typhoon test pilot 1942.  *IWM*

characteristics of Spitfires to beyond 90% of the speed of sound. They were to experience forced landings following loss of propellers and other hazards in the months to come. In America a remarkable character by the name of Cass S. Hough, a colonel in the USAAF, had gained fame from diving a Lockheed P-38 Lightning out of control to what was claimed widely to be the speed of sound; but the Farnborough experts felt that there must have been a fairly considerable position-error in the airspeed system to have produced transonic speed indications at the relatively modest speed at which, they calculated, total energy would have equalled total drag in a vertical dive on that aeroplane.

So it happened that on 16 October 1943 I was detailed for the next of my flights in the Typhoon strain-gauge series which in previous weeks had resulted in reaching a number of odd conditions such as cutting the engine on the ignition switches from full power in a near-vertical dive at 500mph IAS and then, with the tail still in place, repeating the exercise under negative 'g'. On the 16th the idea was to begin to look at all these variations in the last unexplored corner of the flight envelope at the highest combination of indicated

airspeed and altitude which could be reached; and flight test engineer Charlie Dunn briefed me that from a maximum power level at 30,000ft, a push-over into a near-vertical dive should enable us to reach about 450mph indicated at 20,000ft. This he said would do for a start.

It was a day of variable layered cloud as I sat in EK 152 behind the clattering, roaring Sabre engine with the saloon car doors leaking vee-shaped draughts which utterly defeated the efforts of the cockpit hot air system to keep the pilot warm. At 28,000ft there was no clear space in sight for the required dive but I levelled at 31,000ft on top of a cirrus deck and pushed up the power to maximum boost and the phenomenal Sabre RPM limit of 3,750rpm. As speed built up a break occurred in the clouds to port and at the bottom of a quite well defined cloud shaft a bend in the Thames near Eton was visible. The hole looked just about big enough.

23

Setting the instrumentation switches and noting the initial flight conditions on the test pad I rolled down to port, bringing the RPM back slightly as a margin against loss of CS propeller constant-speed control. Rolling out into a near-vertical dive, I trimmed the elevators with a slight residual push force as a safety margin and this time against the anticipated nose-down trim effects of compressibility. At 27,000ft the general noise and fuss was becoming impressive with buffet vibration building up through the controls, seat and cockpit sides — even the motor car windows were vibrating at their natural frequency and it was while observing this with interest that the situation developed suddenly. I was conscious of the controls stiffening up quite rapidly, of the port wing trying to drop and of the aircraft becoming nose-heavy to the accompaniment of violent buffeting and a general feeling of insecurity; and when beginning to bear back on the stick to hold the dive angle from getting too steep and holding off starboard aileron to maintain wings level it was markedly apparent that these actions were becoming progressively less effective. A full two-handed pull failed to reduce the dive angle at all and we were now going downhill and rolling to port with maximum noise, buffet and general commotion, and with no conventional control of the situation at all.

Here was this thing called 'compressibility' about which Philip Lucas had said 'whatever you do don't trim it out of

*Below:* King George VI inspects an RP-carrying Typhoon in 1944 prior to 'D' Day. Sir Trafford Leigh-Mallory 4th from left in group. Sir Roderick Hill 6th and Sir Hugh McEvoy 2nd from right. *IWM*

*Left:* The contrasting shapes of Tempest (top) and Typhoon.

*Right:* A belly-landing after undercarriage trouble. 609 aircraft at Biggin Hill, October 1942. *Air Ministry*

*Above:* The pilot was not seriously hurt in this accident on return from a night 'Intruder' raid.

*Right:* The combat record panel off the author's aircraft PR-G displayed in 1973 at the RAF Museum together with (left) the cockpit panel from 'Widge' Gleed's Hurricane when he was the author's CO in the Battle of Britain at Exeter in 1940.
*The Times*

the dive' as the consequent trim reversal during recovery would probably overstress something severely. So I didn't and throttling right back continued to ride the shuddering and largely uncontrolled device down through 20,000ft until passing about 15,000ft. There as the Mach number dropped at the still nearly constant indicated airspeed the shock waves were supposed to subside allowing control effectiveness to recover.

This indeed occurred and with subsiding buffet aileron effectiveness recovered first, then the nose began to rise under my still heavy pull-force until at last it was possible to ease off the pressure and recover to a level attitude still with the throttle closed, the ASI dropping back from 500mph and, impressively the altimeter steadying at only 8,500ft.

This was the classic pattern of compressibility incident which was encountered subsequently with minor variations according to type on all the final generation of piston-engined fighters and the first generation of jets. But once again the tail had not come off and some still more imaginative flight conditions had to be tested before the Typhoon was finally cleared of any shadow of doubt that tail failures could have occurred as a result of normal or even extreme operating conditions.

In one of the ultimate tests the schedule called up a maximum power dive to 500mph indicated, trimmed out for propeller torque and high IAS effect and then, with the pilot's feet on the cockpit floor and away from the rudder pedals, the engine to be cut on the ignition switches. That this would produce a fin load approaching the design case was anticipated, and the possibility that this might well be the condition that had brought the other tails off did not escape the pilot. It was after all a rather convenient solution as it fitted the background of engine unreliability which had plagued the Typhoon since entry into squadron service in the previous year. But once again the tail did not fall off with me as it had with Ken Seth Smith, and ultimately the cause of the losses was traced positively to random fatigue failures of the elevator mass balance mountings which had resulted in elevator flutter at high speed and the consequent structural failures.

Earlier, when commanding 609 Squadron, it had been possible to put theory into practice and investigate the use for the first time of the Typhoon in a wide field of operations, and prior to this in 1942 to report on its first evaluation for night flying for which purpose it had not previously been considered seriously.

This report, written in the words of a 22-year old went as follows:

*Above:* Mike Brian surveys his flak-damaged Typhoon, Manston 1943. *Air Ministry*

*Left:* RPB hands over 609 to new CO Alec Ingle, May 1942 18 months before meeting him again as PoWs in Stalag Luft III. *Ziegler*

*Right:* A squadron Typhoon in 1944 with bomb racks and the 'clear view' windscreen and canopy. *BAe*

---

*To:* Sqn Ldr G. L. Sinclair, DFC        FOI Air Ministry
*From:* Flt Lt R. P. Beamont
*Subject:* Suitability of Typhoon for Night Flying
*Date:* 25.7.42

Night flying on the nights of 24 and 26 July: Full moon; ⁶/₁₀ths cloud; wind SW 25mph, and ¹⁰/₁₀ths cloud; wind SW 5mph.

### Cockpit Lighting

The three standard cockpit lights (port, starboard and compass) are quite useless as fitted at present, though they can be improved and made usable by painting the bulbs red. However the range of illumination given at present by the port and starboard lights is insufficient, and the addition of two more masked red lamps in the top left and right-hand corners of the instrument panel is necessary.

### Taxying

The view for taxying is comparable with that of the Hurricane and is therefore quite satisfactory. It has, however, become general practice to taxi rather fast in this aircraft and this should be avoided at night as the brakes, though good directionally, are not very positive for pulling up.

The last-minute cockpit check is very simple, as the engine instruments are well placed and the rudder bias, tail trim and flap position can be easily felt.

The complete absence of exhaust glow and sparks is a great asset.

### Take-off

Again the exhaust glare is very conspicuous by its absence — a point which will be greatly appreciated by Hurricane and Spitfire night pilots.

The take-off from Duxford aerodrome was found to be slightly difficult owing to the extreme roughness of the surface, and the aircraft could not be held in flying position for any length of time without being thrown into the air from some particularly uneven part. However, the Macdonald flarepath could be seen clearly at all times and the take-off runs were sufficiently short to create complete confidence. On runways or a smooth grass surface the take-off would present no difficulties at all.

### Handling in Flight

All the instruments are well positioned, but the ASI and the rev counter cannot be seen without the additional lamps previously mentioned.

For instrument flying it is necessary to lower the seat to the bottom position in order to see the Artificial Horizon. This is no disadvantage.

On a number of older type Typhoons, curved perspex quarter panels were fitted to the windshield. Night flying was carried out in an aircraft of this type, and this was a definite disadvantage as the distortion from these panels is of a high order and at the same time there was a large amount of interior reflection from instrument lights and also from the moon when flying away from it.

None of these conditions was found when flying an aircraft with the now standard straight glass quarter panels.

All normal manoeuvres were carried out including aerobatics, and semi-half-rolls as might be used for following evasive tactics, and the aircraft was found to be if anything more pleasant to fly at night than a Hurricane.

### Night Vision

This appears to compare favourably with that of a Spitfire and slightly unfavourably with that of a Hurricane; but when cruising at 285 ASI with both windows down — a condition which is quite comfortable for the pilot — I was quite easily enabled to sight a Wellington at a thousand yards and close with it (with the moon behind it).

Again the complete absence of exhaust glare at any throttle setting was a great advantage. The forward vision will be further improved with the introduction of the 'clear view windshield' now under development.

All night flying Typhoons should be fitted with the standard hood, as the blister hood with the mirror cuts out an important area of search-vision.

### Landing

Very straightforward and simple. The view is good even when making a low approach, and the approach may be made at 120 ASI wheels and flaps down reducing to 100 ASI approximately 100 yards before the glide path indicators (on the Macdonald system) at 30ft.

With the tail down the flarepath is easily seen and the aircraft can be held straight quite simply on the ground.

### General Remarks

The Typhoon should prove satisfactory for GCI under moon conditions, and for Fighter Night, Searchlight Box work etc. Under ideal conditions it is also very suitable for short range intrusion owing to its ability to reach the target area quickly, and to close rapidly with any EA sighted.

The overshooting problem should not be considered against it as speed can easily be lost when the pilot is prepared.

Clear dark night flying with the Typhoon would also be perfectly normal, but of doubtful practicability.

The Typhoon should *never* be flown at night under conditions of rain, as the airstream peculiar to this aircraft causes the hood and windshield to become almost completely opaque even in daylight in the slightest rain shower.

R. P. BEAMONT
Flt Lt

# Hawker Tempest

At Langley in the summer of 1943 the new development of the Typhoon series called the Tempest was on test in three main variants; the Tempest I with uprated Sabre engine, four-bladed propeller and very 'clean' wing-root leading edge radiators; the Tempest II with a Centaurus sleeve valve radial engine and the Tempest V with the uprated Sabre, a longer nose and an extended undernose radiator. All versions had a dorsal fairing to the tall Typhoon fin and the new thin wing which had been designed in semi-elliptical plan form owing mainly to the popular fashion set by the Spitfire. At least some of the aerodynamic specialists maintained at the time and since that a straight taper wing with similar taper ratio, thickness/chord ratio and loading would have achieved the same results but with a lighter structure.

Be that as it may the thinner and cleaner wing combined with spring-tab ailerons gave the Tempest a considerable edge over contemporary fighters in terms of acceleration in the dive, maximum dive speed and lateral controllability. It was in fact the first fighter on our side to have good combat manoeuvrability at and above 500mph IAS — a much sought-after feature to counter the enemy-favoured tactic of one firing pass and a high-speed dive-away.

My first experience was on HM 599, the Tempest I prototype, on 22 June 1943, and at once this felt a livelier, more precise and in some curious way a more aggressive fighter than the Typhoon. HM 599 was on performance testing at the time and for a period Bill Humble and I found ourselves alternately exceeding the existing world speed record of 464mph* as we pushed 'max levels' progressively up to the maximum power altitude at which a true airspeed of 471mph was ultimately obtained. For that stage of the war this was very high performance and it was disappointing that subsequently other operational considerations had to become overriding and resulted in final selection of the Mk V configuration for production with a lower performance.

These considerations were that the wing radiators occupied valuable potential fuel tank space, and they also spread out along the underside of the wing roots where they were highly vulnerable to ground fire. Reverting to the chin-type and lengthened nose radiator permitted the leading edge fuel tanks to be incorporated, but before these aircraft could reach the squadrons an Air Ministry instruction arrived calling for blanking off of the leading edge fuel tanks before delivery, apparently on the grounds that rate-of-climb was now more important than range and endurance, and that the weight of the extra fuel would be critical in this respect.

As a mere pilot this seemed to make no sense at all to me. The rate-of-climb loss with this fuel would have amounted to less than $\frac{1}{2}$ minute to 20,000ft; and the Tempest was unlikely

*Set in 1939 by Deiterle in a Messerschmitt.

in the extreme to be required for high-altitude defence but would most probably be needed for medium level battlefield air superiority combat and ground attack in which range and endurance would be at a premium.

Without the leading edge tanks the Tempest I was fuel-critical as I had already discovered when, concentrating on establishing max level performance points one day I had found myself in the Oxford area with too little fuel left to recover to Langley after only 40 minutes' flying, and had had to make a precautionary diversion for fuel at Abingdon to the surprise of the personnel of this training station and the

*Below:* The prototype Tempest I on test from Langley in 1943. Pilot, Bill Humble. *BAe*

*Bottom:* Tempest I showing the 'clear view' canopy. *BAe*

considerable concern of those at Langley who knew their cherished prototype could no longer be flying once an hour after take-off had passed. Experimental flying, like production testing, was carried out without radio and for communications we relied on the GPO telephone system even in emergency.

This situation was obviously unsatisfactory and I joined with Philip Lucas in lobbying strongly for maximum fuel for the operational Tempest V. A few months later when forming the first Wing* of these aircraft, about 12 arrived from MUs without their leading edge fuel tanks before the fully modified aircraft began to appear, and there was not much that could be done effectively with these early aircraft across the Channel. Later in the summer with modified aircraft, long-range 'drop' tanks arrived to further improve our flexibility and by August we were able to penetrate as far afield as the Friesian Islands and the Ruhr on strikes and bomber escorts.

The testing of the Tempests in the winter of 1943/44 was an exciting time, not so much because of the test programme which for my part was routine and not as dramatic as the Typhoon strain-gauge work, but because of a feeling that I began to develop about this aeroplane. Probably as a result of having had close personal association with the entry into active operations of the Typhoon, I had acquired a fairly comprehensive knowledge of its capabilities and of its operating limitations. In the Tempest we had a direct successor to the Typhoon with most of the criticisms of the latter — many of which I had highlighted personally — either eliminated or much improved. So that I used to look at this sleeker, better proportioned and faster new fighter sitting outside the experimental hangar at Langley with a considerable degree of eagerness to try it in battle. Each flight brought greater enjoyment of and confidence in the crisp ailerons, firm though responsive elevator, good directional stability and damping giving high promise of superior gun-aiming capability and exhilarating performance and with all this, magnificent combat vision with windscreen forward frame members thinned down to a bare minimum and superb unobstructed vision aft of the windscreen arch through the fully-transparent sliding canopy. On every convenient occasion on the way back from tests I would zoom-climb, wing-over and rack the Tempests round in stall-boundary turns simulating combat, looking over my shoulder down the fuselage and under my own tailplane for the first time in our experience. What a fighter this would have made for the Battle of Britain, but what a fighter it was going to make for the Invasion!

Experience with the Typhoon in day and night ground attack had convinced me that a considerable improvement in attack efficiency could be obtained by improving the presentation of the GM 2 gunsight. This item had functioned well in its primary design role of daytime air combat. But when in Hurricanes and later in Typhoons we had started low level operations in bad weather and poor light and at night we had found that the interruption of tracking vision which occurred as the target was lost behind the side frames of the sight reflector, coupled with light-loss through the two reflecting surfaces of the reflector itself, frequently compromised ground attacks. When the full 'ring and range bars plus centre spot' reflections were set up at sufficient brilliance to read, this could be the last straw and sight of a dimly lit target was all too often lost behind them.

*No 150 Wing, Newchurch.

After many frustrating experiences on operational targets across the Channel from Manston and also much realistic experimenting in air-to-ground shoots against wrecks on the Goodwin Sands in bad weather and poor light, I decided to do something. In the absence of any help from the Group Armament Branch who when approached on the subject were not interested, and with the enthusiastic help of the 609 Squadron armourers, a number of 'local mods' were carried out in my own Typhoon PR-G.

The first object was to eliminate all but the aiming spot from the gunsight picture, and this was done by inserting a hollow cylindrical blank up the barrel of the sight. A proof test with guns against one of the Goodwin's wrecks demonstrated as expected no loss of aiming ability air-to-ground with only the spot for reference, and without further delay the modification was night-tested on the next intruder raid.

This turned out to be a moon-period night of full cloud cover over northern France with very little light for target identification. Two trains were attacked and with only the aiming spot dimly illuminated, vision of the target was dramatically improved. But it was still not good enough to make possible completion of attacks in some conditions. In full darkness or rain or mist, targets which were identified through the open side windows or through the quarter panels were then lost when trying to track them past the windscreen frame and the GM 2 reflector bracket into the reduced light transmission area of the gunsight reflector.

Ignoring some quite sharply expressed reactions from officialdom about the unsuitability of windscreen armour-glass as a sight reflecting surface I had a GM 2 sight modified by removing the reflector and brackets and altering the mountings to permit direct reflecting on the windscreen. Checked on the airfield at night we found that although double images of the aiming spot could be seen at high brilliance settings as expected, these were virtually eliminated when brilliance was dimmed down to the levels suitable for night attacks. On the next suitable night I took 'G' with this

Above left: Tempest I with Spitfire-style semi-elliptical wings, and leading edge radiators.  BAe

Above: Prototype Tempest II at Langley, 1943, with Centaurus engine and original fin.  BAe

Right: Production series Tempest II with dorsal fin and bomb racks as delivered to the Chilbolton Wing formed by the author in September 1946.  BAe

Below right: Tempest II on test from Langley, 1944.  BAe

gunsight over to the Lille area and in two train attacks experienced better attack vision than we had ever had before. So effective was this that I gave instructions for all 609's Typhoons to be modified, knowing that such independent action would not be appreciated by superior authority who would, and ultimately did, regard the whole thing as highly irregular.

However as I had not formally reported these intentions to headquarters it was some time before the goings on at Manston sank in at that level, and most of the squadron had been operating enthusiastically for some weeks with the modified sight and with much improved effectiveness, when terse instructions were received to remove these unauthorised modifications. By this time I was convinced that these Typhoon ground attack operations which 609 had pioneered and were still developing had benefited significantly from the improvement in attack vision, and that reversion to the standard arrangement would reduce our efficiency and make the job more difficult than we now knew it needed to be. So I kept the modifications in and accepted the consequences which were soon to show as a mounting number of insistent signals from headquarters. These continued to flow until I left the squadron on 7 May 1943 to rejoin Hawkers where I set about lobbying at once for these improvements to be introduced to the new Tempests.

At this level official activity became more noticeable but after a while we were told that although sympathetic consideration had been given to these troublesome pilot requests, the armament 'experts' had concluded that it would be impractical to manufacture armour glass to a standard of optical accuracy sufficient for direct gunsight reflection.

Repeating that our Typhoon experiences had demonstrated in practice that the specified standards were perhaps higher than necessary in this respect I continued to press for this development. Ultimately the production series Tempest Vs began to be delivered in February 1944 with gunsights directly reflected on to the selected 'Grade A' windscreen glasses, becoming the first day fighters to have this facility. They shared it ultimately with 'Rocket' Typhoons and with some late-series Mosquito nightfighters in response to a similar lobby from the nightfighter empire led by Rory Chisholm of the Nightfighter Development Unit at Ford.

This was a successful outcome and now, about two months before the predicted invasion of Europe, we had a new fighter with a combination of performance and all-round combat vision superior to anything else, on our side.

It was an evocative situation and I was naturally delighted when on approaching the AOC of 11 Group, Hugh Saunders, in February in the hope of getting one of the first Tempest V squadrons, he told me to form the first Wing of these aircraft with Nos 3, 486 (NZ) and 56 Squadrons.

We were soon able to put our new equipment to the test in operations, but prior to these I carried out the first night flight in a Tempest on 5 March 1944 from Bradwell Bay to assess the cockpit lighting and also led a first night formation exercise on 26 April — much to the astonishment of No 3 Squadron who hitherto had considered themselves as a day-only fighter squadron! Then, on the night of 7 May I took my Tempest 'RB' on the first two Tempest operational sorties over France, attacking a train on the first at Lens and another on the second at Evreux.

Our first successful day strike occurred on 21 May when with a formation from 3 Squadron we destroyed a midget submarine and transporter near Courtrai. On 27 May came the first Tempest airfield strike in which I led five aircraft of 3 Squadron in an attack on Cormeilles-en-Vexin (Pontoise) near Paris and destroyed or damaged four recently-arrived Ju 188s in dispersal pens as they were being prepared for a night raid on Southern England.

The Invasion day, 6 June, saw the Tempest Wing on beachhead patrol at dusk, all 24 Tempests returning in formation by night and diverting because of bad weather at Newchurch to Ford where we all landed after midnight except one who got lost and landed at Dunsfold. Then two days later on 8 June Tempests met enemy fighters for the first time when, while leading the Wing over Rouen on Beachhead patrol I took 3 Squadron into a classic 'dogfight' with a squadron of Me 109G6s, destroying three, possibly four.

A week later when flying with Bob Cole* of 3 Squadron at

*Who shot down 22 V1s in the next four weeks.

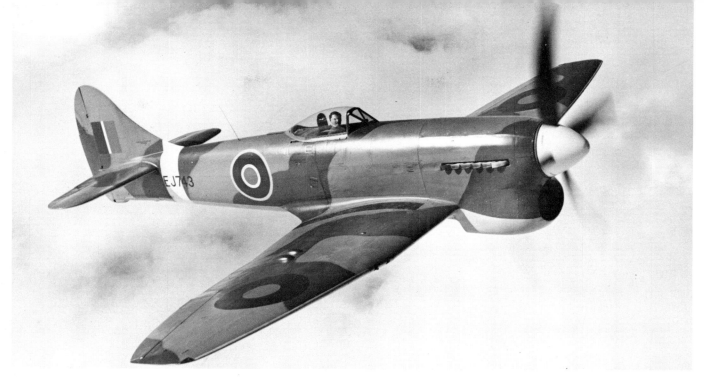

*Above left:* Early production Tempest V with 'long' cannon as delivered to the Newchurch Wing in Spring 1944. *BAe*

*Above:* Later production Tempest V with 'short' cannon, wing leading edge fuel tanks and underwing drop tank system. On test from Langley. Pilot, Cotes-Preedy. *BAe*

dawn on 16 June we shot down the first of the 632 V1 flying bombs to be scored by the Tempests of 150 Newchurch Wing in the next seven weeks. The Tempests were in business and in less than two months since becoming 'operational' had established themselves as the most formidable low and medium altitude British fighters and the most capable type of all against the flying bomb.

In all this activity the combined qualities of this aeroplane were outstanding. In wide-ranging low-level strikes a maximum cruising speed of 365mph IAS coupled with superbly precise controls facilitated target area penetration, and with accurate gun-aiming and the effective use of my strongly-enforced disengagement tactic of 'down on the deck' and round the trees and farmhouses to limit as far as possible the period of exposure to defensive fire, the Tempest began to set new standards for these operations. This policy together with restriction of formations to four or six aircraft except for major set-piece targets or air superiority fighter sweeps, resulted in a high success rate/low loss ratio in conditions in this Invasion Summer of high density defensive fire cover of all significant targets. This was highlighted on 22 May in the mass attack by Fighter Command and fighters of the US Eighth Air Force on communications in the Low Countries.

The Tempests operated from Newchurch in fours from dawn to dusk on that day, and the Wing recorded successful attacks on more than 30 trains and many other road transport targets, without loss or serious damage to our aircraft. Many other fighter units suffered heavily by contrast and the Tempest Wing was called upon to report to 11 Group Headquarters on the tactics employed. We were glad to help them.

The successful summer of the Tempests at Newchurch was a prelude to the final assault on Germany in the winter of 1944-45, when, under the new title of 122 Wing, 2nd Tactical Air Force, and operating before the Rhine crossings from Volkel in Holland with five squadrons, the Tempests went on to establish themselves as one of the most successful ground attack and battlefield air superiority fighters in the European theatre.

The main features contributing to this success were speed, controllability, weapons' accuracy and superior all-round and attack vision. Additional factors were high pilot morale and proficiency following the unique period of gunnery opportunity against the small and fast targets presented during that summer by the V1s, and also the general ease of operation of this big, powerful fighter which had a relatively low accident rate contary to opinions expressed in one rather lurid and often-quoted autobiography. With a wide track undercarriage and effective controls down to the stall the Tempest was less critical to land in crosswinds or turbulence than the Spitfire. On the occasions when owing to defect or operational damage landings had to be made with one main leg down and the other hung up, these were usually successful. In the few fatal accidents under these conditions there were often other adverse factors involved such as a wounded pilot or excessive crosswind. So, in the final battles towards the end of World War II a fighter had emerged incorporating the experiences of the previous campaigns and providing the fighter pilot with a high proportion of the qualities needed at the time.

All-round vision and low obstruction, low light-loss forward vision enhanced by a submerged, directly reflected gunsight ('head-up display' in current technology) had been evolved to meet the specific requirements of operating experience and in doing so had provided the pilot with the most favourable conditions for ground attack and for air-to-air combat experienced until then; advantages which were not maintained in subsequent years.

But the Tempest pilot had no aids to finding his target or to accurate navigation other than the compass, directional gyro and watch, and in the three decades following World War II there was much preoccupation with the development of

'weapons systems' aimed at increasing the 'cost effectiveness' of fighter/strike aircraft by providing self-contained navigation capability with great accuracy and facilities for reducing even small system errors by en route 'update' fixing. The first of these systems came into service in the 1970s but in many cases they appeared in aircraft which had significantly less satisfactory pilot vision than the standards set by the Tempest. Yet the object remained the same — to find and strike the target in as wide a range of conditions as possible. Over a long period successive generations in the Ministry departments concerned failed to identify this as a critical area and to supply vital support in the design phases when company pilots recommended vision improvements at the mock-up stage. Consequently conflicting engineering and equipment requirements have generally been allowed to sway the design compromise in this sense.

In this way the great majority of fighter/strike aircraft developed since World War II have been produced with excessively thick windscreen arches and forward frame members, quarter and centre windscreen panels with vision degraded by the bus-bars of element or conductive film demist systems and by excessive areas of lost-vision due to laminate edge reinforcing. 'Head-up display' sighting units have had heavy metal supporting framework on either side of the reflector glass which, in itself, causes significant light-loss through the reflecting surfaces of the laminates and the coating necessary to provide image contrast. Then, having achieved what is basically a poor standard of forward vision it has become common practice partly to fill in the remaining transparent areas by afterthought-fitting of accelerometers, standby DIs and compasses, incidence gauges and the like. The basis of this process is that in some cases they are essential to head-up reference and in others that there is no room for them elsewhere; and this is all done at the expense of direct, clear vision. The cost of developing a weapons

system of this category has become astronomical in comparison with World War II costs. Part of this is due to the accepted need to achieve a very much higher success rate than was possible with 'manual' navigation, but these systems are at present designed to ensure that the aircraft reaches the target area and when the target has been located a high level of accuracy is achieved in the final attack.

Pending the arrival in service of the next generation true all-weather strike aircraft with 'blind' attack capability the vital link in attacking pinpoint targets is, and is likely to remain in the tactical sense, identifying the target. This must be followed by tracking it visually through the various panels and past any obstructions into the view of the head-up attack display, and then holding it there down to the weapons release or firing point. Target identification is achieved by the pilot looking for it. Thus the whole success or failure of the tactical mission is tied to the pilot being able to 'eyeball' successfully in the conditions prevailing in the last seconds of the attack. These may vary from good light and clear visibility (which can seldom be expected to coincide with important target strikes under wartime pressures), to any combinations of low light and rain, mist or smoke haze. And if the strike aircraft arrives in the target area in anything other than perfect visibility any obstructions in the pilot's forward field of view will further reduce his chances of concluding a successful attack.

The majority of fighter/strike aircraft currently in service in the West are severely and unnecessarily restricted in this way, but technology exists for the introduction of significant improvement in windscreen design. Some examples of one-piece 'wrap-around' windscreens without any metal interpanel frames are already flying in the SAAB Viggen, North American Vigilante, Northrop F-5, and the F-15, F-16 and F-18 series fighters. This principle approaches the ideal for unobstructed forward vision and when coupled with current preoccupation in America and elsewhere with the need to reintroduce 360° fighter fields of view incorporating unobstructed rear vision as well, suggests a return to those times in Northern Europe in 1942/45 when the Fw 190 and the later Typhoons and Tempests set a new style for vision in air superiority fighting and fighter ground attack.

# Tempest Air Combat

The first fight between Tempests and enemy aircraft took place two days after D-Day on 8 June 1944 and involved two squadrons of the Newchurch Wing. Prior to this for some weeks leading up to the Invasion the Wing had been active in strikes against transport and airfield targets and had achieved considerable success without loss. This had contributed to a rapid increase in confidence in the new equipment and to a satisfying rise in morale and aggressive spirit. The squadrons really wanted to get at the Messerschmitts and Focke Wulfs and on 8 June they did.

150 Wing was on air superiority patrol from Le Havre to south of the beachhead at Caen and thence round to Cherbourg. I led No 3 Squadron that day with No 486 (NZ) Squadron stepped up downsun to starboard and the 24 Tempests climbed south-west from Dungeness in clear morning sunlight with only a scattered layer of fairweather cumulus clouds below at about 8,000ft and nothing above. There was little chatter on the radio as we enjoyed the beauty of this summer sky over the Channel. The French coast soon took shape to port from the Somme down to the Seine bay to starboard. I increased to maximum cruise power to cross in west of Dieppe in a shallow dive from 15,000ft to maintain a tactical speed of about 400mph and so reduce the chances of hits by 88mm flak in the coastal defence belt. A brief look down on Dieppe to the left where I had spent an uncomfortable month in hospital in 1940. Then ahead, the great bends of the winding Seine showed where our turning point Rouen had appeared as a dark sprawl against the green and yellow landscape of a rural northern France. Suddenly Blackgang radar warned 'unidentified activity ahead, 15 miles'.

With gunsights switched on, straps retightened and all eyes straining ahead the Wing was ready, but I called to remind them to keep a sharp look out above and behind as well. Then Blackgang again, 'Probably Bandits, 10 miles, 11 o'clock same height or below, heading your way — not positively identified.'

I levelled slightly to avoid losing height advantage and at the next call Blackgang said 'unidentifieds close ahead to port, probably a small formation and below you'. With considerable discipline there was no word from the Tempest pilots as we strained to see something against the mottled background below of farmland and the winding Seine with the built-up areas of Rouen ahead under scattered cotton-wool puffs of cloud. And then they were there, a straggling line of single-seater fighters about 5,000ft below crossing from left to right ahead of us and momentarily silhouetted against cloud. I called 'Aircraft 11 o'clock below, Corncob Leader going down to identify, Harlequin Squadron stay up and cover'.

At about 450mph we were closing fast and when I saw the wing plan form of one of them in silhouette at about two miles range for a fraction of a second I thought 'Damn they're Mustangs' and I warned the others to hold their fire. But then they apparently saw us and broke violently to port with a lot of weaving and general thrashing about, and I recognised them as Me 109Gs and saw black crosses at the same instant.

'Corncob Leader Tally ho! they're 109s, come on in Corncob Squadron, Harlequin Leader cover us.'

The 109 formation of about eight or nine aircraft was now pulling into a tight port turn streaming emergency boost smoke trails. I had to throttle back sharply to reduce our closing speed. Then in a steeply banked port turn I opened fire on the tail-ender. At this stage there were still two other 109s in sight in front of my target and they were all pulling white streaks of wing tip vortices as they tried to turn inside us. But our Tempests had speed and manoeuvre advantage and after missing with my first burst, within one full 360° turn I had closed to about 200yd behind and below him and saw the second burst striking his fuselage and wing roots. This resulted in immediate violent weaving and then the 109 pitched into a dive with smoke billowing and almost obscuring my vision of him as I fired a third burst. This was enough and in a steepening dive I pulled out on to his wing tip

*Right:* RPB demonstrates a 486 Squadron Tempest over his own aircraft 'RB' which was unserviceable. *IWM*

from where I could see that the 109 was well on fire, but the pilot was not visible.

At that moment I paid the obvious penalty for not keeping a look out behind. The Tempest shuddered as there was a loud metallic explosion followed by a smell of cordite and I saw that a ragged hole had appeared in my starboard wing. This was embarrassing and pulling up in a tight spiral climb I peered back through the never more appreciated 'clear view canopy' to see who was under my tail, but whoever it had been was no longer there.

Some confused radio chatter indicated that the fight was still going on somewhere but I could see nothing but two columns of smoke hanging in the air amongst the broken white clouds some miles behind. My No 2 was certainly no longer with me so taking what cover there was among the clouds I took stock of the situation. The hole in the wing had not seriously affected control apparently but it could have damaged the fuel and hydraulic systems. I decided to see if we could get back across the Channel and sort out any landing problems when the time came.

I called Johnny Iremonger to take over the lead with 486 Squadron and to rendezvous the Wing over Rouen and continue the patrol at his discretion since 486 had not been engaged; and I confirmed that I was returning to base damaged and unaccompanied. Someone called from 3 Squadron to confirm my 'flamer' and a 486 Squadron aircraft then called in to say he had propeller trouble and would bale out. As we were quite close to the beachhead area, however, I told him to try for the emergency landing ground which our briefing had indicated would be opened on this day. This he did and eventually landed safely though under fire from enemy ground forces, and he was returned to us by the Navy next day. Meanwhile my Tempest was still flying, though slowly, and the fuel gauges gave normal indications so I headed back north to the French coast and the Channel hoping that there were no more 109s about. After a very long thirty minutes I saw the hazy outline of the South Coast ahead.

Crossing in over Hastings I confirmed to Control that I intended to return to Newchurch where in another ten minutes it was pleasant to see the tents and dispersals of the airfield still bathed in sunshine. There remained, of course, the small matter of whether the undercarriage was damaged and if a safe landing could be made.

Telling Flying Control the problem I brought the Tempest in low over their tented site for a visual check. They reported a large hole on the underside of the wing as well which was not encouraging. However after reducing speed to 110mph I selected the undercarriage down and it locked with comforting green lights. I still did not know if the brakes were unaffected although the differential pressures looked good, and finally a gentle landing executed with more than usual care gave no trouble and we were soon bouncing across the rough Somerfelt tracking taxiway to the 3 Squadron dispersal.

A lot had happened in the past hour and a half and I could not immediately appreciate my good fortune out of concern for the state of RB, and until the Wing was safely back. But a quick look underneath with the ground crew confirmed that the damage was confined to holes top and bottom of the wing and the starboard undercarriage leg fairing completely blown away: RB was repairable. Then Johnny Iremonger came in sight leading the Wing low overhead in reasonable if slightly excited formation and I could see that we had lost no one else.

Whether the 109 leader had got round at me for a wide angle deflection shot while I was busy with the tail-ender or whether I had intercepted some of the shot and shell pouring forth from the Tempests behind me we never discovered, but the Tempests had started their score with four 109s destroyed and two others damaged and we were all satisfied — all that is except the 486 New Zealanders who took some persuading that their Pommie wing leader had not kept them up as 'top cover' to keep them out of the way!

*Left:* Wing Leader, No 150 Wing. Tempest Vs. Spring 1944.

# Tempest Ground Attack

In the neglected garden of the farm cottage at Newchurch which served as Wing Flying Headquarters and dispersal accommodation for No 3 Fighter Squadron, the 'Readiness' pilots were sprawled out in various attitudes of heat exhaustion in the grilling spring sunshine. The 'Ops' telephone shrilled and nearly fell off the windowsill of my office where as Wing Leader I had perched it within reach of my sunbathing deckchair. Identifying myself to the 11 Group Operations staff officer at the other end I said 'What's the form?' and he replied 'We've a target for you near Pontoise if you'd like to try it'. This in deference to the fact that we had only very recently declared our new Tempests 'operational', and Group were not yet sure of our capabilities. He went on 'it is a suspected reinforcement of twin-engined bombers prior to a raid tonight — Johnny Johnston's Wing reported seeing them'.

Though tempted I refrained from asking what the Spitfires had done about it then, knowing that they were most probably on a medium or high altitude fighter sweep and only looking for airborne targets, and I said we would be delighted. Group said that the target areas would be the southern dispersals, I was to take one squadron and yes there was flak, a Form 'D'* was on the way and tactics were at the Wing Leader's discretion.

Checking with the Wing Intelligence Section confirmed the position of half a dozen light flak posts and an 88mm site near the town of Pontoise, and as we would be arriving at about 6pm on what looked like being a perfect summer

*Telexed Operations Order.

evening I planned a run in which would keep us clear of the heavy flak and allow an attack out of the eye of the westering sun. The No 3 Squadron Tempests fired up along their dispersal as I started RB on time, and with their CO Alan Dredge following behind my No 2, we taxied out over Newchurch's undulating Summerfelt track runway with grass already turning brown in the dry weather.

After a check behind at the Tempests lined up in pairs I held my hand up and dropped it forward signalling take-off, and opening up power smoothly to about 90% to leave a margin for the No 2, accelerated down the rough strip with the other Tempest close in to starboard. Undercarriage up and reducing to cruise-climb power in a gentle left-hand climbing turn to allow the others to join up initially in pairs astern, I called control 'Corncob aircraft setting course' and received terse acknowledgement. There would now be radio silence except for operational necessity.

The shining Channel unfolded as we climbed out past Dungeness and at 5,000ft I could already see the grey outline of the enemy coast at Cap Gris Nez. On my brief wing rock to signal 'open out' the Tempests slid out on either side into a four-pair 'search' formation and I looked back with a never-failing sense of pleasure at these slim, purposeful fighters rising and falling gently with their pilots, my good friends, clear in every detail except for their masked faces as they sat high in their clear-vision cockpit canopies. Every sortie was a challenge as it had been since 1939. This was 1944 with the Invasion imminent, and what would today bring?

The radio suddenly broke into this train of thought as Alan Dredge called with falling oil pressure and peeled away from the formation with his No 2, which was standard practice in emergency. I confirmed the action wishing him luck and rechecked the course to our first landmark, the Somme estuary.

Now we were down to six aircraft which reduced our effectiveness and probably increased the risk factor as we would have less guns to bring to bear on the defences. But there were the sand dunes of Le Treport to port and a hazy

*Below:* Re-arming RPB's Tempest 'RB' at Newchurch after a ground attack mission. May 1944. *IWM*

line ahead indicating the French coast stretching towards Dieppe in the south-west. The sky was clear and it was a perfect day for a dogfight.

Control called as we crossed in at 10,000ft with Abbeville over to port and they said 'no trade'*, but I told the squadron to keep a sharp look out in any case as I would now be preoccupied with navigation. I had got to know most of the area well since 1939 but had never been to Pontoise or the Paris area before, and the next five minutes could be critical if I missed the track. But the villages, railways and woods along the track line on my map appeared in the appropriate order and position and suddenly there was the aerodrome of Cormeille en Vexin with a white concrete runway and perimeters contrasting against the green of the airfield grass and the surrounding farmland.

Calling 'Target area to port, going down in 30sec' I pulled the harness straps tight, lowered the seat one notch for gunsight vision, switched on the sight and made a final adjustment to brilliance on the rheostat while searching hard for our targets. At first from 2-3 miles at 10,000ft the airfield looked peaceful and deserted and I wondered for a moment if our effort was going to be abortive but then I saw them, one, two, three and more dark twin-engined aircraft in a long dispersal area among woods well south of the airfield towards a wide bend in the now visible winding Seine.

'OK fellers, targets on the south side. Corncob leader taking left hand dispersal. Spread out echelon starboard and take individual targets. Going down NOW. Make this a good one!'

One always said this but it was redundant as these tremendous fighter pilots could be relied upon utterly and to the ultimate if necessary — this was what it was all about — the sure knowledge of reliance upon the others in the team. Times and values change but these were the values of that time. And this was where the qualities of the Tempest shone. Steady and undemanding in trimmed, cruise formation, it was instantly responsive and well-damped and crisp in manoeuvre so that as I rolled away into a dive to port I knew that as the target area appeared in the windscreen I would be able to track the gunsight on to the selected target smoothly and with little over-correction even in turbulence.

And so it was now. In anticipation of defensive fire I had decided to attack at high speed and so steadied at about

*No enemy air activity reported.

Left: 'RB' repainted with 'Invasion Stripes' for D-Day, 6 June 1944. IWM

Below left: Camera gun frames from 'RB' attacking Ju88 on Pontoise airfield, 28 May 1944. IWM

Right: Ju188 of the type attacked by Tempests at Pontoise. IWM

Below: A section of Tempests taking off on patrol from Newchurch. Summer 1944. 56 Squadron Spitfire Vs in background. IWM

470mph passing 5,000ft. A quick glance behind to see the Tempests lining up to starboard and following closely, and so into the attack! My target was clear now, a black-painted Ju 88 (subsequently identified as a very new 188 version) in a high walled blast pen. A short ranging burst and then hard down on the trigger, ruddering corrections as necessary as the blast pen erupted in strikes with bursts all over the bomber and then a large piece of it flying in the air as I snatched at the stick at the last moment to avoid flying head-long into the target.

Here came the flak, sparks and streaks across the canopy, and grey puffs of smoke and dust from shells bursting on the ground ahead, and continuous flashes from a gunpost up a wooded slope to the left. Now was the time for some really

low flying and with full throttle and propeller in fine pitch my Tempest continued at 50ft or less and about 450mph across runways, past a control tower with gunfire or shell bursts round it, up the side of a hill and jinking round the corner of a village (Pontoise).

Looking back there were columns of smoke from our targets, shell bursts and weaving tracer everywhere and here and there the Tempests jinking after me.

'Keep down low' I called 'and pull up with me at five miles'.

Then it was over and we were climbing homewards at 5,000ft over France in the golden evening sun with the Tempests, all five of them, sliding back into formation. Even from 10,000ft columns of smoke from the target area were

*Right:* 'Digger' Cotes-Preedy, CO of 56 Squadron at Grimbergen, and Volkel. September 1944.

*Below:* With Cotes-Preedy at Grimbergen. *IWM*

*Bottom:* Tempest Wing pilots at Grimbergen, including Cotes-Preedy, RPB, Umbers, on 28 September 1944.

*Below right:* Johnny Iremonger, CO of 486 (NZ) Squadron (Tempests).

*Left:* Morale tremendous! Tempest pilots of 3 Squadron at Volkel. Left, Johnny Cock (87 Squadron, Exeter 1940). At the wheel Spike Umbers.

*Below:* Tempest Wing Leader, September 1944.

still in sight, otherwise the sky was clear and serene over northern France and in our confined cockpits it was difficult to relate the tense excitement that we still felt to the now apparently quiet cruise back to Base. But there could be no relaxing vigilance for the 190s and 109s could well attack anywhere and often attempted radar ground-controlled intercepts at easily identified landmarks such as crossing out points. But on this occasion there was no activity and when control confirmed this I told them 'Not to worry — we had a good Prang!'

With the familiar green-grey vee of Dungeness jutting out towards us ahead I called the Tempests into close formation and we swept across Newchurch, golden in the evening light in a tightly compact group of three pairs before pulling up into a left-hand circuit in starboard echelon for a continuous curve approach and stream landing at 200yd intervals on the rough tracking runway.

Leading the six Tempests back to 3 Squadron dispersal I opened the canopy and unfastened my oxygen mask to breathe in the warm air with its scent of farmland, hot hedgerows and then inevitably high octane exhaust smoke, and enjoyed an almost physical sense of well being. We had struck a good blow at the enemy; had probably saved some lives in a coming bombing raid; had built up further confidence in our new Tempests which had been magnificent, and had lost no one in the process.

I swung RB's tail round in the dispersal sending a shower of dried grass into the air, and cut the engine. One by one the others coughed and spluttered to silence. Then the ground crew, excited by the smoke-grimed gunports, swarmed on to the wing.

As the fitter helped take off my straps he asked 'any luck sir?' and he listened with dawning amazement as I spoke of our attack — then he said 'we didn't think you went on operations — we thought you were only a test pilot!'

# Junkers Ju 88

I saw my first Ju 88 soon after dawn on 24 July 1940 with the 'Readiness' section from 87 Squadron which had been 'scrambled' on interception patrol from Exeter on a glorious summer morning. Climbing our Hurricanes initially towards the North Devon coast through scattered cumulus clouds tinged orange at the tops by the sunrise, it was, to a 19-year old, wonderful to be alive and difficult to contemplate the sombre reason for our being there. Stable anticyclonic conditions with good visibility below cloud and unlimited above presented no weather difficulties for this patrol. My Hurricane, LK-L, was familiar and comforting in its steady instrument readings and engine note. As we levelled at 10,000ft above Barnstaple the orange-gold of the eastern skyline merged into deep purple above, fading into the delicate pale hues of the far distant northern horizon. Below, the land and sea of the Severn estuary lay indistinct in misty mauve shadow between the golden clouds. But we were on serious business and the Controller, for once intelligible in our TR9 radio headsets, in pressing tones instructed that we should turn on to 260° and 'Buster' (the code for 'increase speed') after a positively identified 'Bandit'.

Thirty seconds later he gave warning of other fighters intercepting, and then said, 'Bandit dead ahead of you at two miles, probably below you'. We were turning slightly to the left over Lundy Isle when I saw it, a dark speck against the haze between two brilliant orange patches of cumulus; and calling 'Aircraft 10 o'clock low' I rolled in towards it at full throttle and fine pitch. The aircraft was tracking across from right to left and I had an impression of the high square tail of a Ju 87; but it had no spatted undercarriage and I could then see twin engines — a Ju 88. With twin streams of thin smoke it was going fast in a shallow dive southwards towards Devon, and then from the right a Spitfire appeared firing at quite long range before pulling up and away to starboard.

I assumed that he had finished his ammunition and so continued at full bore until after what seemed a long interval to close the gap I was in firing position at about 300 yards dead astern and in the turbulence of the enemy's wake. We were both doing about 320mph in a steepening dive and I fired a long burst from the Hurricane's eight .303 Browning machine guns and saw some return fire.

The 88 lurched, streamed more smoke and the starboard propeller slowed down. Now down to below 1,000ft we crossed the coast north of Barnstaple and as the German slowed I held further fire because he seemed to be going for a forced-landing. Suddenly an object separated from his fuselage and the rear gunner fell past with a glimpse of white as his parachute streamed at a very low height. Then as I was struggling to stay behind him, the 88 slowed right down and slithered across a field and up a heather slope into a hedge in a cloud of dust.

Breaking sharply round to port through a patch of low early morning mist, I turned back over the field to see a puff of oily black smoke and orange flame as the wreck ignited. There was no sign of life and I had momentary fear that the remaining crew were trapped in the flames, but the second time around and at very low level I could see one man pulling another away from the cockpit and they were soon lying on the ground some distance from the burning wreck. To complete the scene a battered Morris truck coming down the nearest lane proved to be the local Home Guard unit arriving to do their duty. I waved to them and then set course for Exeter where I landed to find that I had seen the 88 much earlier than the other two members of the section who had not been able to catch up after not following me initially. In accord with the practice of the time I reported the engagement to the station intelligence section but did not claim a victory as it was assumed that the first attack, the Spitfire, should have the credit. With the pressure of events that summer and subsequently, more than a decade was to pass before I learnt that the Spitfire had been flown by Bob Stanford-Tuck, one of the top-scoring pilots of the period, operating from Pembrey.

In August of that summer I saw a large formation of 88s at close proximity when we intercepted them on their way to bomb Warmwell, and later in the war had encounters with new versions at night over Bristol and Dover and finally with a very new Ju188 on the ground during an airfield attack near Paris in 1944; but five years were to pass after this first encounter before I came to fly one of these fine aircraft.

At Tangmere in June 1945 following the cease-fire, as a member of the Tactics Branch of the Central Fighter Establishment one had access to the aircraft of the Enemy Aircraft Flight, and having flown their Fw 190 and Me 109G6 I asked the flight lieutenant in charge what was special about flying the Ju 88 night-fighter version which was parked outside and which did not seem to fly very often. He said that he hadn't flown it but that I could have a go if I liked, and here were the Pilots' Notes. He passed me two pages of typescript and said that the flight sergeant would show me how to start it. That together with a look at the cockpit constituted the formalities for my first flight on a bomber-sized aircraft, my only previous twin-engine experience having been a few flights on Oxford trainers and Whirlwind fighters.

Even in the casual atmosphere prevailing this seemed to be taking informality to the extreme, and I wondered whether it would not be better to wait until I could at least talk to a pilot who had flown it. But this seemed to be unlikely of achievement and so on 14 June 1945 I climbed alone up the ladder into the high cabin of this large aeroplane, wondering if what I was about to do was really responsible or was even

*Above:* Ju88 night fighter flown at Tangmere on 14 July 1945. *IWM*

within the practical capabilities of a fighter pilot. In the event the Ju 88 presented no problems. The greenhouse-type construction of the cabin and nose windscreen which from outside seemed to provide a tremendous area of transparency, from inside seemed to consist almost entirely of thick metal frames. It was all sound and solid but surprisingly restrictive in the vision sense.

The controls and instrument layout were conventional but with the advantage of electrical trimming as in the contemporary Fw 190, and the only complexity seemed to be the fuel system which, designed for a bomber with multiple tanks and associated fuel cocks, clearly needed a proper degree of knowledge by the crew. In this case with the 'crew' limited to me, I had been told to 'set the cocks on the main tanks and leave 'em there, and don't stay up for more than two hours.'! This seemed like good advice and so I started the engines under the directions of the flight sergeant shouted through the open hatch below my feet.

The large paddle-bladed propellers revolved readily and sprang into smooth life with a rumble reminiscent of a vintage car, but this soon changed to a higher-pitched and aggressive noise level as power was increased. In fact this turned out to be a noisier-than-expected aeroplane, but that was about the only criticism. On initial taxying in the nose-high, tail-down attitude of this tail-wheel aircraft with its tall main undercarriage there was an awkward feeling that it could easily overswing on the turn, especially down wind; but once lined up on the runway the feeling of being in a much larger aeroplane than one's previous experience had

practically gone, and the 88 felt a compact and well-organised aeroplane.

A short run-up to full power caused the pedal-operated brakes to slip and produced a crescendo of sound that was impressive. I had decided to increase the power progressively on take-off to forestall any unbriefed tendency to swing. This was not necessary and the 88 unstuck at less than full throttle and without any further elevator activity after my initial action to lift the tail conventionally with forward wheel to an appropriate take-off attitude. The initial climb was brisk and I needed to retract the undercarriage before increasing the power to avoid overstepping the undercarriage limit.

Cleaned up, the rate of climb in this light configuration was similar to a Mosquito and the aircraft responded pleasantly to the controls with light ailerons and conventional harmonisation. I noticed that it needed commendably little trimming also, and only when levelling out at 4,000ft and throttling back to cruise at about 230mph* were small tweaks of the elevator and rudder trim switches required. With time

*British standard ASI fitted for trials.

*Above:* The 'Enemy Aircraft Flight'. 1945. *IWM*

to look around the big BMW engines with their annular radiators and large propeller spinners reaching forward of the cockpit and beyond them the long tapering wing tips, were a reminder that this was in fact a 60ft-span aircraft, but it was gentle and undemanding to fly in these conditions and reasonably quiet at cruising power. A look over my shoulder showed that a degree of visibility existed towards the tail through the structure of the top gunner's position, but forward vision was poor and interrupted by the complex metal frame-work of windscreen and canopy.

Rapidly gaining confidence with the aeroplane I tried a few partial rolls, tight turns, rolling pull-outs and dives, climbs and wing-overs; and in all of these the aircraft was stable, responsive and apparently quite viceless except for the noise level which reached a crescendo in dives around 300mph and was distracting.

Returning towards Tangmere I was about to slow down to look at slow speed behaviour when I noticed a Mosquito in the circuit below. Thinking it might be Bob Braham, also a member of the Tactics Branch and the leading exponent of long-range Mosquito fighter tactics, I rolled down toward him and increased power; and it was immediately apparent that it was Bob and that he wanted a fight!

The Mosquito wound into the turn in my direction, and with full throttle and fine pitch I pulled the 88 into a vertical bank after him. The results were impressive for although I did not know the aircraft it was easy to hold firmly on the opposite side of the circle to the Mosquito and begin to make progress towards getting on his tail. Braham got down to work then and took the Mosquito on to its stall boundary

with wings rocking perceptibly, but I could still see him in my forward arc. I was not far off getting into a firing position but after a number of descending full power turns over Tangmere which had the station out watching, I felt that discretion had to be the better part. I was getting into areas in which I could not possibly know the 88's characteristics; so I eased up and out of the turn and Bob Braham was promptly round on my tail.

It had been a remarkable demonstration of the flying and manoeuvring qualities of the Ju 88 and I suddenly felt very much at home in it, but there was still the landing to come. This interlude had used up a fair amount of fuel, not to mention adrenalin, so I decided to have a brief look at handling in the landing configuration and then return to base. Again the Ju 88 behaved impeccably with undercarriage and flaps down and when turning on to 'Finals', keeping the traditional 'plus 5mph' over the Pilots' Notes figure until safely over the threshold, I found that this big aeroplane could be steered on the approach as gently and responsively as any fighter. Levelling out and closing the throttles slowly, a gentle rumble indicated that the main wheels were already on the runway owing to slight misjudgement of height from the high cockpit while considering whether to go for a classy '3-point' landing. I swallowed my pride and easing the wheel forward to prevent any bump-induced excursions back into the air, completed a smooth, uncomplicated and classic 'wheeler'.

This flight and another the next day were enough to show why the 88 was regarded by the Germans as their best large aircraft of the World War II period. The performance of this night-fighter version when matched against the latest Mosquito of 1945 was remarkable when it is realised that apart from increased power in the night-fighter version, the basic 88 airframe was largely unaltered from the 1940 bomber version.

It remains in my rating as one of the best heavy twins of all time, and a very pleasant flying experience.

# Focke Wulfe Fw 190

One day in 1943 a German fighter pilot reported that he became lost after a combat with Spitfires over the Channel near Weymouth. Whether he was really lost or whether, as rumour had it at the time, with a recently injured back he was not anxious to continue his personal war, did not alter the fact that he landed at the first aerodrome he saw which was the Training Command Station of Pembrey in South Wales. From there the story gained in the telling, and with reason. It was said that Pembrey, being in the Fairwood Common Sector whose Commander was none other than the redoubtable 'Batchy' Atcherley, was not surprised when the latter drove over to collect his prisoner. The German had remained silent since capture and on the way back Atcherley, rested his service revolver rather pointedly on his knee. The car then hit a pothole and a round went off through the side whereupon the prisoner is quoted as having said in perfect English. 'You should be more careful with that — it might hurt someone!'

Another part of the story concerns the aeroplane — it was the first intact Fw 190 to reach this country and on 1 June I was invited to fly and report on it at Farnborough. This was an intriguing assignment as I was taking part in testing the Tempest series developments of the Typhpoon at the time, and there was much interest in the reports coming in of increasingly frequent encounters by Spitfires with this formidable new German fighter.

Seeing the Fw 190 for the first time there was an immediate impression of power and strength with a simplicity of line marred only by the high, stalky main undercarriage. The latter, together with the short, squat fuselage suggested that ground stability might be a problem, which it certainly was. To a fighter pilot a point of major interest was the rear-vision canopy. Unlike the practice in the Me 109, Spitfire, Hurricane and early Typhoon, of rear vision severely limited by canopy framework and rear fuselage lines, the 190 had a superb one piece moulded transparency from the windscreen arch right back to a few feet forward of the foot of the fin. When in the cockpit I found that the practical rear vision area included not only either side of the fin but also below the tailplane. This was reverting almost to the days of open cockpits in this respect and was a very valuable combat feature.

The Aero Flight pilots had established the basic handling and systems characteristics for a briefing which seemed almost too simple when one considered the well-instrumented cockpit with flight and engine instruments calibrated in unfamiliar KPH, metres and kilogrammes. The critical references were red-lined and I was assured that as far as the fuel system controls were concerned I could 'leave 'em all on'.

Once strapped in there was an immediate impression of rightness. This was a cockpit which exactly fitted the fighter pilot. It was the first we had seen to adopt the two consoles and centre panel' arrangement, and it was immediately apparent that this was condusive to a logical and well-proportioned lay-out. Also new to us and a significant improvement was electrical trimming, the stick-switch-operated longitudinal trimmer being especially appreciated. I noted with approval low static-friction control circuits and the comfortable positions of the controls relative to the sitting

*Below:* The first Fw190 to land intact in UK. Pembrey 1943. Later flown by RPB at Farnborough on 13 September 1943. *IWM*

*Above:* The same aircraft at Farnborough being flown by RAE Chief Test Pilot 'Willie' Wilson. *IWM*

position. The coaming and windscreen seemed a little high until the gunsight was switched on when it was seen to be at exactly the right level.

On start-up the big 14-cylinder radial engine made noises reminiscent of a vintage Bentley accompanied by much acrid exhaust smoke, but it settled down to rumble with comforting smoothness. The view for taxying though restricted over the big engine was better than from a Spitfire, which was just as well as there was a very strong tendency to ground loop if one allowed the nose to swing from a straight taxying path. The tailwheel had a castoring lock incorporated which was operated by pulling the stick fully back, and was used to prevent swinging and the ground-looping which could apparently also very easily occur on the landing run.

Take-off was straightforward with torque reaction from the big propeller easily countered with rudder. The contrast in view from the steep tail-down position to that in the take-off attitude was striking, and suddenly any sensation of restriction of awkwardness was gone in this high-sitting wide-field-of-view cockpit with controls and instruments easily reached or seen. The 190 leapt off the short N/S runway at Farnborough into a strong southerly wind feeling every inch a fighter aeroplane. This impression increased throughout the flight — light, responsive and dead-beat lateral control gave a high rate of roll at combat speeds and only heavied-up significantly above 500kph. The elevator control was in good harmony with aileron and light enough to pull high 'g' easily without overcontrolling (or 'pilot-induced oscillation' as it became titled in later times). The rudder was unobtrusive but satisfactory for countering the directional changes resulting from sharp power variations with the big BMW engine. The latter itself was smooth and responsive to throttle and clearly maintained power and a high rate of climb at 30,000ft where

it seemed likely to create problems for even the latest marks of Spitfire.

Rolling into dives the 190 gained speed rapidly while retaining dead-beat directional damping, and the gunsight bead could be placed firmly on a simulated target and then tracked accurately throughout the speed range checked from about 300 to 550kph IAS. From low level to 20,000ft in high rate rolls, tight turns, steep climbing turns and wing-overs it proved to be a formidable fighter aeroplane and attractive to fly with visibility all round which had great operational significance. It was only in the accelerated stall which produced a sharp wing-drop and in the steep ground attitude and proneness to swing violently on landing that serious criticisms could be made.

When settling into the currently traditional curved approach on to 'finals' for the Farnborough short runway I was very reluctant to bring back this extremely pleasant and potent fighter. I felt it would give us many headaches in the months ahead in the hands of experienced pilots. But I also felt that inexperienced pilots might have trouble with it, and it was comforting to realise that the Typhoon would probably out-turn and out-perform it at heights below 20,000ft, while the latest Spitfire (Mk 9) could probably just about match it in performance at 30,000ft, though not below. It seemed to me that the 190 would be able to outdive both of them, but that our new Tempest might have the edge on it there. In fact as I taxied back in with the canopy open amid gusts of exhaust smoke I felt a growing conviction that it would be no bad thing to be on a 190 squadron at that point in the war. Our two best fighters in service could cope with it, and that the Tempest V which we were hoping to make operational before the coming invasion would be superior in everything except rate of climb below 20,000ft. Above that height the 190 was clearly going to give us problems.

Later with 122 Wing from Volkel in combats using the Tempest V these theories were soon substantiated, and although the 190 was a major succeess in the Luftwaffe it was never a serious worry to a Tempest pilot — providing he saw it first!

46

# Messerschmitt Bf 109

In July 1945, following the Ju 88 sortie and a refresher flight in the Fw 190 which, though enjoyable, seemed less impressive than it had at Farnborough in 1943 before my two years of Tempest flying, I noticed with interest that the Tangmere Enemy Aircraft Flight had an Me 109G. Enquiries revealed that it was indeed serviceable but that few pilots seemed to want to fly it.

Since the earliest days of encounters with 109Es I had wondered about this legendary aeroplane because it seemed to have some severely limiting features such as its stalky, narrow-track undercarriage and what looked from a distance like an almost inpenetrable array of metalwork around the cockpit where a good fighter should have clear, unobstructed transparencies. So on 12 July I took a look at the Tangmere Me 109 Serial No VD 349. At close acquaintance it brought back very sharply the time on D-Day plus 2 when I had first seen a G6 at close range while firing at it over Rouen. Then I had an unpleasant feeling that its pilot could not possibly be seeing me as I attacked owing to almost nil rear vision, although from his violent manoeuvring he obviously knew I was there. Now, as I climbed into the narrow cockpit, fixed the harness and closed the slide-opening canopy, the effect was almost claustrophobic. The windscreen arch and heavy armour glass front panel were cased in extremely thick metal frames, and the canopy itself seemed to consist more of metal than of perspex. By comparison with the efficient ergonomics of the Fw 190, the cockpit layout was untidy and revealed its longer development history with modifications and bracket adaptors in profusion.

The engine proved rough and raucous and taxying was even more of a problem than in Spitfires due to the long, high nose and miniscule windscreen panels. But once on take-off with full power and the tail up it began to feel more like a fighter.

In the air the G6 showed pleasantly conventional control and stability up to about 350mph but above this the controls heavied up markedly, especially the ailerons which became almost immovable at much above 450mph. It was small wonder that the Spitfire IXs had been able to cope very well with the 109G.

Climb performance was good and obviously superior to the Tempest above about 20,000ft where its turning performance was also better, but in all low and medium altitude comparisons it was clearly inferior to the Tempest, being at least 50mph slower at low level. It had one feature giving it a clear advantage over all Allied fighters in the period however. This was a fuel injection system in place of a curburettor that permitted sharp pushovers to negative 'g' which could not be followed by our fighters as they suffered engine cutting in these conditions.

Pushing the 109 sharply over from steep zoom-climbs into vertical dives maintaining full power throughout was an interesting manoeuvre which we had always wanted to be able to do, especially in 1940 with the odds against us. Now with nothing more unpleasant resulting during combat manoeuvres with stick hard forward — than showers of grit and debris from the cockpit floor, the 109 anticipated the 'weightless' manoeuvres of astronaut training 20 years later. It was interesting to feel that this aeroplane could undoubtedly be a threat in the hands of a particularly skilful fighter pilot, but that the same pilot could have done much better with a Tempest V or the later marks of Spitfire.

It was immediately apparent that its negative 'g' capability gave the Messerschmitt a powerful evasive manoeuvre which we could not follow right to the end of the war. We could and often did half-roll after them keeping our engines at full power under positive 'g' as they pushed over, and caught up with them that way.

For the rest I found the Me 109 a constricted, noisy, half-blind fighter with very heavy controls above medium speeds. Although it was always interesting to fly a new type and especially one from the other side, after a few more wing-overs and tight turns over Tangmere I felt that a low altitude at least I would have preferred a Tempest, a Typhoon or even a 190, and at high altitude a Spitfire IX. So setting up a curved approach into Tangmere to keep the runway in view, I landed tail-up in a prevailing 10kt crosswind and found the Messerschmitt delicate but controllable with rudder in these conditions until easing the stick back lowered the tail wheel to runway contact, and then the landing roll was completed by looking sideways at the runway edges with the nose blocking all straight-ahead vision.

In taxying round the corners of the perimeter track the G6 rocked delicately on its narrow undercarriage. I realised that if a fighter pilot had nothing better to compare with the Me 109 he could well have developed a respect and liking for it, but to those of us who had benefit of better vision, higher performance and easier landing and ground handling it was an inferior fighter. I now readily understood why the sight of them had worried us far less than had Fw 190s from 1942 onwards.

*Below:* Me109G as flown at Tangmere on 12 July 1945. *IWM*

# The Strains of War

In World War II life for many people became moulded into a rigid pattern as they found themselves tied to day-to-day existence in factory, office or the armed forces. Often cut off from home and family many lacked even the reassurance of regular telephone contact. These circumstances brought into sharp relief extremes of emotional experience — illness, the birth of a child, indefinite separation, lack of certain knowledge of the safety of loved ones — to a point where existence became sharply concentrated on the daily task. The continuity of personal life became virtually suspended 'for the duration'.

My own experience was no exception. In 1941 I had got to know a WAAF Cypher Officer rather well in the cockpit of my single-seater Hurricane on the way to a dance at RAF Pembrey for which rather irresponsible action I was subsequently and quite properly court-martialled. We married in October 1942 after we had decided that if we did so and she should eventually have to leave the WAAF in the event of a baby appearing, at least we should be able to spend my leaves together. This indeed occurred and during 1943 we were able to set up house at Uxbridge while on my second tour as a Hawker test pilot. Baby Carol was fit and noisy; Shirley was preoccupied rather proudly with her first house, her baby and her husband. An equally proud husband, father, and test pilot of the new Tempest, felt life was good indeed and the months flew by until early 1944 when it became clear that the 'Invasion' was a final certainty for the coming spring.

Torn between the calls of the Service and home and of undoubtedly strong personal desires in both directions, I talked this over with Shirley. With her unfaltering courage she agreed that I must break our idyll and return to Fighter Command — and if they would have me — for the final battles to come. She knew, of course, that my current post of Service test pilot at Hawkers could automatically have been extended to the end of hostilities as a 'reserved occupation', but she never mentioned it. When I returned from visiting AVM Sir Hugh Saunders at 11 Group Headquarters to ask for a job with one of the first Tempest squadrons with the news that he had charged me with forming the first Wing of these new fighters with three squadrons, she was very happy for me and totally successful in masking her other thoughts about the implications. Closing our first and only home in February 1944 I took the family in my old Rover down to the bungalow at Hindhead. My parents had rented it while my father continued reserve service in the Army, our family home at Chichester being let. I then left to begin the exciting task of forming the first Tempest V unit with 486 Squadron at Castle Camps in Suffolk.

The weeks passed swiftly until by the end of April we had two squadrons trained on their new Tempests and installed on an advanced airstrip laid on farmland at Newchurch on Dungeness, with the enemy coast less than eight minutes away. First Tempest actions against ground targets were quickly followed by D-Day, the beginning of the invasion of Europe. The first Tempest air combats came two days later and then the Tempest's battle against the V1 flying bombs began. There were few visits home that summer. On the last of these on 5 July 1944 I flew my Tempest to Lasham, destroying a V1 flying bomb near Eastbourne on the way, and that afternoon drove Shirley from Hindhead to Hartford Bridge* where I had been summoned to a Field Investiture. After the ceremony we met King George VI in the Mess with Queen Elizabeth and immediately came under the latter's spell and her supreme ability to make even the most self-conscious enjoy talking to her.

Shirley looked tired that evening and I thought that the fact that my name had been cropping up quite frequently in the Press in connection with fighter operations was probably not helping to prevent worry at home. But the tempo of events continued to accelerate and after an August devoted to ground attacks in Holland and daylight bomber escorts into Germany, the Wing was at last posted to 2nd Tactical Air Force in Belgium. I led 60 Tempests out from Matlaske in Norfolk to Brussels Grimbergen on 28 September with considerably mixed feelings. This was the ultimate point in my association with the Tempest — to be leading the first squadrons out to join the final attack on the enemy mainland and it was also a fitting finale to the first act in 1940 which had ended for me with a hurried flight back from France in a KLM DC-2. But in the hectic recent operations and preparations for the Wing departure there had not even been a chance to visit Shirley and the baby.

Our first operations after arrival at Grimbergen in the tense atmosphere of the front line immediately involved successful combats with Fw 190s over the Rhine. Then after a few more hectic days over the Dutch salient and nights in very liberated Brussels we moved on again on 1 October, this time to Volkel. This was the most forward major airfield in the Dutch salient and within range of German artillery which shelled us punctually every morning. We were now back at grips with the hottest part of the war and my aeroplane was hit by flak on the way in to my first landing at Volkel. Two days later I had what was to be my last encounter with enemy aircraft, destroying an Fw 190 at over 500mph in the Reichwald forest area.

On 5 October I headed Tempest RB west from the battle zone for a 48hr leave and landing in the dusk at Dunsfold in the uncanny peacefulness of Sussex, was soon with the family at Hindhead. In the quiet, deeply close walk over the heather

*Now Blackbushe aerodrome.

48

next day I told Shirley that my third tour of operations was almost complete. It would be my last as Philip Lucas* was arranging with the Air Ministry for my return to Hawkers for experimental test flying as an attached RAF pilot until the end of the war. After that I would be offered a job as a civilian test pilot. In a few weeks I would be back in England and we could set up house again. Shirley was obviously happy at this but looked pale and tired and with difficulty I persuaded her to admit that she felt unwell. Unusually for her she did not want to walk far and we went slowly back making plans and able to see excitingly for the first time a real future for us as a family. Next morning we sat close in the taxi taking us slowly through the hazelnut-laden autumn-hued lanes through Chiddingfold back to Dunsfold. We said goodbye outside the Flying Control building, and I made her promise to see a doctor without delay. She promised, said 'come back soon' and let me walk out to the Tempest. I taxied out conscious only of the small figure still standing by the car on the tarmac.

In an hour the greens and russets of the English fall had given place to a cold grey sky and the flat featurelessness of Holland in winter. I was soon taxying in a drizzle of rain over the rough brick rubble-surrounded dispersal areas of Volkel among the bombed-out hangars with *Rauchen Verboten* still emblazoned on shattered walls and the mounds of recent hastily dug graves alongside crashed Dakotas and Horsa gliders.

Six days later on 12 October 1944 the engine of my Tempest stopped during a ground attack operation in Germany north of the Rhine near Bocholt. The remainder of the war provided plenty of time for consideration in various prison camps of what Shirley might be needing and of what I might have been able to do for her in other circumstances, and for writing to her my one permitted letter per week. Not one of her's nor of anyone else's ever reached me.

On 27 May 1945 I stepped on to Oakley aerodrome near Oxford out of one of many hundreds of Lancaster bombers engaged on recovering PoWs and savoured once again the poignant tranquillity of England in so stark contrast to the atmosphere of horror and destruction prevailing over Europe.

Disengaging myself from the hordes of ex-Kriegies* and reception personnel as soon as decently possible I found the Mess and a telephone. Thinking that my parents and Shirley might by then have returned to Chichester I called Lavant 61; almost immediately my father's voice replied and I announced my whereabouts. I heard his voice call out to my Mother 'Dots, he's back!' and then say 'How am I to tell him?' Shirley had died the previous week in hospital near Hindhead.

At this very moment of realisation that it was all over — the war with Hitler finished and in our favour and the daily likelihood of abrupt decease or injury ended; at the moment of savouring this and the very freedom of being able to go where I wished to go in my own country which at that moment was only to my family; at this brief moment of sharing a victory, I had lost my own private world.

In the void that followed it was beyond my imagination that I could before long meet someone who would create a wonderful family and home for us which endures and gains in strength and warmth more than 30 years later.

---

*Deputy Chief Test Pilot of Hawkers.

*Kriegsgefanger — POW.

# Gloster Meteor

During the early months of 1944 rumours were rife on the subject of jet fighters. Intelligence reports showed increasingly frequent references to sightings of Me262s and 163s over Germany with their reportedly fabulous performance. In this country it was known that the Meteor I was having a difficult time in development and was being subjected to special attention by the RAE at Farnborough. Additionally a new and very secret development was heard to be going on at Hatfield, and one day when on a test flight from Hawkers at Langley I had seen a spidery twin-boom single-seater quite literally snaking through the sky at a speed which was well beyond the capabilities of my Typhoon. This was the prototype DH Vampire.

With the Tempest operational and much going on across the Channel in May and June we had heard no more about the Meteor until shortly after the beginning of the V1 flying bomb battle in which my Tempests were heavily involved. I then learnt that 616 Squadron were moving in to Manston with Meteors commanded by Andrew Macdowell, 'to counter the flying bomb'. This was interesting as although the Tempest V was doing well against the V1s, greater speed could clearly be an advantage.

Making contact with Manston I was told that, as was only to be expected with a new aircraft, there were serviceability problems. A few days later I flew across from Newchurch and taxying over to the East side of the airfield, parked my Tempest alongside two of these brand new jets. It ought to have been an impressive experience but somehow it was not. The low, thin-fuselaged, blunt-nosed profile was not enhanced by an awkward looking high tail, with two bulges at mid-wing on either side were distinctly more reminiscent of beer barrels than of aerodynamically-refined engine nacelles.

Macdowell's briefing was simple and casual. The Meteor it appeared was a straightforward aeroplane in most respects but had some limitations as a fighter. It was slow to accelerate and decelerate and it was very fast — but by the time it had reached its maximum IAS of about 480mph it was fuel-limited and needed to land! I was warned to expect a long take-off and flat climb and to give myself plenty of room on the approach to get the speed off.

The cockpit with its deep hole effect and upright sitting position was surrounded by the heaviest iron-to-glass ratio windscreen and canopy structure I had seen on a fighter since the early Typhoon. All this coupled with control runs creaking with static friction did little to improve the first impression. But the engines were a different matter. The starting cycle began with a mild whine followed by a dull boom of light-up and then only a subdued, smooth hum as idling RPM stabilised. It was difficult for a hardened piston engine pilot to believe that an engine was running at all with none of the usual heavy propeller and engine vibrations or acrid exhaust gases, and only steady figures on the engine instruments and a smell of paraffin to prove it. With the second engine lit, taxying was a dual experience of new sensations. The tricycle undercarriage eliminated any difficulties and tendency to swing and provided vision completely uninhibited by the nose, but getting going at all required a large proportion of the available power and a comparatively long wait while the Derwents wound themselves up. By the time we had reached Manston's long runway I had come to several conclusions about this aircraft, most of them uncomplimentary. Take-off was completely undramatic with a quiet hum from the turbines and the tricycle undercarriage running true until the nosewheel lift speed — in later years to be jargonised as 'rotation' — was eventually reached. A strong pull was needed here and as the Meteor whistled into the air it was immediately apparent that its control forces on all axes were heavy, even at low speed while the undercarriage was retracting.

With power set at max continuous we lumbered quietly round the circuit gaining speed and height slowly until at 4,000ft, realising that this was no Tempest or Spitfire in climb performance. I levelled out to gain speed while checking gunsight and safety catch as this flight over Kent would be well into 'Flying Bomb Alley' which Sector Control radio advised was currently active. With the nose slightly down speed increased steadily with no fierce acceleration to about 480mph IAS, faster than I had been in level flight before and still increasing. The engine noise level was imperceptible beneath the rising airflow noise and the stiffening controls confirmed that we were not only going fast but that we had no operational manoeuvrability worth mentioning at that point. Throughout this acceleration a small-amplitude short-period directional oscillation had been apparent, and this was a case of 'classic snaking' which would clearly affect gun aiming.

The fuel gauges were already below 'half' and so it was necessary to haul this projectile round and aim it back at Manston, slowing down on the way to check at low speed the basic stability and control responses which proved to be conventional. A long, flat approach to Manston with the turbines humming quietly was the only pleasurable part of the sortie, except for the landing. This was simple with a pleasantly responsive elevator flaring to a gentle touchdown on the soft-action main undercarriage, followed by the still unfamiliar pitching on to the nosewheel for a nose-down full vision landing roll with no swing at all. It had been an interesting experience and I was readily convinced that gas turbines would become the power for the future when more thrust could be made available. In the meantime it seemed that the Meteor could be regarded as a useful test bed for its jet engines but not by any measure as suitable for fighter

*This page:* Meteors of
616 Squadron at Manston,
Summer 1944.   *IWM*

operations as they were at that stage of the war. Furthermore I felt that the cumbersome twin engine, high tail configuration was unlikely to be capable of development into a truly effective fighter aeroplane, although with greatly increased power/weight ratio it might make a useful interceptor/bomber destroyer.

In the final outcome, despite praiseworthy efforts by the squadron, the operations carried out with the Meteor from Manston were in the nature of window-dressing. Only 23 V1s were destroyed in the whole Meteor operation. Similarly when they moved out to the Dutch bases in the last months of the war these aircraft did not have significant success against the multiplicity of air and ground targets then available.

In subsequent developments with increased power later marks of Meteor gave good peacetime service in the RAF while remaining heavy, relatively unmanoeuvrable and curiously unsuitable for their intended role as front-line fighters. With stable and docile general handling qualities, however, they gave good service for hack duties such as target towing, instrument rating training and weekend transport for the next two decades.

Meantime I was delighted to remain on Tempests, but after the war in 1946 I took part in developing the Mk IV Meteor at Gloster's airfields Brockworth and Moreton Valence. This work led to an interesting series of tests on a special Mk IV prepared for an attack on the world's airspeed record in the summer of that year.

The aircraft, EE 549, had uprated engines and a strengthened canopy, and it was hoped to achieve a comfortable margin with it over the exciting record of 606mph set by Wilson and Greenwood in a special Meteor III in the previous year. The rules required that the aircraft's speed should be observed over a measured course at low level as the mean of two runs in opposite directions. As the RAF were to carry out the attempt with a special High Speed Flight formed at Tangmere for the purpose, it fell to Gloster's as the Contractor to clear the aircraft under test conditions so as to provide a margin of safety above the Service requirement.

An increase of at least 10mph was needed to set a new record and so we programmed a limited handling clearance

to 620mph (true) or more if possible. In a series of exhilarating low flights down the Severn estuary from Moreton Valence in June and July of 1946 at times rendered difficult by heavy turbulence, we established that 612-618mph TAS (depending on the air temperature at the time) was practical at 100ft or so in level flight. Clearing a handling margin above this was less easy as it was apparent that at these speeds the Meteor was encountering the onset of compressibility trim effects in addition to buffet vibration and very loud airflow noise round the cockpit. In shallow dives from about 1,500 to 100ft over the mudflats, passing Avonmouth and Weston-super-Mare in seconds, the controls at upwards of 600mph were already heavy and slow in response and levelling out required a two-handed pull on the stick.

I was determined however to establish the optimum condition which might be encountered by the High Speed Flight. In a final sortie on 9 July, after a run at about 600mph down to 150ft to check atmospheric conditions which proved smooth and ideal in very hot sunny weather, I pulled the Meteor up in a wide climbing turn to the west over the Severn off Avonmouth. After tightening down the harness adjusters and checking instruments, I set up a diving turn at full power from 2,000ft back down the Severn from the Aust ferry at approaching the handling Mach limit for that height of 0.79. Straightening out over the mudflats with heavying controls we continued the shallow dive until passing 500ft at about 605mph indicated and increasing. With buffeting, wind roar, heavy vibration and near solid controls it was time to level out but at that moment the Meteor suddenly changed trim, pitching nose-down with the Machmeter touching 0.8.

With the two-handed pull that had now become vitally necessary to avoid bouncing off the Severn, I could not reduce power. There was a brief moment in which with

maximum possible pull force on the stick the Meteor continued its apparently unchangeable flight path down to what now looked like an inevitable impact point only seconds ahead. Then the nose began to rise and, at something under 100ft which seemed altogether too low for comfort at that speed, we levelled out with the ASI showing about 608mph.

The Meteor was not going to go faster than that at low level and survive. We returned rather gently to Moreton Valance for a somewhat sweaty debriefing with a very happy flight test engineer, Fred Sanders.

When corrected for position error, instrument error and met temperature (+27°C), the true speed achieved looked like 632mph. We were well satisfied that this had explored an adequate margin for the RAF attempt under official record conditions, and that a set Mach limit of 0.79 would keep them out of trim-change trouble at low level. But as often happens in the world of aviation, the facts were not allowed to remain plain. The following morning we were horrified to read headlines in the Press that Gloster's had reached 632mph beating the world's speed record, and naming the pilot.

In an excess of zeal Gloster's sales department had on hearing of this flight the previous night straight away telephoned the Press. We now had a situation in which the firm were seen to be claiming something before the customer had his opportunity to establish a record with his own equipment. It was all embarrassing and unnecessary. When Gp Cpt Teddy Donaldson subsequently set up a creditable

official record of 616mph in EE 549 from Tangmere later in the year he did not seem to appreciate our small part in it!

Finally after joining English Electric in 1947 I flew a Mk IV in an interesting programme of research into the effects of compressibility on high altitude intercept manoeuvrability. Even the Meteor IV had insufficient altitude performance to enable us to simulate realistically the manoeuvres which would be necessary for successful interception of the new B3/45 jet bomber under development at Preston. These tests were to lead directly to the establishment at Warton of Britain's first supersonic flight research and fighter development programme. The following reports tell their own story.

*Above:* RPB testing the record-breaking Meteor in 1947.   *BAe*

*Below:* The world's first speed record-breaking Meteor. Moreton Valance 1946. Pilots, Greenwood and Wilson.   *BAe*

## Report on the
## Handling and Performance at Altitudes
## above 40,000 feet

During the months of September, October and November 1947 a series of flights was carried out on Meteor IV, EE545, for the purpose of recording control forces at 40,000ft and above with varying CG positions, and during these some information of considerable interest with regard to the general problems was obtained. That the operation of conventional military aircraft at altitudes above 40,000ft will entail the overcoming of many obstacles not encountered in practice hitherto is not yet generally appreciated. The Meteor IV can provide some excellent examples of these obstacles by virtue of its ability to reach these altitudes with relative ease.

The operational ceiling of the aircraft is quoted as 49,000ft, but as conclusive evidence of controllability limitations has been obtained between 40-45,000ft, and as two thirds of the fuel available is used on a climb to ceiling necessitating upon arrival at that point an immediate descent, no attempt was made to obtain complete evidence over the last 3,000ft. Four check flights to between 46,000 and 47,500ft were, however, made.

Firstly it was found that at 40,000ft the aircraft suffers loss of elevator control in compressibility at $M=0.815^*$ or 248kt IAS (buffeting and instability occurring from $M=0.79$), and that it stalls at 220kt IAS, $M=0.74$, at $2\frac{1}{2}$g indicated.

Further, at this altitude the minimum speed at which the aircraft could be trimmed, but at which it could not be manoeuvred effectively in any way was found to be approximately 165kt, $M=0.68$. At this condition the stall occurred at $1\frac{1}{4}$g.

At 40,000ft therefore the aircraft has a practical speed range of only 60kt and manoeuvrability is reduced to gentle turns at accelerations up to $2\frac{1}{2}$g most carefully executed in order to avoid the inevitable stall from which recovery at this altitude is by no means the simple low altitude procedure for reasons described later.

This speed range is reduced to less than 40kt at 45,000ft and to even less with further increase of altitude.

Above 40,000ft operations in the Meteor are limited by:

(1) A narrow speed range diminishing with height.
(2) An acceleration range of $0-2\frac{1}{2}$g, again diminishing with height and with Mach No.
(3) Extreme sensitivity to angles of dive.

In this third case the sensitivity referred to is both a function of (1) and of the low drag of the aircraft, which allows a rapid increase in speed for relatively small angle of dive.

To describe a typical case. With the aircraft cruising at say 220kt, $M=0.745$, an almost imperceptible change of trim to about 5-8° nose-down will increase the ASI in a few seconds to 245kt or $M=0.81$, a rise of 0.065M for an increase of only 45kt and a change from cruising conditions to semi-loss of control in compressibility.

Complete loss of control occurs at 0.825M approximately, and the only way of ensuring that the aircraft does not reach this condition is never to allow a situation to occur in which the nose drops more than a few degrees below the horizontal for the following reasons.

*All references to Mach No are approximations of the Mach No except those quoted from flight reports.

In a case at these altitudes where the speed has risen to $M=0.79$ and is increasing owing to the attitude of the aircraft, the pilot has two courses of action open to him — (i) to reduce RPM or (ii) return the aircraft to level flight.

But (i) is impractical, for a reduction of RPM produces a pronounced nose-down moment and only aggravates the condition; and (ii) is often impossible as follows.

At $M=0.79$ the aircraft is pitching longitudinally, the elevator control is becoming progressively heavier and less effective until at $M=0.825$ (a rise of only 25-30kt in a matter of seconds) the nose drops away as elevator control is lost, dive is steepened and all control is lost at $M=0.84$.

At this point it may be said that application of the dive brakes at $M=0.79$ to $M=0.8$ has, in most cases, prevented complete loss of control by limiting the Mach No, but the effectivness of this action is governed entirely by the angle of the dive to which the aircraft is already committed before application of this control.

That this matter of angle of dive is the essence of the problem of operation at these altitudes may be seen from the following:

A fighter flying at 220kts IAS ($M=0.745$, true speed approximately 450kt) will have a bomber, flying at the same conditions and altitude, in sight for a relatively short period, and the final part of the curve of pursuit will, of necessity, take place through a sharp angle, sharper, that is, than is likely to be obtained at a maximum acceleration of $2\frac{1}{2}$g.

At the same time the overtaking speed of 50-100kt necessary for interception at lower altitudes is not available and a margin of, at the most, 25kt is left for this purpose owing to the limitation of compressibility, in addition to the fact that the increased Mach No reduces the available acceleration and therefore the effective curve of pursuit.

Therefore, in the case of the bomber having a compressibility limitation equivalent to that of the fighter, the curve of pursuit interception can no longer be executed.

In illustration of the narrow limits of control left to the pilot at these altitudes the following instances which occurred during the Meteor trials are quoted.

### (1) Flight No 15

'. . . A final attempt to attain 3g at $M=0.65$ at 41,000ft resulted in a stall and half flick roll during the recovery from which the nose dropped until a 30° dive was attained at about 40,500ft. The Mach No rose rapidly and at 0.80M indicated (0.825M true) the elevator became ineffective accompanied by considerable fore and aft pitching.

'By this time it had not been possible to reduce the angle of dive beyond 20°, and this steepened as elevator control was lost until $M=0.835$ indicated was reached (0.86M true) at about 38,000ft. At this point dive brakes were applied and by 31,000ft control was regained as Mach No dropped below 0.8.'

### (2) Flight No 17

'. . . After the last test speed was increased slightly to $M=0.74$ indicated (0.765M true) at 43,000ft and visual contact was discontinued while notes were checked.

'During this process apparently the nose fell away slightly as the aircraft suddenly began to produce the normal effects of compressibility and by the time recovery action could be taken the Machmeter registered 0.8 (0.825M true) and the elevator was becoming ineffective in the usual manner.

'As the nose was dropping uncontrollably it was necessary to reduce thrust, but as this would only produce a further heavy nose-down change of trim Mach Nos were once again reduced effectively by the use of dive brakes to M=0.8 (true) and control regained with the loss of only a few thousand feet on this occasion.

'During this episode an earlier impression was confirmed that in addition to the longitudinal control loss the aircraft suffers from a lateral oscillation in compressibility which can but be described as alternate tip stalling and can be felt through the ailerons, which, unlike the elevator, retain a small degree of control up to at least M=0.84 (true).'

From the foregoing, therefore, it would appear that:

(1)   The stall, a normal flight condition at lower levels, cannot be allowed to occur at these altitudes, for the angle of dive reached in recovery would result in loss of control in compressibility before level flight could be regained.
(2)   Dives to gain speed for interception are out of the question owing to compressibility.
(3)   Turning circle is limited to a very small acceleration range.
(4)   The margin of overtaking speed is limited already by compressibility. (In full throttle, level flight, the Meteor reaches 241kt IAS at 39,000ft, M=0.785, at which condition compressibility trim changes and pitching are already in evidence.)
(5)   The ability of the future fighter or bomber to operate closely to its limiting Mach No at high altitude, an obviously essential feature, will be limited to the extent to which thrust can be reduced in emergency, and more especially by the effectiveness of the dive/air brake or other speed reducing control with which it is fitted.
(6)   In future the ability of a fighter to intercept a bomber by the curve of pursuit method at upwards of 40,000ft will be governed entirely by two factors:
a  It must have a lower wing loading at the moment of interception and, therefore, a greater margin of manoeuvrability, and
b  it must have a higher Mach No limitation to enable it to overtake the bomber.

R. P. BEAMONT
November 1947

---

Memorandum from W. E. W. Petter
To W/C BEAMONT
Subject Meteor Flight Tests
Our Ref WEWP/EMC          Your Ref

Mr Ellis
W/C Beamont,
Mr Creasey.
RTO
18 Nov 1947

Following our recent conversation, and on further thought, I think it is very desirable that we should get in an interim report to the Ministry on the important discovery we are making of the high and low speed limitations of the Meteor at altitude. This, for the following reasons:-

1    We are establishing that the Meteor is entirely useless for interceptions at heights exceeding 40,000ft. It is essential that this should be known by the Air Staff and a suitable fighter produced, if one is not already in hand, if there is to be any chance of dealing with bombers such as the B3/45.

2    It gives us a chance to demonstrate to ourselves and the Ministry that the B3/45 will be considerably better in regard to these limitations, both high and low speed.

3    It reinforces the case for getting on with the B35/46 design as proposed by us, rather than waiting for several years to obtain a few more knots, since the chances of intercepting, even at our cruising speed and altitude, seem to be pretty remote.

4    It demonstrates a valuable piece of research flying and allied thinking.

I attach a very rough draft and curve showing the form which I think this report might take. The figures shown are not exact and I would ask Mr Ellis to revise these and get a realistic curve for discussion by all of us as soon as possible, and after the minimum number of further essential flights.

Copy to: Mr Page.                          Chief Engineer,
                                          Aircraft Division.

From: Group Captain G. Silyn-Roberts, AFC,
                Experimental Flying Det,
                        Royal Aircraft Establishment,
                        South Farnborough, Hants.
                        18 Dec 47.

Dear Petter,
Very many thanks for your letter of 15 December, enclosing your paper on the High Altitude Flying Tests you have carried out on the Meteor IV. I was most interested, particularly as in the operational requirement stage of the B3/45 some three years ago, I drew the attached curves in order to illustrate to DOR quite unofficially that there appeared to be a theoretical limit to the operational height of present-day aircraft bounded by the limiting Mach No and the stalling speed. You will recall about the same time that we had some difficulty over putting across the idea that an

aeroplane designed to operate at very high altitude could be built economically in structure weight only if it was accepted that factors could be lowered, so that full fighter factors would be realised at operational height whilst something akin to bomber factors would be realised at low altitude.

It seems to me that until we have gone through the sonic barrier the only possible relief is in the direction of lower wing loadings.

Again thank you very much and best wishes for Christmas and the New Year.

Yours sincerely,
(Sgd) Silyn Roberts.

Air Ministry,
King Charles St,
Whitehall, SW1
18 December 1947

My dear Petter,
Thank you very much indeed for your letter, WEWP/EMC/43/1 dated 15 December 1947, to which you attached the notes discussing the results of the high flying tests which you have been making with the Meteor IV.

These are of very great interest indeed, and I hope you do not mind, but I have made extracts and passed them on to Fighter Command because I think that they will be invaluable.

As you know, we are doing interception experiments at CFE in an endeavour to obtain some basic data for use in the future and so far these tests have been carried out at 35,000ft. It is obvious, however, that they will be running into a very different story when they go higher. A warning such as these notes will save them a lot of trouble.

Thanking you once again and wishing you a very happy Christmas.

Yours sincerely,
(Sgd) J. Boothman.

Royal Aircraft Establishment,
South Farnborough,
Hants
18 December 1947

Our Ref: Aero F/MBM/126.
Your Ref: WEWP/EMC/43/1.

W. E. W. Petter, Esq,
The English Electric Co, Ltd

Dear Petter,
Limitations on High Altitude Flying.
Flights on Meteor IV Aircraft

Many thanks for the notes enclosed with your letter of 15 December 1947. The results obtained are of very great interest to us, and we would welcome being kept in close touch with the experiments.

I feel that you are doing a first class piece of exploratory work, and the pilot in particular deserves congratulations for the able way in which he is tackling a very tricky job. I am sorry I was unavoidably away from the RAE when he recently visited us.

With best wishes for Xmas and the New Year,

Yours sincerely,
(Sgd) M. B. Morgan,
Superintendent,
Aero Flight Section.

Ministry of Supply,
P.D.S.R. (A),
Millbank,
London, SW1
2 July 1948.

Dear Petter,
We shall shortly be sending to you officially requirements for a design study which we should like you to prepare of a transonic aircraft.

This design is intended in the first place to obtain research

information at speeds from M=1 to M=1.4, and I think it is unlikely that the aircraft in its first form will be suitable for operational use. We shall however, be asking for alternative designs, one accommodating cannons and the other without. We shall also be asking for alternative designs with and without seat ejection.

The choice of power plant for this aircraft will be dominated by the endurance of the aircraft. We are asking for sufficient fuel to provide for take-off, climb to operating height (45,000ft), 10 minutes full throttle and 15 minutes economical cruising. We are also asking for descent under power to sea level, and a reserve of 80 gallons.

I should like you to look into this question and let me know whether you will be prepared to undertake a design study. I am very anxious to go ahead with the construction of a transonic aircraft on these lines as quickly as possible, and should therefore like to have the alternative design studies within the next three months. After receiving the various design studies I hope we shall be able to go ahead with two designs placed with different firms.

Mr Vessey could let you have more information on what is required if you wish, but I hope I have given enough in this letter to help you to decide whether you would like to go ahead or not. I should be grateful for an early reply.

Yours sincerely,
(Sgd) H. M. Garner.

ROYAL AIRCRAFT ESTABLISHMENT,
FARNBOROUGH,
HANTS.
DRAE/27                                18 October 1948.

Dear Petter,
Very many thanks for your letter of 14 October, enclosing three copies of your report on your flight work at high altitude. This is a most valuable piece of work, especially in view of the projects now under development.
Kindest regards,
Yours sincerely,
(Sgd) W. G. A. Perring.

E. W. Petter, Esq,
The English Electric Co, Ltd,
Aircraft Division,
Warton Aerodrome,
Nr Preston.

*Below:* The second record-breaking Meteor EE 454. Summer 1946. *IWM*

# North American XP-86

During a Ministry-sponsored visit to America in 1948 to gain experience of experimental jet bombers and fighters prior to the forthcoming B3/45 (Canberra) trials programme, I first carried out the required visit to the British Joint Services Mission in Washington and there heard the latest information on the military prototype scene. It was thought that the Boeing B-47 and Martin B-48 would not be available for me, but that the B-45 Tornado might be at the North American base at Muroc Lake in California. Also I would be able to fly a P-80 Shooting Star and a P-84 Thunderjet at Wright Patterson Air Force Base.

The thought of Muroc was intriguing as I knew that North American had the prototype XP-86 (later named Sabre) there on its initial programme which had begun less than six months previously, and which had just received world-wide publicity as being the first military aircraft to reach supersonic speed and the second aircraft only in the world to achieve this, the first being the Bell X1. With nothing to lose I approached W. Perring, the Director of the RAE who was in Washington at the time, with the suggestion that some flight experience of this aircraft would be more valuable than the rest of my programme put together. He agreed to try it on with the Pentagon. I continued with the planned programme, flying a P-80 and a P-84 at Wright Field. I surged the engine of the former badly when trying to overshoot from the first landing which had burst a tyre. This did not improve my standing as a 'limey' visitor with the redoubtable Colonel Al Boyd who commanded the Flight Test Centre. His response when I went to report the affair next day was to say, 'Don't apologise — it's a sign of weakness'! He was not too anxious to let me continue with the P-84/Thunderjet but was persuaded by USAF test pilot Major Dick Johnston. Johnston later became Chief Test Pilot of General Dynamics and project pilot of the F-102, F-106, B-58, and F-111 programmes.

The test pilots at Wright Patterson were a collection of enthusiasts who later made great names in American military test flying — Johnston, Pete Everest and Russ Slegh. It was interesting to find that they had a great respect for British standards in military and test flying. My performance in the P-80 hardly came up to expectations, but the Wright Field test pilots continued to give me full support and this probably had a critical effect on subsequent events.

Successfully negotiating the P-84 which I flew from Wright Patterson on a cloudy day, I was glad of its radio compass. It enabled me to fly a full flight envelope in a strange environment with unintelligible RT and out of sight of the ground, solely by reference to bearings to the Wright NDB.

Navigation aids were not often found in fighter aircraft at that time and I was impressed with the degree of self-reliance which a radio compass could give.

On the following day I was to fly from Dayton to Muroc, and that night a signal came from Washington confirming 'flights as necessary' in a B-45 and possibly one-only flight in the second prototype XP-86. This was really good news and I resolved to make the most of it.

The flight to California in a World War II B-25 North American Mitchell was notable for the din (I had no helmet) and for 2,000 miles of sunshine and magnificent visibility. No maps were visible in the cockpit and navigation was solely by 'beacon-hopping' with the radio compass. Muroc Air Force Base, the embryo Edwards of today, consisted only of a group of buildings and a hangar in the middle of a vast white salt lake. It had two exceptionally long runways marked out on the lake bed, and another group of buildings on the north side at the North American base.

As the B-25 joined circuit in the late evening sun I could see, standing out against the white concrete apron at North American, a squat shape with highly swept wings which I did not immediately recognise. It was the XP-86 and at that moment the one aircraft in the world I wanted to fly more than any other.

After a briefing by North American's project pilot on the 86, George Welsh,* and the flight test engineers, I was scheduled to fly at 7.00am on the following day. The briefing had covered current limitations and what would be practical in a single sortie and it had included brief references to the corner points achieved only recently of 650mph at low level (establishing a new world speed record) and Mach 1 at 28,000ft in a dive. Stability and control was said to be adequate in both conditions. So, while my new North American friends were suggesting a climb to 30,000ft to conserve fuel, then a shallow dive to Mach 0.9 followed by general handling in the descent and a high-speed run to about 575mph at 2,000ft before rejoining circuit with X lb reserve of fuel, I was already working out a possible alternative. This was to be a unique flight and certainly the first opportunity for a British pilot to see at first hand what supersonics were all about.

Later in my quarter instead of getting in as much sleep as possible prior to rising again at 5.00am, I went back over my briefing notes and worked out fuel consumptions for a number of different flight patterns. The issue could be critical and the XP-86 was far too important an aircraft to be put at risk, especially under these conditions by a 'guest' pilot. Nevertheless it seemed to me that there would be no navigation problems in the clear air over the Mojave Desert. It should, therefore, be practical to climb in a wide circle round Muroc to about 35,000ft learning as much as possible

*Killed in 1953 when a prototype F-100 Super Sabre ran out of $N_v$ under supersonic roll-coupling conditions.

*Above:* The XP-86 over the Mohave desert in 1948. Pilot George Welsh. *North American Aviation*

about the handling in the ten minutes this would take, then dive as fast as possible to 20,000ft. Following this manoeuvrability and slow-speed handling could be assessed while descending round the dry lake and at 10,000ft a decision could be taken on whether there was sufficient fuel remaining for a maximum speed run over the low level course marked out on the lake.

This worked out well in the event. As we drove out over the desert to the North American hangar in the brilliant orange dawn light I felt confident that it would, but that it would be inappropriate to mention these plans in detail to my hosts. During the strapping-in procedures and pre-flight checks I became uncomfortably conscious of a problem — the sun glare on the blazing whiteness of the salt lake floor was difficult to cope with without dark glasses. The tinted visor on the rather cumbersome 1948-style USAF helmet did not seem a practical alternative — at least for take-off and landing. This proved to be the only embarrassment in flying the XP86.

The large roomy cockpit had a rather haphazard lay-out of instruments and controls, the windscreen was too far forward and restricted vision by British fighter standards. The foot-operated rudder pedal brakes were a little difficult to use after our lever-operated systems. Aside from these minor criticisms the aircraft was simple and straightforward to fly. Its 'solid' and rather 'dead' feel at low speeds longitudinally was immediately reminiscent of its stable predecessor, the P-51 Mustang of World War II fame; but there the similarities ended. Lateral control by power-boosted ailerons was over-sensitive at low speed and produced a spectacular rate of roll up to high combat speeds. In prototype form the XP-86 was underpowered. Its take-off and climb were unimpressive by comparison with the Meteor IV with which I was then accustomed, but its acceleration in the dive was a new experience. One could readily appreciate that with a bigger engine this would become a first-rate fighter with performance possibilities in excess of 100mph more than the current straight-winged jets.

Mach 0.95 was reached quickly in a shallow dive at about 27,000ft but, as briefed, compressibility effects could be felt in the form of mild buffeting and lateral trim changes. A moderate increase in the dive angle produced no more speed increase — the drag rise was clearly making itself felt. With fuel state adequate and no navigation problem as Muroc dry lake was directly underneath I decided to go for the bull's-eye. I zoom-climbed back to 33,000ft for another level acceleration to 0.9 while monitoring the rising JPT with throttle adjustments within the briefed limits. This engine sensitivity and extra pilot work-load to control it was unusual. From the earliest days of jet engines Boscombe Down standards had required the UK engine manufacturers to provide automatic engine temperature limitation. This facility together with surge-free handling characteristics throughout the practical operating portion of the flight envelope, rendered British military jet engines superior to their American counterparts at the time and for many years subsequently.

After a final check round the cockpit — and with a conscious thought that although supersonic flight had been done before in this aircraft it had not been done often and I did not know how thoroughly, — I rolled away down-sun to avoid the glare and into a dive of about 30°. By 30,000ft the Machmeter registered 0.98 and there was some buffeting and right-wing-low trim-change. I trimmed this out with the stick trim-switch and still at full power pushed the nose down further.

At 0.99 the right wing wanted to go down further and a nose-heavy trim-change began to show and then with the altimeter unwinding rapidly, buffeting suddenly reduced. The M-meter showed 1.01 and on commencing the pull-out I found longitudinal stick force much increased and response in pitch quite low; but the latter returned quickly to normal as I throttled back and the speed came off fast in the transonic high-drag region. As no Machmeter/ASI 'jump up' had

59

occurred (or I had not seen it) it was probable that we had not gone fully supersonic, but we had undoubtedly reached transonic speed and with the fuel state reducing fast and much work yet to be done that had to be enough.

In a leisurely spiral descent to 12,000ft general handling and approach to the stall proved straightforward and confidence-making. Then the fuel decision point was reached and there was just suffiicient for a high-IAS run. At full power the remaining height was lost in a diving turn to line up with the five-mile black oil line marking the measured speed run across the lake bed, and during the turn power had to be eased momentarily to restrain this eager fighter. At 600mph and 500ft the XP-86 was rolled smoothly and precisely out on to the straight and again with full power held down to about 300ft AAL* as the ASI wound quickly up to 650. Bringing power back smoothly this condition was held for an exhilarating few seconds across the desert under precise and responsive control though with a fairly high level of noise disturbance going on. Then it was time to ease off in a quiet and relatively gentle climbing turn round into the landing pattern. With the fuel now looking on the low side I slowed to undercarriage speed. Handling in the approach was impeccable — I had got used to the lateral sensitivity. I did not appreciate the poor forward view permitted by the heavy windscreen frames and panel laminates. Here was another military aircraft with the glass/iron ratio all wrong looking forward (although vision to the rear was good) in the pattern which developed in the post-war decades. Vital combat vision was being sacrificed in the interests of structural integrity and manufacturing convenience as speed demands increased.

Descending towards the landing area on the salt lake bed, dazzling white in the morning sun, it became apparent that landing judgement might be difficult. In fact after passing 200ft at about 150mph depth perception was virtually lost. It said much for the basic stability and control that a very passable arrival was achieved by gently flaring and easing power back until, with nose high and 125mph on the ASI, the mainwheels rumbled on the salt and we were there.

To a pilot straight out from a dull UK June the intensive reflected sun glare and lack of contrasting features made Muroc a uniquely difficult area for the judgement of distances. I even found it rather difficult when taxying back to the North American base to be sure of avoiding obstructions.

There was a mixed reception in debriefing when I said that the aeroplane had behaved so well as to enable me to take a look at the two corner points — it had not been specified that I should not do so, but then again it had not been specifically said that I could. Some repercussions were to follow from this flight and that it was to attract interest was very soon evident when on leaving North American I was taken over to the USAF Officers' Club for some refreshment. As we entered, a brick-red suntanned USAF captain appeared and my escorting officer said 'I'd like you to meet Chuck Yeager'. Advancing with the traditional cheerful grin and outstretched hand I met a strong stare which after a while looked away with the words 'Is this the Limey that's been flying the 86!'

This courageous test pilot who had only recently become the first man ever to fly faster than sound and survive, in the Bell X1 rocket research aeroplane, had not apparently been afforded the opportunity to try the XP86 and was understandably rather sore about it!

*Above Airfield Level.

60

---

Flight report on North American No 2 XP-86, No 598, at Experimental Flight Test Section, North American Aviation, Muroc Lake, California, on 21 May 1948

There was no possibility of more than one flight in this aircraft and, therefore, an attempt had to be made to gain a large amount of information in a short period of time. The following is a description in chronological order of the main events of the flight.

*Take-off*

This was made with 30° of flap and slats open. Initially some difficulty was experienced in lining up for take-off owing to the fact that the nosewheel castoring action was hindered by the crust of the lake bed at slow taxying speeds. Nosewheel steering, which was not connected, will eventually eradicate this.

Acceleration was slow as the aircraft is underpowered with the TC.180 engine. The nosewheel was lifted at 110mph and the aircraft flown off smoothly and easily at 140mph at a sharp angle of attack.

Retraction of the undercarriage required considerable trim adjustment, nosedown, and this was accomplished simply with use of the stick slide-switch controlled horizontal stabiliser. The ailerons were very sensitive on take-off and the aircraft could be rocked laterally with them from 110 upwards. Slats were locked at 350mph and the climb started at 380mph IAS. The climb to 35,000ft at full power (controlled to JPT) occupied some 15 minutes and this was used generally to assess the pilot's position, control 'feel', etc.

Briefly, impressions gained were as follows:

Controls are well harmonised. The cockpit layout is quite good. Visibility is good to the side, above and rear, but poor forward for the type, owing to the heavy structure of windscreen and quarter panel frames.

The aircraft handled excellently and one did not have any reason to feel that the airframe was other than perfectly orthodox.

At 35,000ft, 255mph IAS the gallons-left counter showed 250 galls US (JP 700° at maximum power). It was, therefore, impracticable to continue to 40,000 as planned, and tests were begun from this point.

Speed was increased to $M=.85/30,000$ft. At $M=.9/29,000$ft aileron and rudder control were excellent and a 10lb elevator force reversal was in evidence, nose up. This was held until another reversal occurred returning trim to normal at about $M=.94$, and at $M=.97/23,000$ft a further reversal had produced a heavier nose up moment which was comfortably trimmed out with the stabiliser.

A further run was made from 36,000ft and according to the Mach Meter unity, or a little over was reached at 29,000ft, partially trimmed with a slight lateral roll in evidence and with some minor buffeting at the tail. The aircraft was perfectly comfortable at this condition.

The drag rise does not make itself really apparent until $M=.95-.96$ is reached, at which point the dive angle must be increased considerably for further increase in speed.

Before descending, $3\frac{1}{4}$G was pulled at $M=.88/30,000$ft and only minor buffeting was felt at this point. A steady dive was then carried out at $M=.85$ from 28,000ft to 10,000ft at a shallow angle and approximately 80% power. The controls were used vigorously and with fighter manoeuvrability effect at these conditions.

The dive brakes, operated by slide switch on the throttle, were operated during this dive at $M=.85/20,000$ft. Reaction was smooth with a 10-15lb nose up moment and deceleration rapid.

At 10,000ft speed was reduced and the machine stalled in the 'Clean' condition, slats locked 'in'. Stability approaching the stall was of a surprisingly high order; sensitive aileron control remained to the last and after a gentle but adequate stall warning buffet beginning at 140-45, the stall occurred at a very steep angle of attack at 131mph. The right wing tended to drop, but this was held easily and recovery affected in approximately 1,200ft without any attempt to cut things fine. By this time fuel was becoming low and some high indicated speed runs were made to the lake.

During a circuit of the north base at 560-580mph all controls appeared to be so adequate as to give an impression of flight at a much lower speed, and for this reason I decided to make a fast run across the high speed course up to the speed at which the tail parachute castings under the stabiliser should begin to set up buffeting.

As soon as the aircraft was turned on to course at 580 and height lost to 3,000ft (ASL) at full throttle, the aircraft accelerated remarkably quickly in the shallow dive and the ASI soon reached 650mph. Power was reduced and the aircraft eased up out of the rough air at this point again without any control difficulties other than the necessity for use of the horizontal stabiliser as the elevator stick forces were rather high.

Immediately following this 600mph IAS was held in a turn and through several quarter rolls to assess controllability under these conditions. This was of a very high order indeed.

Fuel shortage made a landing imperative at this point, and this was carried out in a normal 'Spitfire approach' manner, keeping power at 80% and speed at 1.4X stalling until well into the final approach.

At this point I remembered that I had not unlocked the slats, but having stalled satisfactorily without them, I continued the landing, touching down easily at 140mph and by trimming the stabiliser fully 'tail down' held the nosewheel off until 100mph was reached.

The brakes applied at 90mph were smooth and powerful and were held full on from 70mph to standstill without subsquent overheating.

There was no tendency to fading and the firm's Test Pilot says that the brakes, which are of the multiple disc type, may be used fully from the moment of touch down without over-heating.

Judgement of distance on the dry lake was difficult, but on this occasion the landing run, which could have been shortened, was of the order of 16-1,800yd from touch down, which occurred approximately on the aiming point. The use of slats would have reduced the landing speed by 10mph or more.

*General Notes*

1  The TG.180 suffers from lack of acceleration and deceleration and over sensitivity to throttle movements at all altitudes. In all handling characteristics it compares unfavourably with the obsolescent Derwent and Goblin. With its doubtful 4,000lb SLT the aircraft is underpowered.

2  The overlarge ailerons provide lateral control even during the take-off runs and are inclined to be over sensitive on take-off in the hands of the new-comer. With power boost they provide an exceptional measure of control up to high IAS's and Mach No. Rates of roll were not taken owing to the X category of the aircraft. But the impression gained was that they would compare with the P-84 (360/3½secs) at 500mph and out-roll it at 600mph IAS by a fair margin.

3  Longitudinal trimming by the stick-switch operated adjustable stabiliser is satisfactory throughout the range of speeds and Mach Nos which I was able to experience. At altitude at high Mach Nos it is not too sensitive, but provides that rapid trim adjustment which is an essential flight control under such conditions. At lower levels it is, of course, slower in operation, but adequate.

4  At no time in the flight could I detect snaking, though without a gun sight assessment of the flight path is difficult.

5  Apart from the obvious ones of the high Mach No/ASI, the most significant feature of this aircraft is, I feel, its ability to be manoeuvred operationally at Mach Nos of .9 and more, even to the extent of quite high accelerations, and rates of roll.

A further flight to 40,000ft in this connection to assess accelerated stability would have been of great value, but was not possible unfortunately.

6  The cockpit is generally a great improvement on previous US practice, in that the windscreen, IF panel, stick and engine controls are all appreciably nearer to the pilot, and some attempt has been made to achieve 'sense grouping'. There is still room for much improvement along the latter lines, however.

Two items rating special mention are the directly reflected Radar gunsight, which leaves unobstructed the view forward through the armour glass panel, and the flap selector lever which operates along a quadrant inboard of the power control, calibrated in degrees of flap setting. The lever action is smooth and the desired flap settings can be achieved progressively and instantaneously without the necessity for observation of another indicator or dial lever.

According to the NA test pilot this feature was very popular, but steps had been taken to provide a different system in production, for some reason unknown to him.

Engine Data
TG.180
Max rating: 4,000lb static (generally accepted as 3,800lb or less) at Airflow: 73lb/sec
rpm: 7,600
Turbine Temperature: 1,500°F
Compressor inlet temperature: 59°F

*General Notes*

The performances quoted above are makers' estimates for the TG.180 engine (3,800-4,000lb SLT). Therefore, with the TG.190 (general electric) giving 5,200 SLT and considerably more with methanol-water, there is no doubt that the performance will be more in keeping with the capabilities of the airframe. The aircraft flew for the first time with this engine during my visit, after one straight hop of about 3 miles on the lake. The pilot reported everything to be very satisfactory.

The next development, the XP86C is being prepared for great range. It will be equipped with the Pratt and Witney 'Nene' giving over 6,500lb with after burning, and is to carry 1,800galls (US). This will provide, in theory, a combat radius of 1,000 miles, including 5 minutes after-burning. An initial rate of climb is quoted at 13,000fpm and a gross take-off weight of 'approximately 20,000lb'.

*Spinning*

The spinning trials carried out during my presence and conducted with direct broadcast by VHF from the pilot, G. Welch, to the office of the Chief North American Flight Engineer, were apparently completely successful. They were taken to five turns each way, CG forward, on 19 May, and five turns each way, CG aft, on 20 May. The characteristics were described by the pilot as excellent, it being only necessary to take off a small amount of elevator from the fully up position for recovery within one turn. The spin is fast at about 1 turn/4 secs and the attitude nose well down.

*Mach No and High Speed Performance*

The North American Test Pilot has flown the aircraft to M=1.05 at 30,000ft at which point buffeting and longitudinal trim changes are in evidence, together with the lateral rolling tendency. Both can be trimmed out, and there may be a possibility of reaching a higher figure.

There has been a slight variation between the high Mach number characteristics of the two aircraft used so far.

Mach numbers of .96 at 15,000ft and 640mph IAS at 7,000ft have been reached without any sign of trouble, and it would appear that the figure of 650IAS at 3,000ft achieved in this flight was

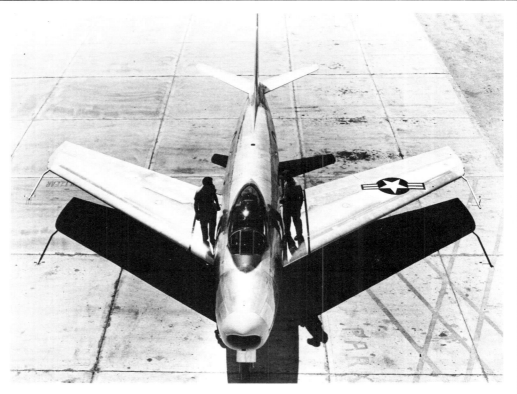

### XP-86 *flight report continued*

slightly higher than had been reached before. There was certainly no indication of trouble at that point.

At 30,000ft 3g has been applied at M=.92 and no great tendency towards buffeting reported.

No information is available yet with regard to accelerated stability above 40,000ft, but the general feeling seems to be that the very high range of usable Mach number will compensate for loss of $C_L$ with sweep back at altitude.

At least with adequate power it would appear to be assured of an adequate usable speed/g range up to 50,000ft, in spite of its relatively high wing loading.

### Cockpit

During my cockpit check-out I was agreeably surprised with the layout. The windscreen, instrument panel, etc, were far nearer to the pilot than is normal US practice. The stick is positioned so that it can be held with fore-arm on thigh, another unusual feature, while the instrument grouping was reasonably satisfactory in nearly every way.

In general it gives that feeling of being one with the machine, so essential for the full confidence and, therefore, efficiency of the pilot, and so often lacking in modern aircraft.

This particular aircraft was fitted with a 'radar reflecting gunsight', which was fitted below the foot of the front armour glass panel and did not interfere with forward view in any way (TA-1A radar Range Finding GS +AN/APG-5A (M×215).

The cockpit pressurisation sealing appeared to be a little primitive, much use being made of a bostik compound everywhere. The system was not connected and I could not check its operation. North American say they are experiencing very considerable trouble with all aspects of cabin pressurisation, especially in connection with the XB-45. They have, of course, only just begun.

Pressurisation is by airflow from the final stage of the compressor at 10lb/min for 'full cool' or 14lb/min for 'full heat', routed through an after-cooler and a turbine refrigeration pack or a bye-pass. Control is by thermostat.

No external de-icing arrangements are made, and internal de-frosting of the windscreen and single skin free-blown hood is by ducted hot air as above. It appears that North American have solved the problem, hitherto so accute in fighter circles in this country, of actually ejecting hot air from a heating system.

Externally the aircraft is well finished with the exception of the main intake duct. Inboard of the moulded nose ring this is a riveted tunnel, the skinning of which is of poor quality.

All aircraft are delivered unpainted as no fillers or paint suitable for use at high speed in rain, etc, have yet been developed.

### Services

Hydraulics are preferred by North American to electrics as they are, in their opinion, lighter, more flexible and 1/10th the cost. They have no interest in pneumatics.

(North American consider that 3,000lb pressure is high enough and troublesome enough for the moment, and they have had some success with aluminium hydraulic cylinders with chromium plated pistons, dust and dirt being excluded by means of micro-filters.)

### Conclusion

The P.68 is an outstanding aircraft in that
1   It can achieve Mach No exceeding unity.
2   It is fully operationally controllable at up to M=.97 at least, above 20,000ft and gives the impression of being even aerobatically controllable at M=.9.
3   It is more probably capable of development to IAS of 700mph or more.
4   With its extremely high performance capabilities, it is an unusually pleasant and straightforward aircraft to fly — possibly more so than most earlier jet fighters on both sides of the Atlantic.
5   It is not merely a research aircraft, in which field and that of record breaking it is likely to shine, but is a standard fighter aircraft in production for the USAF who should experience no functional difficulty in operating it

I could find no one who was prepared to suggest the effect of the firing of the six .50 MG's in the nose at M=1.

# The Supersonic Era

In the immediate postwar period the first generation jet fighters, Gloster Meteor, de Havilland Vampire, Lockheed Shooting Star and Republic Thunderjet, and the first jet bombers North American B-45, Boeing B-47, Martin B-51 and the English Electric Canberra were under development. They all encountered in varying degree at around 80% of the speed of sound 'compressibility' characteristics which were remarkably similar to those of the faster propeller-driven fighters. It was becoming apparent that the problems associated with stability and control at transonic speed were of a standard rather than of a random pattern. For example when an experimental project pilot on the Meteor IV prototype at Moreton Valance in early 1946, I had encountered buffet onset at about $M=0.79$, heavy elevator force at $M=0.8$ and wing dropping and nose heaviness with heavy buffeting above about $M=0.81$. In the Vampire these symptoms occurred earlier in the $M=0.75$ to $M=0.79$ range. It was also becoming clear that the relatively clean lines and low drag of the early straight wing jets were not enough in themselves to enable full use to be of the potential performance with the jet engine. The RAE and a number of firms in this country, and North American among others in the USA, were evolving solutions based largely on captured German information. It suggested swept-back wings with thinner sections as the path for the future. But while the aerodynamicists were confident that they knew about the behaviour of air flow at the speed of sound and how to deal with it, this knowledge had not yet reached hardware form. Pilots continued to experience buffeting, nose heaviness, wing dropping and loss in control effectiveness at high Mach number with each new aircraft. Only the critical Mach range varied between aircraft, not the basic symptoms.

What was happening, and this was well understood by the late 1940s despite popular impressions to the contrary, was that as the air flow compressed with increasing speed the aerodynamic centre of pressure moved aft giving a corresponding and powerful nose-down pitching moment. At the same time local shock waves reduced the effectiveness of elevator and aileron, in some aileron cases asymmetrically. Thus the pilot could gain a false impression that the more he pulled on the stick to recover from the dive the more the nose wanted to go down. Much interest developed at the prospect of swept wings but in 1947 tragedy struck. Geoffrey de Havilland was killed while exploring the transonic region in the DH 108. The 108 was an ambitious project incorporating the relative uncertainties of swept wing aerodynamics and tailless stability in one development. This did more than a little to cloud the issue of transonic controllability. Although the accident did occur under transonic conditions there was some doubt as to whether it was caused by the effects of compressibility or by the basic marginal longitudinal stability of the tailless configuration, or a combination of the two.

Plans for a supersonic research aircraft of a very viable concept inspired by the RAE and to be built by Miles were shelved by the 1945 Labour Government. The published grounds, erroneous on both counts, were that supersonic research flying would be too dangerous and could be done adequately with models. Thus Britain was left out of the running and by 1948 the USA had begun successful supersonic flight research in the Bell X1 flown by Chuck Yeager. It had also started the flight development programme of the world's first swept-wing transonic fighter, the North American P-86 Sabre. In spring 1948 when I flew the second prototype of this aircraft over the Californian desert it confirmed the sequence of symptons that we had been experiencing with minor variations over six years of flight research but with much less severity than with the straight-wing aircraft. The buffet onset was well delayed by the swept wings and did not occur until $M=0.93$; a nose-down trim change began at $M=0.95$ and then as $M=1.0$ was reached flight became smooth and on this aircraft control was retained albeit with some loss of effectiveness.

Aviation had arrived at a new threshold and the gateway was open! Meanwhile in England John Derry of de Havilland had been exploring the flight envelope of the second DH 108 which had been modified following loss of the first with Geoffrey de Havilland. By the time I returned from California he had reached $M=1.0$ in a dive — the first British aircraft and the third in the world to do so. The development of swept-wing fighters had continued rather more slowly at home and by this period only two programmes of importance had emerged. Hawker had produced the 1072, a swept-wing version of the 1067 with a conventional 'straight' tail, while Supermarine had yet to fly the prototype of the swept-wing Swift series.

Although having a critical Mach number slightly higher than the straight-wing fighters of the time the 1072 was limited by its 'straight' tail. Then in 1949 the Chief Test Pilot of Hawker, 'Wimpy' Wade, lost his life in the 1081 development of this prototype in a high-speed dive.

The English Electric design office had by 1948 become convinced that there was abundant evidence to show that if the wing was thin enough and swept enough with a thin, swept tailplane mounted low enough relative to the wing to minimise the effects of wake and down-wash at high incidence, the end result could be a fully supersonic aircraft with adequate and even good standards of stability and control at both high and low speeds. They began design work on such a vehicle under Ministry contract F23/1949 for a supersonic research aircraft suitable for development into a fighter. This was to be the predecessor of the Lightning. Much more, however, was to be heard in the field of supersonics before the Lightning arrived.

By 1951 the Supermarine Swift programme was underway and with it the Hawker Hunter, a fully-swept development of the 1072. Ultimately the Hunter was to become an all-time classic subsonic fighter/ground-attack aircraft. But then a new phenomenon appeared — the news media became aware of supersonics. Both the Hunter and the Swift had shown the by now conventional transonic compressibility characteristics in dives (like those of the Sabre) in the hands of Neville Duke and Mike Lithgow. Their arrival at the Farnborough display in 1951 was heralded with supersonic booms aimed directly at the crowd and this was repeated daily throughout the Show. Overnight, test pilots became supermen in the writings of the columnists and in the torrent of words from the 'air correspondents' and others. Their wives were subjected to earnest inquisitions on how they contrived to calm the shattered nerves of their supersonic husbands — luckily most of them merely said 'feed the brute'. Somehow the media failed to note that the state of the art had derived from many years of progressive development flying and was not a case of 'instant supersonics' in the '50s.

Supersonic flying had in fact been going on in America since 1947. Nevertheless the sun shone at Farnborough at the beginning of that decade and the media lost no time in making hay. By 1952 a film was produced named *Sound Barrier* which undoubtedly set out with sincerity to do justice to the subject. In the event however it proved to be such an extraordinary amalgam of factual inaccuracies sensationalism and poor taste as to have most probably caused at least some of the people listed as 'advisers' in the credits to be horrified at their part in it. For those of us in the business it was intriguing to see a Chief Test Pilot portrayed having hysterics in his office following a brush with 'compressibility'. But then which of us might not have done so if faced with the film's solution to the supersonic problem, to 'reverse the controls and push out of the dive'!

Nonetheless the film caught public imagination. Drama was heaped on drama and at the Farnborough display of 1952, the Pilots' Tent, normally a holy of holies reserved only for pilots and officials, was invaded by the producer of the film with most of his staff and cast. The atmosphere became charged with tension as boom followed supersonic boom and the film world clutched their drinks. Then real tragedy did strike in the accident to the DH 110 when structural failure occurred at a moderate speed in a tight turn killing Derry and Richards and a number of people in the crowd. There was then no way of convincing the film makers, press and radio that this was not yet another item in 'the fiercesome toll of the Sound Barrier'.

*Below:* Classic supersonic shape. P1. 1945.  *BAe*

This period of hysterical euphoria did much to provide the public with a distorted image of the calm, hard-working, stalwart individuals who had formed the hard core of transonic flight development over the span of years from 1942 to 1948 both in the air and on the ground. It was to be many years before this taint of sensationalism was overcome.

To many people even 20 years later, the phrase 'sound barrier' still conjured up a vision of a sensational and dramatic period in test flying. High subsonic exploration in the period 1942-48 was indeed a time of probing into the unknown. To the pilots most involved in this country including Philip Lucas and Ken Seth Smith of Hawker, Jeffrey Quill of Supermarine, Martindale and Zurakowski of the RAE and Geoffrey de Havilland of de Havilland, however, it had been all part of the fascinating job of aircraft development. They saw it as no more hazardous than other aspects of the work. In fact over the whole of the relevant period the fatal accidents which could be related in any way to transonic testing numbered significantly less than those incurred in routine flutter testing, structural testing, or spinning and other stability and control tests. The trial and error phase had ended with the successful introduction of the P-86 Sabre in 1948. This aircraft set the pattern for the compressibility characteristics of the first generation of high subsonic performance fighters with the transonic dive capability which followed it like the Hunter, Swift, Mystère and F-84F.

It was perhaps inevitable that the first public showing of aircraft capable of being dived at the speed of sound would attract ballyhoo. This in fact was still going on when the true supersonic era began in 1954 with the advent of fully supersonic fighter prototypes such as the F-100 in USA, the P1 in England and Super Mystère in France. Over the next few years new unknowns were resolved in the extension of performance to twice the speed of sound and in establishing on the way acceptable standards of systems engineering and stability and control in fully supersonic flight. This development in its turn bringing problems in lateral stability, inertia coupling, thermal effects and engine intake flow stability. These proved to be quite critical areas in fact and more accidents occurred in this phase before all the facts were established than in all the earlier probing up to $M=1.0$.

Finally by 1960 in the development programmes of the F-104, Lightning and Mirage, acceptable standards were achieved and set for $M=2.0$ operations in service and the way ahead for supersonic military aviation and for the supersonic airliner of the future had been established.

*Below:* Transonic shock-waves round a Lightning at low level.  *BAe*

# English Electric Canberra

Friday, 13 May 1949 ushered in a new era in aviation — that of the high altitude jet bomber — with the first flight of the English Electric Canberra.

There had been earlier attempts at this breakthrough in technology with the Arado 234, a German light jet reconnaissance bomber before the end of World War II, and the Martin XB-48, Boeing XB-47, North American B-45 and other American experimental prototypes in 1948. Without exception, however, these had combined inadequate power initially with excessive wing loadings which had resulted in severely limited operational performance in terms of altitude and manoeuvrability and, in most cases, range.

The Canberra prototype, VN799, with an initial test take-off weight of less than 30,000lb had a wing loading of about 27psf, and with 6,000lb thrust initial rating from each of the two Rolls RA1 engines a lively performance was expected. We were not disappointed. On initial tests it was even possible to carry out straight hops on the 1,900yd Warton runway to check three-axis stability and control response. These were completed satisfactorily up to 100kt, becoming airborne up to 15ft at around 85kt without even overheating the brakes during the resulting braking runs.

The first flight was in fact almost an anti-climax with no incidents or defects other than some sharp variations in rudder hinge moment and response. These resulted in modifications to the horn balance area before flight 2. So uneventful was flight 1 that with the limitation imposed by the suspect rudder there were very few events to record as can be seen from the flight report at the end of this chapter. The overriding impressions were of a straightforward and simple aeroplane with conventional stability and response to controls, exceptional smoothness and lack of high noise level from engine or aerodynamic sources. It had that indefinable impression of engineering and aerodynamic integrity that all pilots recognise in the description 'a pilot's aeroplane'. When these features were considered against the performance estimates for the BMk2 production standard — of range in excess of 2,000 miles, altitude above 50,000ft, speed greater than Mach 0.8 and IAS limit 500kt — our hopes that this would prove to be a world-beater grew to conviction. Within a short period these predictions had all been exceeded comfortably. We had dived a standard BMk2 to M=0.85, climbed to 55,000ft, and set new records for direct crossings of the Atlantic. These were followed subsequently by the first

*Far left, bottom:* 'TC' — the requisitioned garage in Corporation Street, Preston, which was English Electric's design office for the B3/45 Canberra in 1947.  *BAe*

*Above left:* Canberra prototype VN 799 on preparation for flight. April 1949, Warton.  *BAe*

*Left:* Roll-out clearance.  *BAe*

*Below:* Roll-out, 1949 style. *BAe*

*Top:* First engine run. Note rounded rudder and dorsal fin, both modified later. *BAe*

*Above and left:* Canberra prototype, first straight 'hops'.

*Below left:* Canberra Flight Certificate.

*Right:* First flight sequence to undercarriage retraction. 13 May 1949. *BAe*

## CERTIFICATE OF SAFETY FOR FLIGHT.

*From :—*                                    *To :—*

Inspector in Charge, A.I.D.,          The English Electric Co. Ltd.,
The English Electric Co. Ltd.,              Warton Aerodrome,
East Works, Preston, Lancs.              Nr. Preston, Lancs.

I HEREBY CERTIFY that the aircraft defined hereunder :—

| Type. | Engine(s). | Serial No. or Registration Mark. |
|---|---|---|
| B3/45 Prototype | RR.Avon R.A.2. | A13/A617963  A14/A617964   VN.799. |

has this day been inspected including the engine(s), the engine installation(s) and instruments and is in every way safe for the undermentioned flight(s) :—

Purpose of flight(s) Initial Taxying & Flight Trials in accordance with schedule of Flight Tests & Design Certificate dated 5/5/49.

Authority* Contract 5841/CB6(b).                                      To take place

from WARTON Aerodrome with Mr. R.P. Beamont. as Pilot.

NOTE.—Any alterations, repairs or adjustments made to this aircraft subsequent to the issue of this certificate renders it invalid, and no further flight may be made until the certificate is renewed.

Signed.                                                      Date.

1 INITIAL TAXYING (LESS SEAT CHARGES)          7TH May 1949
3 INITIAL TAXYING (LESS SEAT CHARGES)          8TH May 1949
2 TAXYING & HOPS (LESS SEAT CHARGES)          9TH May 1949
    & HOPS                                  11TH May 1949
5 Flight & Taxying &                         12TH May 1949
6 1ST Flight &                               13TH May 1949

(*13706—7251)  Wt.40659—3381  5M Pads 1/44  I.S. 700     *Contract, A.N.D., etc.

68

out-and-back crossing of the Atlantic in one day by any aircraft, this time in the Mk5 prototype VX185. One bonus resulting from this unique design concept of a bomber/reconnaissance aircraft with performance well in excess of current fighters was that in order to achieve adequate controllability at the maximum design speeds with conventional manually-operated controls, the latter turned out to be exceptionally powerful for a bomber aircraft in the medium and lower speed range. The predicted rate of roll of 45°/sec at 300kt and a normal acceleration limit of 5g were soon proved, and so we decided to take a look at aerobatics.

The idea did not meet with universal enthusiasm as some design people took the view that this was a bomber aeroplane and not to be trifled with. This view was also shared by the official inspection department. Both areas had to be reassured. We had first to explain the design capabilities relative to the comparatively unsophisticated manoeuvres we had in mind. Ultimately we had to remind the doubters that the official Ministry Approval of the Chief Test Pilot vested full responsibility in him for flight safety within the formal limitations once he had signed for the aeroplane.

A few of us in Flight Test had felt from early in the programme that if the aeroplane flew as well as predicted it would present us with a unique opportunity to exploit in public and sales demonstration a degree of manoeuvrability that had not been seen in a bomber aircraft since the Boulton and Paul Sidestrand of the '30s, or in jet bombers at all. And so it happened. One evening in July 1949 I took the prototype 799 discreetly away from the Warton area and began to develop quarter rolls progressively into 360° rolls, and similarly zoom climbs and wing-overs into the first half-loop and roll-off-the-top. The 360° rolls, gently barrelled in deference to the as yet untried negative 'g' qualities of the fuel system, felt smooth and elegant though demanding rather heavy wheelforce to sustain. Looping plane manoeuvres were a different matter. Elevator forces were high at the initial entry speed of 400kt, speed was slow to drop off and quick to recover on the way down with this very 'clean' design. The first time I committed the aeroplane to going over the top instead of winging over from a 45°-50° climb, I was very conscious of the value to the Country and to the Company and its employees of this prototype. I was now committing it to a manoeuvre from which it might enter a spin from an accelerated stall which we had not yet investigated, or suffer a number of other misfortunes including double engine flame-out if I did not get it right first time. I also remembered keenly that I could not expect universal support in such an outcome.

The Canberra sailed over the top easily first time having gained about 5,000ft in the process, and was rolled out at 220kt precisely as the nose came down on to the horizon having maintained full power all the way from the initial pull up. With practice 100kt or so was taken off the entry speed resulting in much tighter 'roll-offs' with height gains of 3,000ft or less. Ultimately we were able to get down to a bad weather drill at low fuel state for 'rolling off' under a 2,500ft cloud base. I practised a co-ordinated show linking rolls and rolls-off-loops with a semi-stall small radius turns and tight circuits at 4g/250kt in order to present as much of the aeroplane as often as possible in a few minutes. I then tried it out over Warton. There was much subsequent enthusiasm but already some critical rumours of 'hazarding a valuable prototype'.

If this attitude had gained ground there can be little doubt that an embargo could well have been placed on aerobatics in

*Left:* Low-level flypast of Canberra prototype on Flight 2. *BAe*

*Below:* Rudder modified after Flight 3. *Flight International*

*Left:* The Canberra team after First Flight. L to R: Don Crowe, Dai Ellis, Harry Harrison, Alf Ellison, Teddy Petter, RPB, Denis Smith, Freddy Page, Hugh Howat. *BAe*

this new generation military aircraft which might have had a lasting and significant effect on its future. So I played safe and only flew decorously when in sight of Warton for the remainder of the summer's test programme and divulged no detailed plans about the forthcoming public debut of the Canberra at Farnborough. Privately Dai Ellis, Chief Aerodynamicist, and Dave Walker, Chief Flight Test Engineer and the test observer who would be with me in any case, knew and enthusiastically supported the plot. Teddy Petter the Chief Designer had a twinkle in his eye and didn't want to know.

In the event, at the 1949 SBAC Display, the prototype's showing of performance and manoeuvrability, excelling at most points the year's crop of jet fighters, became a talking point in aviation circles and set the scene for the next few years. The Canberra became a popular feature of international air displays in the 1950s and we were called upon for much sales demonstration flying at home and abroad, in addition to the heavy test programme. Once the basic philosophy had been established of emphasising the low wing loading and the for that time high power-weight ratio by using relatively low speeds in keeping the aircraft low and close to the onlookers, the Canberra was an almost ideal demonstrator. Exceptionally good engine and airframe serviceability combined with docile handling and good cockpit visibility, especially in rain, enabled it to be flown as and where required with complete confidence — and sometimes with considerable added enjoyment when weather which proved too difficult for the other jets did not stop us. But it was never necessary to resort to tricks or marginal manoeuvres to attract attention. By frequent and hard practice, making opportunities at the end of almost every test flight, we established a balanced sequence from take-off to touchdown. It aimed at keeping as close to the onlookers as possible throughout, and ringing the changes only by varying speed and altitude within rolls, wing-overs, roll-off-loops, and fast and slow flypasts. The only exception to this strict rule of adhering to the conventions was that I used the trimming tailplane to relieve the heavy elevator control forces at high speed or in sustained turns. On occasions I also throttled the inner engine to achieve a 'cart-wheel' effect when winging-over from a steep climb after take-off back down the runway for the first low run. This manoeuvre used to intrigue Oliver Stewart, the SBAC commentary broadcaster, who reckoned

*Left:* Flying the first pre-production Canberra B2 over the Pennines in 1950. *BAe*

*Centre left:* Testing the Canberra to 450kt with canopy removed. 12 April 1951. *BAe*

*Bottom left:* The Canberra's first overseas demonstration. Antwerp 1950. L to R: J. Taylor, A. Sheffield, Strang Graham, Joe Sarginson, RPB, Bob Hothersal, Freddy Page, D. Davenport, Harold Chapman, Jack Potter. *J. Walton*

*Below:* B Mk8 close-up. August 1954. *BAe*

*Above:* Delivery of the RAF's first jet bomber, Binbrook 1951. RPB, Wally Sheen, Pat Connelly. *BAe*

*Left:* The RAF's first jet bomber squadron, No 101, Binbrook 1951. *Flight International*

*Below left:* Pat watches a Canberra demonstration by her husband at Warton with (left) Esme Watson, Tommy Evans and Peter Hillwood. *BAe*

*Top right:* Arrival at Gander, Newfoundland after record Atlantic flight, 31 August 1951. *Glenn L. Martin Co*

*Right:* Arriving at Martin Airport, Middle River, Baltimore, after the Atlantic record flight. Meeting the Martin Company President Glenn L. Martin. *Glenn L. Martin Co*

that it produced a radius of turn which looked less than 500yd.

Demonstration flying became a major feature in the early development period of the Canberra, but not without incurring some problems and disadvantages. Although possessing these remarkable qualities of manoeuvrability, performance and relative ease of operation under adverse weather conditions, it was primarily a bomber aeroplane with suitability matched control forces so that in fighter manoeuvres at fighter speeds control forces were very heavy indeed. Similarly the spring tab control system, while more than adequate for the specified task, was rather spongey and imprecise for some demonstration manoeuvres. These factors, when added to the greenhouse effect produced by the bubble canopy with no cool-air conditioning, resulted in working conditions for the pilot which fell far short of ideal on a hot and turbulent day. Demonstrating a Canberra could be a very sweaty experience; so much so in fact that under sustained high 'g' rivulets of sweat would run down into the pilot's eyes causing a salty and dangerous distraction. To overcome this I fitted a pad of absorbent material under my

*Top and above right:*
Demonstration at the Martin
plant. 1951.   *Glenn L. Martin Co*

*Right:* Taxying in after
demonstration.
*Glenn L. Martin Co*

*Below:* Testing a Martin B-57
version of the Canberra.
Baltimore, 1953.
*Glenn L. Martin Co*

lightweight tropical helment, and also carried an additional pad stuffed into the harness webbing for a last minute face-wipe before take-off. With these measures and constant practice we were able to keep the Canberra in the forefront of world aviation in the early 1950s. In the process we aroused much interest which was followed by world-wide export sales, in addition to achieving a degree of over-development of the pilot's biceps.

Ministry of Supply,
Aeroplane and Armament,
Experimental Establishment,
Boscombe Down,
Amesbury, Wilts.

14 November, 1949

Dear Petter,

The Canberra passed over my office just after 12 o'clock today on its way back to you after a very successful preliminary set of handling trials at Boscombe.

The report on the aeroplane is being prepared and should be available in the near future. I cannot wait to tell you, however, that the Squadron pilots have made a special point of emphasising the help given by Beamont in his discussions with them. He has apparently been very frank in telling them the doubtful points as well as the good points, and I don't think we found anything concerning the handling qualities of the aircraft that had not already been mentioned to us beforehand by your pilot. This happy state of affairs is very much appreciated and I hope it will continue in our future work on the Canberra and its successors.

We shall be ready to discuss our findings with you on Monday 28 November. Can you manage this date?

With kind regards,
Yours sincerely,
Ivor Bowen.

W. E. W. Petter Esq,
The English Electric Co Ltd,
Aircraft Division,
Warton Aerodrome,
Nr Preston, Lancs.

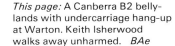

*This page:* A Canberra B2 belly-lands with undercarriage hang-up at Warton. Keith Isherwood walks away unharmed. *BAe*

77

## THE ENGLISH ELECTRIC CO. LTD.
### AIRCRAFT DIVISION, WARTON AERODROME, PRESTON

FLIGHT No. :   1.
SHEET No. :
DATE :   13:5:49.

# EXPERIMENTAL FLIGHT REPORT

AIRCRAFT TYPE   B3/45      CREW:- PILOT   W/Cdr. Beamont.

AIRCRAFT SERIAL No.   VN.799.      OBSERVER   -

OBJECT OF TEST :—

               First Test Flight.

TAKE-OFF LOADING :—

| | | |
|---|---:|---|
| TARE WEIGHT | 20,337 | LB. |
| FUEL 825 Galls. | 6,650 | LB. |
| FUEL EXTERNAL TANKS | - | LB. |
| OIL | - | LB. |
| CREW | 200 | LB. |
| BALLAST | 690 | LB. |
| TOTAL | 27,877 | LB. |

TYRE PRESSURES:—

| | | |
|---|---:|---|
| MAIN | 72 | LB/SQ. IN. |
| NOSE | 60 | LB/SQ. IN. |

C.G. POSITION AT TAKE OFF   1.469 ft. aft of datum – 19.615% M/C

TIME OF FLIGHT   10.46 hrs. – 11.13 hrs.

AIRCRAFT CONDITION (MODIFICATIONS etc.):—
Aircraft in Experimental Condition with 108 lb additional ballast on ballast box.

Fuel distribution:-
No.1 Tank 500 Galls.
No.2 Tank 300 "
No.3 Tank 25

DISTRIBUTION:—
Chief Engineer    Mr.Page.
Mr.Ellis.    Mr.Harrison)
R.T.O.    Mr.Crowe )
Flight Observer.    Mr.Smith.

PILOT R.P.Beamont.    DATE 13:5:49.

---

All services were checked before flight and found satisfactory. Engine figures:

| | | | |
|---|---|---|---|
| 7,800 | 600 | 40 | 45 |
| 7,800 | 620 | 38 | 40 |

Brakes: main pressure — 440lb
Tailplane: 1½ divisions from nose down
Isolating switches on.
Power for take-off: 7,500/7,500
Flaps down
Time: 11.54 — zero

The aircraft was flown off normally at approx 90kt and, as the speed exceeded 120kt IAS, full nose down trim was insufficient to trim out the subsequent nose up trim change. At 200ft power was reduced and the undercarriage retracted satisfactorily. During this operation a slight yaw to port occurred, a correction for which was made by application of right rudder.

After approx 2in of travel involving a low control force and a very small rudder reaction, the rudder control lost effectiveness in a manner which suggested over-balance in that control forces were suddenly reduced to zero, and no further rudder reaction was noticeable. This condition was corrected rapidly by left rudder pressure and the aircraft climbed straight ahead to approx 5,000ft. Flaps were retracted satisfactorily at 170kt after holding the aircraft in trim by a 20-30lb push force together with full nose-down trim. This resulted in a mild nose down trim change and the aircraft was trimmed hands off at 245kt IAS, tailplane 2 graduations up from 'nose down'.

Right rudder was again applied, this time at 200kt, with the same results as before, plus the additional impression that, following on the sudden reduction of starboard rudder force to zero, a sharp minus force occurred until held and reversed with port rudder.

During this test it was confirmed that during the over-balance condition a slight tremor could be felt through the rudder system though not through the airframe.

At this condition of flight (245kt, 5-6,000ft, time: zero plus 3), the tailplane actuator was found to operate satisfactorily, though with some lag, and the aircraft was satisfactorily in trim at a tailplane setting 2 graduations up from full nose down.

At zero plus 8½ an ASI check was made with a standard Mk V Vampire with the following results:

B3/45 — 245kt          Vampire — 245kt

The Vampire reported all doors and fairings closed.

At zero plus 12 further investigation of the rudder condition was carried out at 210kt, 6,000/6,000rpm, 6-8,000ft, and the condition was confirmed without variation from the previous test, the general impression being that the rudder was effective through the very small angles either side of neutral and over-balanced outside those angles. This condition naturally restricted the scope of the test, but before descending the other controls were checked at this flight condition as follows:

Ailerons firm and positive in action with heavy wheel forces for large angles.

Elevator well in harmony with ailerons; positive and firm in action and response. Possibly slightly less positive than ailerons. A slight tremor was noticeable with jerky application which was probably spring tab effect.

The tailplane actuator was checked at this point and this, though smooth and effective, suffered from an initial lag of between 2-3 seconds between operation of the switch and a noticeable response. This is undesirable but need not interfere with the early flying.

At zero plus 14 it was decided that the test should be discontinued owing to the rudder condition which did not promise an adequate measure of control for the single engine case, and the descent was begun. During this it was noted that the aircraft lost speed very slowly at idling rpm and in fact would not do so at any appreciable rate of descent. The flap speed of 140kt was not reached until zero plus 15½ after a descent from approx 5,000ft to approx 2,500ft, and when flaps were applied the resulting nose up trim change could not once again be completely trimmed out with tailplane. A normal half circuit was made, the undercarriage being lowered at 120kt satisfactorily with the warning lights operating within a period of approx 15 seconds. This did not produce a noticeable trim change.

During the crosswind leg and the first part of the final approach at 115-110kt the aircraft handled easily apart from the rudder condition, control being maintained without the use of rudder; but during the last 1,000yd of the approach at 110kt IAS, rough air was encountered which set up a series of yaws which could be felt in phase on the rudder but which could not be corrected or controlled by its use; an attempt to do this resulted in recurrence of the over-balance condition.

The hold-off and landing was normal apart from an excess safety speed, and after cutting the engines 500yd short of the runway at 100kt/20ft, the ASI was still reading 100kt at the moment of touchdown 7-800yd further on. The brakes were used quite severely and retarded the aircraft adequately without undue temperature rise.

*General Impression*

Apart from the rudder conditions described, the aircraft handled smoothly and easily. All services operated satisfactorily although in the case of tailplane actuation some alterations may be necessary. Engine behaviour was satisfactory, and no engine handling was carried out owing to the circumstances of the test. Both engines and airframe were remarkably quiet in flight and the noise level in the cockpit allows excellent radio reception.

As was to be expected from the loading condition, the aircraft was stable longitudinally and appeared to be so directionally in smooth air conditions. Rudder and aileron trimmers were set at neutral for take-off and were not required throughout the flight.

During the approach it was noted that up to its maximum range the tailplane actuator keeps pace with the nose up trim change caused by flap operation, so that provided the airspeed is kept below 130kt stick-free trim can be retained during the full operation.

*Work Before Next Flight*

(1)  Inspect brake assemblies and check Thermo-couples.
(2)  Remove flap system stop for full travel.
(3)  Mark tailplane dial graduations 0-9 (to suit), top to bottom.
(4)  Investigate rudder control.

R. P. BEAMONT
Chief Test Pilot

*Left:* The first production Canberra Mk 9 ready for structural demonstration by RPB at Warton on 21 September 1960. *BAe*

*Below left:* Testing the first Canberra for Argentina. Samlesbury 8 April 1970. *BAe*

*Right:* Adjacent photography. *BAe*

*Above:* Demonstrating the first Canberra for Argentina at Warton on 13 May 1970 — the 21st anniversary of the Canberra's first flight. *BAe*

*Right:* After the demonstration. *BAe*

*Below right:* Nudging the Canberra prototype in for adjacent photography. June 1949. *BAe*

# Short SB5

While English Electric were evolving the P1 in the early 1950s to the F23/49 Air Ministry specification the RAE at Farnborough had had misgivings about the P1's aerodynamic design concept. They had persuaded the Ministry to procure a 'cheap' research aircraft on which to test their theories about the control and stability of a highly swept wing and, in particular, the effects of tailplane position relative to this wing. English Electric had maintained throughout that the pitch-up problems plaguing the current generation of transonic fighters were due to their tailplanes being in the wrong relative position. They were either level with the wing trailing edge and directly in wing wake downwash or in some cases were the newly fashionable high positioned 'T' tail which in English Electric's view was even worse. It was liable to result in proneness to the 'deep-stall' characteristics which did subsequently result in tragic losses during the development of Javelins, F-104 Starfighters, Victors, Tridents, BAC 1-11s and others with this configuration. The selected English Electric tail position was as low as possible on the rear fuselage in relation to a high shoulder wing with 60° leading edge sweep angle. RAE thought it to be so unconventional as to be strongly questionable and even dangerous. Thus to investigate the whole low speed stability problem the Short SB5 was designed as a minimum cost, low performance test vehicle with facilities for ground adjustment of wing sweep from 50° to 70° in stages and for variations of tailplane position from high 'T' tail to the low 'P1' position. The conservative policy of the RAE was that the SB5 first flight would be in the 'safest' configuration of 50° sweep and 'T' tail which English Electric did not consider safe at all for stall investigation!

The SB5 was finally assembled at Boscombe Down in 1953 and then flown in this configuration by Tom Brooke Smith*. He found that if he kept well away from the stall boundary it was a safe and reasonable aircraft to fly, albeit with heavy and coarse 'manual' controls and severely limited climb performance which reduced to virtually nil as thrust equalled drag at about 8,000ft. He also found a curious lateral characteristic of wing rocking and associated variations in aileron hinge-moment felt through the stick during slowdowns through about 135kt KIAS. This intrigued the aerodynamic specialists as it was the first full scale demonstration of the anticipated swept wing leading-edge vortex. This had already been identified in wind tunnel tests and illustrated in water tunnel tests at Warton, and much hope was placed for its theoretical stabilising effect on swept wing control at high incidence.

*Short's Chief Test Pilot and later to become the world's pioneer test pilot of successful jet vertical take-off and landing.

With the P1 first flight approaching it was considered advisable that we should obtain some prior experience on the SB5 and so I reported to Boscombe Down on 11 August 1953 for a briefing by Brooke Smith. The machine looked more like a piece of marine engineering than an aeroplane with very basic lines round the nose, tail and cockpit and with thickets of mushroom-headed rivets all over it. With one 1,500lb thrust Viper engine and few associated instruments, a fixed undercarriage, two-position flap selection and virtually nothing else, briefing was soon completed and Brooke Smith warned me not to 'over-rotate' on take-off as this could lead to a thrust-equals-drag situation and no take-off!

*Below:* Short SB5 in first high-tail configuration. 50° sweep. Boscombe Down 1953. *Short Bros*

Similarly I was warned of the high rate of descent which would result from rapid increase in induced drag if I reduced speed on the approach without corresponding increase in thrust. This was a valuable first insight into the delta (or highly swept wing) induced-drag effects with which the military aviation world was to become familiar in the next decade.

In common with the rest of the aeroplane the cockpit was very basic with cable-operated controls that rasped with static friction, a coarse and heavy-to-operate canopy locking mechanism and a cumbersome-looking heavy framed canopy with small windows permitting a rather restricted view of the outside world. For test purposes the stick was fitted with a stick-force measuring head with a grip consisting simply of a round metal ball surmounting a dial for stick-force read out. The ball was too small to provide sufficient grip to cope comfortably with the high manual control forces at the top end of the performance range, although this was an

*Above:* SB5 with final 70° wing, and the high tailplane.  *RAE, Bedford*

*Below:* SB5 in low-tail configuration and with wing tufts for airflow investigation.  *RAE, Bedford*

*Right:* SB5 in final wing and tail configuration.  *Short Bros*

awkward and limiting feature it did not seriously interfere with the primary task of low speed investigation.

The SB5 proved to be an interesting aircraft to fly and I enjoyed all my 23 flights on it in 1953 and 1954. During this period we developed a chord-wise slot to control the leading-edge vortex pattern relative to the aileron. This modification was applied to the P1 prototype in time for first flight and has been incorporated in all Lightning aircraft since.

The SB5 was a fascinating 'trainer' for the low speed handling of highly swept wings. Its high induced-drag characteristics were so exaggerated by the low power/weight ratio that marked variations in speed could be produced at fixed power settings (generally full throttle) merely by slightly increasing or decreasing angle-of-attack with the stick. On hot summer days at Boscombe Down the take-off proved interesting with acceleration to unstick often requiring 2,000 yards. The subsequent climb-out was acutely dependent on reducing the take-off incidence otherwise it would not climb

at all, and a height gain of only 1,000ft in the first five miles was a not uncommon occurrence. On these occasions the climb to an initial test height (the practical ceiling) at 6-7,000ft would take about 20 minutes at full power. By this time there would be barely sufficient fuel left for the tests if, as was usually the case, these were either accelerated stability points or slowdowns below the Minimum Drag Speed. Either of these would result in a high sink rate even at maximum power. Because of all this the tests had to be positioned so that the end of the resultant steep spiral or flat nose-high descent was suitably adjacent to the approach end of the runway. This in turn caused some problems with and for Boscombe Air Traffic Control at times, especially in marginal weather.

In fact the SB5 never really felt like an aeroplane but more like an interesting 'boiler plate' exercise. However it did provide valuable aerodynamic data in support of the P1 configuration. In later years, when modified with 70° sweep and full length cambered leading edge, it provided invaluable support for slender delta research for the Concorde programme in conjunction with the HP 115. In this configuration I flew a series of tests on it again at RAE Bedford in 1964, this time with an Orpheus engine giving twice the power and a much more reasonable performance.

# English Electric P1

In parallel to the Canberra design activity and before the first flight of the prototype, work was already in progress at Warton on the next project. Teddy Petter and his team had become incensed by Government procrastination over supersonic research policy and the decision in 1947 to discontinue progress towards manned supersonic flight which left the field wide open to Russia and America. Being convinced that this decision was wrong, that the future of aviation lay in supersonic flight and that this was now already within the practical state of the art, the team had worked up an effective lobby with the OR* Branch of the Air Ministry. Early in 1949 the latter in conjunction with the Ministry of Supply issued specification F23/49 for a supersonic research aircraft with potential for development into a fighter. The specification was written round a Warton proposal for a radical design with a very much higher wing sweep angle than any previous experience, exceeding 60°. It had a high shoulder wing relative to a low tailplane to ensure against the pitch-up instability problems at high $C_L$† which was then widespread among the current subsonic fighters, and had two conventional 'off the shelf' axial flow engines.

At that period, as in subsequent years, there was a refreshing amount of interchange between designers and the pilots at Warton. On the basis of my one recent flight at transonic speed in the prototype XP-86 at Muroc I was regarded as something of an expert in this field. In discussion of the practicability of operation at supersonic speeds I had told them that provided they could eliminate the loss of elevator effectiveness in ability to control transonic 'compressibility' trim changes and similar loss of aileron effectiveness in 'wing drop' — almost standard characteristics of the then current subsonic jet fighters with relatively thick wings — I could see no operational reason why flight at supersonic speed should not be practical. Smooth responsive control had also to be maintained through the transonic compressibility region. Aerodynamic experts Ray Creasey and Dai Ellis showed even more enormous enthusiasm for this work than they had over the Canberra. Their feelings then on the benefits of low wing loading and high power/weight ratio had so closely matched my own. They assured me that with suitable wing shape, irreversible powered flight controls and the right wing-to-tailplane relationship it would prove possible to reduce compressibility effects and transonic trim change to negligible proportions. This combination could furthermore be expected to maintain 'fighter' manoeuvrability beyond the speed of sound.

The powered flight control was a new field in itself. I had already developed some strong opinions in this area based on experience with the conventional 'manual' systems. I was convinced that circuit stretch, mechanical 'back-lash' or lost-motion, excess static friction or dynamic friction resulting from structural flexing, were all effects which a good control system could well do without. To this end I had, since flying the FW 190 in 1942, become a strong advocate of push-rods to replace cable runs for flying controls wherever practical. In long discussions with Ellis and the systems designers a policy for the power control engineering and 'feel' system was

*Operational Requirements.

†Lift Coefficient.

*Below:* 1954 GA drawing of the prototype P1 showing the leading edge slots. *BAe*

*Right:* Preparation for first flight. Boscombe Down, Summer 1954. *BAe*

*Below right:* RPB 3rd from right. *BAe*

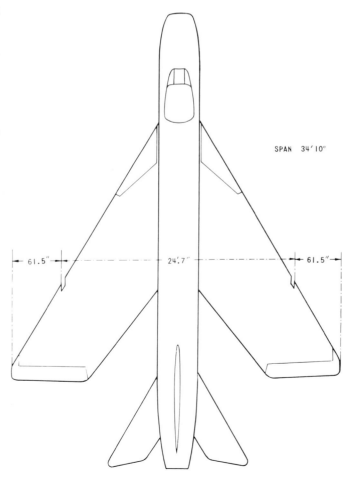

SPAN 34′10″

61.5″    24′.7″    61.5″

hammered out. I recommended that with lost-motion and friction reduced to the lowest practical levels, the projected 'q pot' feel system should be designed to give the lowest possible stick-force-per 'g' commensurate with the structural limitations and with keeping clear of pilot-induced oscillations. A simple spring back-up might be practical if the basic aircraft stability and damping characteristics proved good enough. This view, which was generally held at Warton, was by no means a universal one and the subject was hotly debated by various authorities at the time.

A symposium was held by the Royal Aircraft Establishment Farnborough at which aerodynamic and controls experts exchanged views with test pilots from Industry and the Services. Some quite remarkable red herrings were raised which were allowed to confuse this important issue for some years. Perhaps the most misleading was the theory that a powered control must have a strong and positive break-out force measured in pounds to prevent 'overcontrolling' by the pilot. The most surprising one was that self-centring would not be necessary as pilots could learn to fly without such a luxury — and this from the RAE itself!

My view was that self-centring was as essential to provide a sensible 'feel' as it is with car steering, and that 'break-out' forces and associated system friction levels needed engineering to 'ounces' rather than 'pounds' to provide smooth control lacking in 'notchiness'. As our view did not immediately prevail, Warton soldiered on along its own lines in this as in other aspects of the design. One such was low tailplane aerodynamics — against the weight of much influential opinion. In the outcome this was justified by producing a quality of stability and fine control in the P1 and Lightning series which set a standard for the 1950s still unsurpassed for this class of aircraft even in the 1970s.

The design stages and prototype build of the P1 was a fascinating period at Warton and busy for me because during 1950-54 we were also much preoccupied with the development flying of B2, PR3, B5 and B8 Canberras, together with massive Canberra production testing. Introduction of the aircraft to the air forces at home and abroad called for various support activities such as long distance flights and international and customer demonstrations. Nevertheless a supersonic fighter for the RAF was something that had a magnetic attraction for me

86

*Below:* Roll-out for engine runs.  *BAe*

*Below left:* First engine run. 11pm at Boscombe Down in July 1954.  *BAe*

*Right, top to bottom:*
Taxying out for Flight 1.  4 August 1954.

Ready to go.

'Rotate'.

Airborne.  *All BAe*

and I found the time to work closely with the programme. In the process I identified some disturbing features. The planned fuel capacity of the P1 was to be 5,000lb in integral wing tanks and it did not take a computer or a mathematical egg-head to work out that with two 9,000lb thrust engines working at power to sustain climb to the tropopause and then a max level performance acceleration, the fuel would not last long. I calculated it to be about 25-35 minutes with allowance for missed-approach though not sufficient for a practical weather diversion. The suggestion, frequently repeated to the Design Office, that this was an impractical amount of fuel on which to base a major flight programme was met with an unusually uncompromising negative. The negative was unusual inasmuch as this was one of the few occasions in which pilot advice on major issues was not acted on at Warton in time to be of maximum benefit. It seemed that some genius was countering the pilot's 'pessimism' by quoting the engine company's brochure specific performance (optimistic in the outcome) for optimum cruise conditions only. He was coming up with a figure, unfactored for performance testing, overshoot and diversion margins, of 'endurance over 1 hour'. As a result of this the question of navigation accuracy began to assume abnormal significance in the absence at that time of surveillance or recovery radar at Warton. As was conventional up to then provision had been made only for dual VHF radio and main and standby compasses. When I asked for airborne fixing facilities such as radio compass/DME there was a shocked silence. In the event we began flying without these aids. After experiencing the critical fuel shortage expected and having to plan reduced flight test schedules to match 25-35 minute practical duration with consequent severe limitations on usable weather, a decision was made to fit a radio compass during the first suitable lay-up.

The first flight of prototype VX 760 was due in mid-summer 1954. Prior to this it was hoped to experience some aspects of the slow speed stability and control of the wing configuration in the Short SB5 experimental aircraft which had been designed by RAE specifically to investigate the viability of our planned low tailplane-to-wing relationship in comparison with the high tailplane position strongly advocated by the Aero Department at RAE. (See Chapter 12).

These flights provided immediate evidence of a problem and unique opportunity for establishing a cure before even flying the P1. Brooke Smith had established that at a specific high angle of attack a sharp wing-drop occurred in the SB5. Repeated tests of this at about 145kt confirmed that the vortex from the 60° leading edge was sweeping outboard in what was to become recognised as classic 'Delta' pattern and affecting the lift distribution and hinge-moment on the aileron. As this was a manual control circuit the vortex effect was transmitted to the pilot as a step in hinge-moment at the point of wing-drop, with control returning to normal if incidence was increased beyond this point. There was some uncertainty for a while about why these characteristics occurred on one wing on one occasion and the other on a second but not always repeatably. Then it was realised that with rather low $N_v$ * giving low weather-cock stability coupled with a high friction rudder circuit the SB5 did not trim out directionally very precisely and that this could result in the wing vortex patterns being asymmetric.

The Farnborough authorities said 'Ah, the P1 will have to have fences', but the Warton experts had other ideas. Wishing to conserve performance and also needing to

*Directional stability derivative.

accommodate a fuel system inward-vent valve on the wing leading edge, they contrived a chord-wise slot at about mid-span which while acting as a pressure fence would produce less drag than a fixed fence and also incorporate the vent valve at its base.

This was schemed and applied to the SB5 and I found immediately that it had cleared the wing-drop and reduced the hinge-moment change to negligible proportions. The power controls of the P1 could be expected to mask any residual effects in any case, and this was so in practice. The P1 flew from Boscombe in August 1954 with these pressure slots in the wing leading edge where, apart from a later programme to optimise size and shape, they have remained throughout the life of the later developments of Lightning.

From its first flight the P1 was a resounding success, exceeding Mach 1 on its third flight as befitted the country's first fully supersonic aeroplane. Even with its early cold thrust engines (ie without reheat) it ushered in a new era in military aircraft performance as I recognised when pulling up into a maximum performance climb for the first time — it really was like a 'Homing Archangel'.

Once minor modifications had been made to aileron gearing and in static balancing of the aileron and rudder circuits the prototype set a new standard of precision in flying controls. This, coupled with the predicted qualities of longitudinal and lateral stability and adequate though marginal Nv resulted in a sweet-to-fly aeroplane which rapidly became popular with test and Service pilots. In the process the P1 brought about a significant change in attitudes toward supersonic flight which no longer seemed a remote and probably unsatisfactory regime for operational flying. The optimists had been justified and enthusiasm for the P1B fighter version soared.

Before this however a number of milestones were achieved by the P1 in addition to the satisfactory proving of its design envelope. First was the firing of 30mm Aden guns at

*Above:* Prince Bernhard of the Netherlands sees the P1 at Boscombe, with the author. *BAe*

*Left:* Lord Nelson, Mr Duncan Sandys, Prince Bernhard, RPB, Freddy Page. *BAe*

*Above right:* Testing the prototype at Warton. December 1954. *BAe*

*Right:* The debriefing team at Warton. Left to right round the table, RPB, Atkin, de Villiers, Eaves, Dyke, Smalley, Cundick, Horsfield. *Flight International*

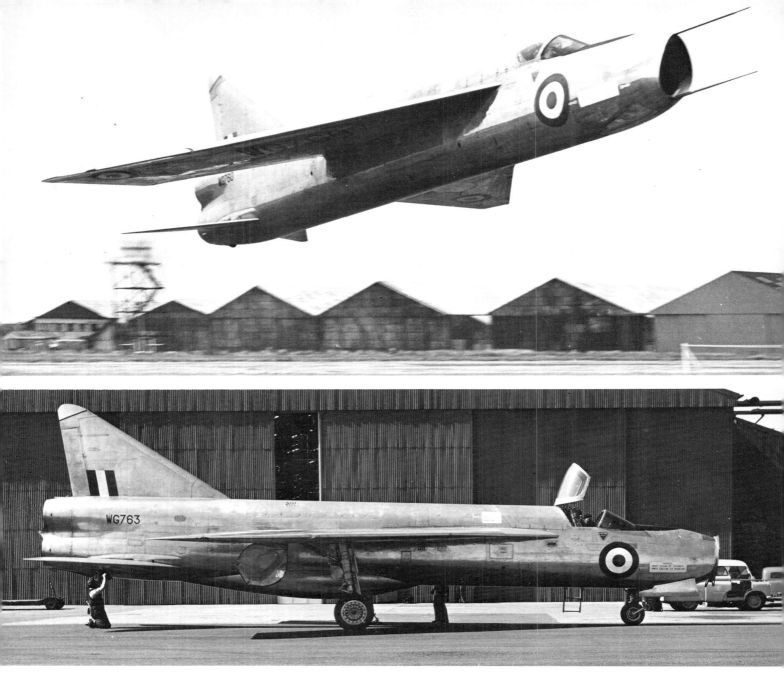

*Top:* Press Day at Warton, 1955.  *Aeroplane*

*Above:* Roll-out of the 2nd P1 prototype with additional external fuel tank and twin 30mm Aden guns.  *Crown Copyright*

*Right:* Classic supersonic shape, 2nd P1 prototype on first air photography. Gun ports in nose. *Crown Copyright*

92

supersonic speed and second the installation of a fixed nozzle reheat system. The latter enabled stability and control investigation to be made from the initial performance boundary of about Mach 1.1 out to beyond Mach 1.5 where Nv was measured at 0.015/1g and considered too low for normal operation. This gave immediate emphasis to the one area requiring major development, and three further increases in fin size had to be introduced subsequently to cater for the increased 'external' stores and higher performance of the later marks of Lightning. But these advances were not achieved without some disasters. Two fin failures occurred at supersonic speed in the test programme in the following years, the first causing Johnny Squier a long uncomfortable night afloat on the Irish Sea in his dinghy after ejecting from the T4 trainer prototype. The second seriously injured Jimmy Dell and flight test engineer Graham Elkington when a similar failure occurred on the T5 trainer prototype.

The P1 development programme from August 1954 to spring 1957, though notable for its overall success was not without moments of hilarity and sometimes mild drama. During the supersonic gun-firing programme authority had been obtained to use the Eskmeals artillery firing range which extended out to sea from the Westmorland coast conveniently close to Warton. There had been strongly expressed objections locally from a senior and retired Army officer who lived nearby, but despite careful planning of communications and operational details it was not long before Desmond de Villiers contrived to drop a number of 30mm rounds in the senior citizen's garden — resulting in abrupt cessation of the trial. On another occasion in the programme we were occupied in extension of the flutter envelope to the highest IAS practical subsonic. This meant at the lowest height commensurate with reasonable safety and precautions against noise disturbance. Accordingly I had set up the previously proved speed at 575kt/800ft in the Morecambe Bay area, increased to the next test point of 585kt. I selected the gun trigger to 'Fire' for firing the 'Bonker' explosive exciters when at the very moment of firing an enormously loud explosion occurred. The aircraft bucked and I could not see at all. First reactions were that I had succeeded in blowing the wing or tail off or something like it.

Then I realised that I was still in the cockpit, the explosion hadn't stopped, I still couldn't see and that unless I did something adequate to the occasion we would most likely hit the ground or water very shortly. Trying to see resulted in a frighteningly painful reaction. I realised that I was sitting in a 550kt or more draught and that the windscreen or canopy must have gone together with my helmet and visor. So, still with eyes necessarily tightly closed I began to ease back the power and the stick together on the basis that higher was safer. There was also the thought that if I couldn't control the situation and needed to eject, height would also be an advantage. The noise level and buffeting reduced as the speed came down and it was a relief to find that I could begin to see again, though somewhat painfully. We were still flying and in a 30° bank climbing through 4,000ft with about 400kt on the ASI. The windscreen was still in place but the canopy had disappeared. A routine May Day call was now in order but was frustrated by the fact that my helmet was missing and connecting wires and pipes were threshing round my face threatening further injury. This limited the options and so I set about finding the course for base and assessing the damage and the chances of making a normal landing.

At less than 250kt and with the harness loosened to lean well forward under the protection of the windscreen conditions were adequate. I was still experiencing much discomfort in the eyes for reasons which were explained later. The aeroplane seemed otherwise serviceable so, to the relief of a slightly surprised air traffic staff, the P1 was brought in to Warton to a normal if draughty landing after what was probably the fastest open-cockpit flight in history up to then.

I was met on the tarmac by the ambulance and a very concerned nurse with an enormous glass of brandy. Had I taken it, it would certainly have caused further incapacitation, and it wasn't until some time later that my eyes became so painful as to suggest professional attention. This time the nurse did have her way when it was discovered that my eyeballs had received a liberal distribution of glass fibres from the shattered insulation blankets of the cockpit.

The cause of canopy failure had been self-release of the locks, but the reason for this was not easy to establish. Two more canopies were lost before the cause was found, both experienced by de Villiers who on one of them achieved the distinction of becoming the world's first open-cockpit *supersonic* pilot. Urgent redesign action followed, but despite assurances from the Design Office that all would now be well, the test pilots tied their helmets and masks on with extra lashings of string for some time.

Overall the tone of the P1 programme was of great success and confidence for the future as indicated by the absence of serious problems in the report on Flight 1.

*Below:* The P1 landing after a Farnborough display.

94

THE ENGLISH ELECTRIC CO. LTD.
AIRCRAFT DIVISION, WARTON AERODROME, PRESTON

FLIGHT No. : **1**

DATE 4.8.54

# EXPERIMENTAL FLIGHT REPORT

AIRCRAFT TYPE ___F23/49___          PILOT ___W/C R.P. Beamont___

AIRCRAFT SERIAL No. ___WG 760___     NAVIGATOR _____

OBSERVER _____

PASSENGER _____

OBJECT OF TEST :—

General Handling on Initial Flight

TAKE-OFF LOADING :—                    FUEL (GALLS)

TARE WEIGHT _____ 21,443    LB.    2288 lb Port
FUEL _____ 4,576    LB.    2288 lb Stbd
MISCELLANEOUS Removable Equipment 298 LB.
CREW _____ 200     LB.
BOMBS, FLARES or BALLAST  450    LB.

TOTAL  26,967  LB.

TYRE PRESSURES:—              OLEO PRESSURES :—

MAIN      240   LB/SQ. IN.     MAIN ____435  LB/SQ. IN.

NOSE_____ 200   LB/SQ. IN.     NOSE ____160  LB/SQ. IN.

C.G. POSITION AT TAKE OFF  7.740 aft of datum 35.04 s.m.c.

TIME AT TAKE-OFF  09.58

TIME AT LANDING  10.31         TOTAL  00.33

SPECIAL FLIGHT LIMITATIONS:—

4th August 1954

F23/49   WG 760   Flight No 1   4.8.54

*Weather Conditions*

Dry runway; light variable wind at 90° to the runway, backing; 6/8 high cloud; small amount scattered low cloud; visibility 4-5 ml in slight haze. Runway 24.

A full cockpit check was carried out which revealed no defective items except for the leg straps on the Mk 3 ejection seat. The individual leg harnesses had been checked previously but the lacing had not been completed during previous checks. On coupling the lacing in accordance with the maker's instructions it was found that the lacings were required to interconnect between the left and right leg. With feet on the rudder pedals this resulted immediately in a severe restriction of backward control movement. After re-checking this case it was decided that flight could be accepted without the leg harnesses owing to the existing speed limitation and the circumstances of the flight.

Radio checks with the Tower and Flight Test van were satisfactory. Stopwatch failure soon after initial tripping prevented a time record being taken of the flight. Instrumentation was switched on after start-up.

Take-off was made with flaps down and without any attempt to lift off at the lowest possible speed. After lifting the nose wheel at approximately 120kt the aircraft became airborne easily with slightly under full elevator at approximately 145kt. The attitude was checked immediately on becoming airborne with a small amount of forward stick, and as the aircraft gained speed it became progressively 'nose up' in out-of-trim.

The undercarriage was selected up at approximately 160kt and power was reduced to maintain approximately 200kt in a shallow climb. The undercarriage retracted rapidly with slight asymmetry which caused a small lateral displacement. This was over-corrected with aileron control, which under these conditions was very sensitive, but the resultant oscillation was damped immediately by centring and momentarily relaxing stick hold.

The undercarriage locked home before 200kt and as speed was gradually increased above this point buffet was noticeable from the flaps.

As IAS exceeded 250kt the flap blow-back device operated and the flaps returned to neutral with the selector down. This resulted in further 'nose up' out-of-trim and full 'nose down' trim on the indicator was not sufficient to return to in-trim flight.

Speed was reduced to 200kt, the flap selector moved to 'up' and then at 190kt selected to 'down'. Flap operation was normal and it was noted that there was little buffet from flaps below 200kt. Flaps were retracted at 210kt.

At this speed nose flap only was selected and apart from a very slight 'nose down' trim and no other effects were noted. (Lessening of the existing 'nose up' condition.)

With flaps retracted power was increased and altitude increased to 8-9,000ft. IAS was increased progressively up to 400kt and at this point there was no buffeting or roughness. The ailerons, which were noticeably sensitive became progressively more so with increase in IAS with the result that lateral damping seemed to be rather lower than desirable. Releasing the stick in all cases damped out the lateral oscillation immediately, however, and it was thought that much of this over-sensitivity in lateral control resulted from the fact that the pilot had at all times to hold a small but noticeable 'nose up' out-of-trim force.

Height was increased to 13-14,000ft and speed increased to 400kt IAS/.75. Under these conditions the lateral control remained very sensitive but adequate. During a course alteration to avoid a cloud layer, the nose was depressed slightly and speed inadvertently increased at idling power to approximately 440-450kt. This was reduced as soon as level flight could be resumed.

Dive brakes were checked at 300-400kt at 13,000ft over approximately 2°-4° of movement. In each case after the initial slight 'nose up' trim very heavy buffet began. This was associated with an erratic directional characteristic which immediately resulted in an erratic rolling displacement due to yaw. These circumstances were not regarded as satisfactory and the tests were discontinued subject to further progressive investigation at low speeds.

During the climb it had not been easy to control the air conditioning with the cold air unit, as with this there was a tendency either to be too hot or too cold. The cabin air ram valve was opened and found to produce a pleasantly distributed flow of cooling air. This was kept open at all times during the flight except for a short period at 14,000ft where was closed to test pressurisation, which was found to be satisfactory at this height.

During the descent the inner surface of the centre armoured glass panel became misted with the NESA switch switched at 'half'. Switching the NESA system to 'full' cleared this condition in a few minutes.

During descent with power reduced to idling considerable difficulty was experienced in obtaining a consistent rate of descent while keeping IAS below 400ft. This may tend to be a minor limiting factor in flight test operation if the present dive brakes prove unsatisfactory.

With the fuel state at 1,000/1,000lb it was decided to return to base, and during this some difficulty was experienced at a critical point in obtaining homing facilities from Boscombe.

Once the circuit had been regained circuit manoeuvrability at 350-250kt proved excellent with vision forward and sideways rather better than on the Hunter. Turns at and up to 2½g were comfortably executed with nose flap up and with nose flap down turns up to 2g at 250-300kt again were positively stable.

In a proving flight of this description a detailed appraisal of feel is not possible, but the increase in feel forces on the tailplane control with increase in IAS seemed to be precisely suitable.

The undercarriage was selected down at 230kt and locked rapidly with green indicator lights at 210kt. There was asymmetry in this operation which resulted in the expected lateral displacement and corresponding momentary over-correction with aileron. This case is similar to that experienced on the Hunter.

Flaps were lowered at 200kt and in doing so returned the aircraft to in-trim longitudinally, still with full 'nose down' trim. A final turn was carried out at 200-190kt and speed reduced. Speed was reduced to 160kt at short finals and the throttles returned to idling. A normal hold-off was made crossing the boundary and a final check comfortably and easily executed at 150kt. The touchdown was smooth at a reasonable attitude with excellent vision of the runway at approximately 140kt.

The parachute was streamed at approximately 135kt and this operated with a delay of the order of 2 seconds. There was an immediate 'nose up' pitch and weather-cock yaw to starboard requiring approximately full port rudder to hold. This condition was easily controlled and once the nose wheel had returned to the runway light wheel brake was applied to bring the aircraft to a standstill. The parachute jettisoning operation was satisfactory. At standstill the port wheel thermocouples indicated 160°C.

During the flight a PE check was carried out with the pacing Canberra WH 775 and this gave 195/195kt at 8,000ft.

*Summary*

From this short flight the following main points were clear:
(1)   The main services functioned satisfactorily with the exception of the dive brake which gave indication of heavy buffet, even at the small angles employed.
(2)   The trim actuators were satisfactory on rudder and aileron, but that on the tailplane control provided inadequate 'nose down' trim.
(3)   Longitudinal and directional static stability was positive in all flight conditions experienced so far. The aircraft was neutrally stable laterally with adequate damping, stick free.
(4)   Tailplane feel and response was entirely satisfactory under all conditions and there was no sign of over-sensitivity leading to pilot-induced oscillation. Aileron response and spring feel was very sensitive and powerful and required a light touch to prevent fairly continuous over-correction. It was not easy to apply this light touch owing to the necessity of holding off 'nose up' out of trim force throughout the whole flight, with engines above half power. This condition may be less noticeable when the longitudinal trim range has been adjusted suitably.
(5)   The power control circuits were remarkably free from noticeable friction or backlash.
(6)   The engines were used as required and no detailed attention was paid to engine conditions beyond observing the limitations. They responded normally and entirely satisfactorily to all requirements.

In this short flight the aircraft proved to be pleasant and straightforward to fly with the take-off and landing operations lacking in complication. The over-sensitivity in lateral control will require careful observation during subsequent tests.

*Defects*

Martin Baker seat lacing restricts travel of stick.

Insufficient nose down trim.

Check No 1 and 2 radio on 122.5 and 131.3mcs.

R. P. BEAMONT
Chief Test Pilot

# P1B Lightning

By the spring of 1957 the P1 programme had produced so much valuable information and successful results in tests of the basic aerodynamic configuration that there was little doubt that the fighter version would be satisfactory in this respect, but there was much to be done to prove it. The P1B followed a nearly identical aerodynamic configuration to that of its predecessor aft of the cabin pressure bulkhead. The significant external differences were limited to a deeper nose section with raised cockpit and improved rearwards vision areas, a centre-body intake with housing initially for test instrumentation and subsequently for the intercept radar, a dorsal spine from the canopy to the foot of the fin accommodating starter system components and controls, and revised jet pipes with reheat nozzles.

Internally it was a very different aeroplane. The Rolls-Royce RA24R engines, each giving nearly 15,000lb SLST* with reheat, provided the aircraft in its initial light-weight configuration with a 1 to 1 power-to-weight ratio — a potential unusual even now in the late 1970s, which was unheard of up to then in the 1950s. An air data computer, the first in a British fighter, supplied signals to the control system, flight instruments, and ultimately the weapons system.

The prototype XA 847 again had the inadequate fuel capacity of the P1 of about 6,000lb. The design office party-line was that 'with the better specific fuel consumption and much greater thrust of the RA24, fuel economy will be much improved'. It was — up to a point — and we began to improve our average test flights to 30-40min in the P1B which, though better, was still a long way short of a practical fighter endurance. It also made test flying an inefficient matter of frequent short flights.

XA 847 flew over 30 flights in the two months following first flight and cleared its initial design envelope to Mach 1.8, covering the first Service release point of Mach 1.5 by a good margin. By the end of 1957 it had become clear that this aircraft would set new standards of performance and fine controllability. Mach 2 was already in sight as a practical goal for development without major redesign work, but the fuel situation remained an enigma. After many more flights of groping back to Warton following only half an hour's test work to arrive with 800lb in the tanks or barely enough for one safe overshoot, circuit and landing and no margin for diversion, I wrote a paper expressing the view that for operational flexibility in any role the P1B needed considerably more fuel. I also made it clear that it would not stand a cat-in-hell's chance of achieving export sales unless we were able to more than double the existing internal fuel capacity.

That was in 1957.

*Sea level static thrust.

*Below:* Lightning P1B prototype at Warton. April 1957.   *BAe*

*Above:* Joining the photographic Meteor on Flight 1, 4 April 1957.
*BAe*

*Above right:* Going in to land on Flight 1.   *BAe*

*Below:* Preparation for first flight.   *Flight International*

Eventually in 1963 the Air Ministry accepted our proposals for retrospectively increasing the internal fuel capacity of the Mk 3 Lightning then entering service to 10,000lb. Shortly after this overseas customers began to make enquiries. These led to the Saudi Arabian interest which became the basis for the biggest single British export order on record at that time, with follow-up orders which totalled more than 1,000 million pounds sterling over the next ten years. It was a strange paradox that the company which had made its name in postwar aircraft design with the Canberra, one of the most flexibly operating military aeroplanes of all time, should have spent the next decade failing to recognise that it was likely to kill its own supersonic fighter project stone dead by not developing the fuel system.

In flight XA 847 was superb with crisp, precise controls resulting from three years' development and perfecting on the P1. There was a total absence of 'PIO'* tendencies throughout the flight envelope which was soon extended to Mach 2. In October 1958 the P1B became the first British aircraft to make Mach 2 and achieved this speed regime without dependence on autostability on any axis. Pitch and yaw autostabilisation was provided subsequently for weapons aiming accuracy but the whole initial flight envelope

*Pilot-induced oscillation.

clearance to Mach 2 was completed safely before the autostabilisers were even available for trials.

With increased weight over the P1 prototype (approximately 30,000lb in comparison with the P1's 26,700lb) the effect on the induced drag of the semi-delta wing in the landing configuration was more noticeable as a need to balance incidence with power in the classic delta manner. With the responsive, surge-free and powerful RA24 engines, however, this was no problem.

A rate of climb of 30,000ft in two and a half minutes and low level acceleration to 700kt/Mach 1.1 in two minutes from brakes-off tended to sort out the pilots. Stability and control was such that once the pilot had become rate-adapted to this mode of progress confidence was gained rapidly. It became clear that although the Lightning would double the performance of Fighter Command at one step from the Hunter as had the Canberra from the Lincoln in Bomber Command, the transition would be straightforward. We were confident that with such superb handling qualities 847 would have an easy passage through its Boscombe Down trials. This it did with one notable exception.

'A' Squadron pilots reported that due to high induced drag, allegedly inadequate speed-stability and poor response to ailerons at the firm's recommended approach speed of 175kt, Boscombe would recommend a visual approach speed of 185kt and even faster for instrument-approach conditions. This was a sharp divergence of opinion and it had serious implications on programme costs and on clearance into the Service. The Company's figures had been arrived at to provide a margin for Service conditions over the 165kt approach and 150kt touchdown speeds pronounced practical under test conditions by Company pilots. The recommended 175kt approach fitted well into the Auto-ILS design datum speed for the production aircraft for which the autopilot system design had already been finalised. Approach speed increases of the order proposed by Boscombe would in accordance with the 'square of the speed' law seriously degrade the landing performance. They would compromise specified landing distances and brake, wheel and tyre design margins, as well as the design datum speed for the autopilot-coupled ILS mode. The debate was lengthy and not satisfactorily concluded for some time, neither side seeing good reason to give way. This argument thus became an

*Above left:* P1B on test from Warton. Ventral tank fitted. *BAe*

*Left:* Lightning take-off! *Flight International*

*Above:* P1B Farnborough Display 1957. *BAe*

example of the difficulty of achieving efficient compromise on all occasions between strongly held opposing views on qualitative matters.

With the more elaborate instrumentation systems of today there is less chance of misinterpretation because less is left to qualitative judgement. In this case, however, the Lightning's initial clearance was compromised by Boscombe's insistance on an excessive instrument-approach datum speed. The initial autopilot throttle datum had to be modified to suit the new figure and then remodified back to the makers' original 175kt, all at the taxpayers' expense when reason finally prevailed some years later.

Boscombe also made strong criticism of the cockpit instrumentation with which we agreed whole-heartedly. Development of the OR 946* system had not kept pace with the aircraft programme and the flight instrumentation did not match the performance of the aircraft. Particularly criticised was the CSI† which gave IAS and IMN on one dial with a confusing and indistinct presentation. In the year following the first P1B flight, during a visit to California to evaluate Century-series fighters I became conscious of the fact that although having received prior warning from authorities in this country that the American counterpart CSI made by Kollsman was 'even more unsatisfactory'. I had flown four different advanced prototypes in the course of a week at Palmdale and Muroc. In each of them I had used the Kollsman instrument which had at no time proved difficult to read, interpret, or to be otherwise unsatisfactory. This instrument presented IAS conventionally round the dial and IMN digitally in a window which gave sufficient information

*OR 946 was the Operational Requirements specification for the flight instrument system.

†Combined Speed Indicator.

to show trend as well as actual Mach number. This presentation seemed entirely satisfactory and a possible solution for the Lightning. Accordingly arrangements were made for one of these instruments to be obtained and fitted to a Lightning. We carried out a trial at Warton which was completely satisfactory and then delivered the aircraft to Boscombe whose pilots also reported favourably. The Kollsman was not procured however and the matter was dropped. The reason, we were told, was that Air Staff policy required that the OR 946 system must continue to be developed as planned.

Some years later a completely new system of OR 946 'Strip Speed' display was introduced. Once again it was at considerable cost to the taxpayers of course, and again it proved quite unsuitable without lengthy and expensive modification. Even when finally it came into service in the Mk 3 and subsequent Lightnings, this instrument was in some ways still inferior to the Kollsman.

Expansion of the flight envelope of XA 847 to 700kt IAS and ultimately M=1.9 was, however, made with a number of constraints in relation to predicted buzz-boundary trouble and to the probable effects of thermal stress on critical areas and equipments at the skin temperatures to be expected at twice the speed of sound. In the event ram temperature indication was provided with a 'never exceed' limit set at 115°C. This proved to show a small but adequate margin of safety at Mach 2. Rolling manoeuvres were also strictly limited owing to known low NV with the prototype fin.

At the other end of the envelope 700kt/1.1 provided us with our first supersonic flights at low level. Ultimately Mach 1.05 at 500ft or less over the sea was an impressive experience for the first few times in 1959. Here also the trials were relatively trouble-free. Later in the programme, however, when clearing 'corner points' we did encounter problems with impressive engine 'bang' surges under these conditions. There was also a reduction in aileron effectiveness due to a combination of wing flexing and adverse yaw.

Within a year of first flight the basic standard of control, stability and performance of the P1B had been accepted for the Service. A mammoth development programme totalling 21 prototypes and pre-production series aircraft was gaining momentum to clear the full and very advanced weapons system. At that stage the performance capabilities of this remarkable aircraft were approached only by the F-104 and the Mirage, and both of these aircraft had inferior qualities of stability and manoeuvrability.

Fifteen years later the Lightning Mk 6 and Mk 2A in the RAF and the Mk 53 export version in Kuwait and Saudi Arabia, remained the fastest reacting interceptors in service in the western world. They had by then proved their superiority in combat manoeuvrability over their equivalents in current service — including the Mirage, Phantom and Starfighter.

But this achievement was not reached without problems. These included the loss of four development Lightnings from Warton from which Squier, Dell and Elkington, Knight, and Cockburn all ejected safely with the reliable assistance of our good friend Jimmy Martin*.

Major milestones in the P1/Lightning programme were the initial flight of 847 and first flights to Mach 2, as recorded in the following reports:

*Sir James Martin, designer and manufacturer of the world's finest escape system, the Martin Baker ejection seat.

*Right:* 2nd prototype P1B with Firestreak missiles. 1958. *BAe*

---

### THE ENGLISH ELECTRIC CO. LTD.
### AIRCRAFT DIVISION, WARTON AERODROME, PRESTON

FLIGHT No. : 1,

DATE : 4.4.57

# EXPERIMENTAL FLIGHT REPORT

AIRCRAFT TYPE ___F23/49___  PILOT ___Mr. R.P. Beamont___

AIRCRAFT SERIAL No. ___XA 847___  NAVIGATOR ___-___

OBSERVER ___-___

PASSENGER ___-___

OBJECT OF TEST :—

    P1B Prototype

    Initial handling

TAKE-OFF LOADING :—  FUEL (GALLS)

| | | | | | |
|---|---|---|---|---|---|
| TARE WEIGHT & Eqpt | 23,616 LB. | 426 lb , | Residual | ( 54 gal ) |
| FUEL | 4,535 LB. | 2,267.5 lb | port-usable | (287 gal ) |
| MISCELLANEOUS | LB. | 2,267.5 lb | stbd-usable | (287 gal ) |
| CREW | 208 LB. | 4,961 lb | Total | 628 gal |
| BOMBS, FLARES or BALLAST | 578 LB. | | | |
| TOTAL | 28,937 LB. | | | |

TYRE PRESSURES:—  OLEO PRESSURES :—

MAIN ___260___ LB/SQ. IN.  MAIN ___425___ LB/SQ. IN.

NOSE ___240___ LB/SQ. IN.  NOSE ___330___ LB/SQ. IN.

C.G. POSITION AT TAKE-OFF ___7.877' aft of datum 33.73% SMC___

TIME AT TAKE-OFF ___12.51___

TIME AT LANDING ___13.18___  TOTAL ___00.27___

SPECIAL FLIGHT LIMITATIONS:—

    See Design Certificate.

---

F23/49   XA 847       Flight No 1       4 April 1957

*Alterations since Taxi No 1:*

1  No 25 2-stream brake parachute installed (Type 7 High Speed Stream). All taschengurts removed; 15ft 9in cable with clamps fitted; eye end with modified ferrule and side plate assembly; shroud lines from skirt to keeper 16ft 0in.

2  Checks carried out during engine runs of Alternator and Turbine warning light failure; found satisfactory. No action.

Prior to flight checks. After connecting parachute and seat harnesses, it was found that the loose adjustment portions of the lower port straps together with buckles overhung the canopy jettison handle and obscured vision of this. Direct access to this handle was also obstructed by these straps.

The aircraft oxygen hose was not clipped to the starboard lower seat harness.

The emergency oxygen bottle had no separate manual operation and it was apparently intended that the pilot should operate this by pulling on the cable. This did not appear to be a practical operation owing to the geometry of the cockpit and of the cable concerned, and this limited the altitude for the subsequent flight.

Engine starts and checks were satisfactory and all warning lights and indicators were 'out' with engines at 31-54%, JPTs 540/480°C.

Hydraulics: 3,000psi
Flap operation and indication satisfactory
Dive brake operation and indication satisfactory

In taxying with engines at 31/54% there were no further system warnings, with the exception that No 1 oil pressure blinker showed an intermittent 'white'. This was eliminated by increasing to 35%.

Take-off was made with engines at 100/100% and was smooth and straightforward with acceleration of a similar order to No 1 with reheat, but without the usual high noise and vibration level associated with that engine installation.

Undercarriage retraction was smooth and symmetrical and the climb away was held steeply in order to maintain speed below 300kt initially.

Power was reduced to 70/70% at approximately 5,000ft and all systems checked before reaching 10,000ft. No abnormalities were found and the climb was continued to 27,000ft.

At this height at 0.8 IMN power was reduced and at 70/70% a sharp increase in noise level occurred of a type normally associated with cabin venting, canopy mal-fitting or other airflow noises. It was found that this noise increase was associated with engine speed and would come in as power was reduced to 70% and stop on increase above 70% at will.

A maximum cold thrust acceleration was carried out reaching 1.13 IMN, 495kt IAS, 25,500ft, and power was then reduced slightly to 80%. At this point the noise increase occurred again, and deceleration from M=1.0 and the subsequent descent at 0.9 was accomplished by employing half dive brake with engines maintained at 80%, in a spiral descent at 2-3g.

The increased noise level condition did not occur below 15,000ft where both engines could be throttled to idling.

Dive brake checks were carried out up to 400kt IAS and 0.9 IMN and these were found to be very effective. There was no buffet or noticeable trim change up to deflection in excess of 50%, but at approximately 75% on the gauge, buffeting began which at 400kt was quite severe. Associated with this buffet was a mild, erratic directional wander. At all points, reduction of dive brake deflection to less than 75% eliminated this directional characteristic and reduced the buffet to negligible proportions.

Subsequent use of the dive brakes for closing into formation with the chase aircraft demonstrated their efficiency in this role.

During descent fuel contents were checked at 1,100/1,100lb at 0+17 and an idling descent was continued into the circuit.

General control characteristics in this flight had been almost identical to those of the first and second prototypes with unmodified wings, and aileron control had the old characteristics of slight over-sensitivity at transonic speeds. Buffet thresholds under 'g' seemed to be virtually identical with those of the first prototypes without modified leading edge. Transition through Mach 1 occurred without buffet or vibration and with even less trim change between 0.9 and 1.0 than on the previous aircraft.

The nose up trim change characteristics were quite normal and undercarriage lowering occurred with more symmetry and therefore less disturbance than on the previous prototypes.

The final turn was made at approximately 200kt and characteristics on the approach were normal until, when initiating the hold-off at approximately 170kt IAS, the rate of change in pitch from full tailplane deflection was found to be rather less than that of the previous aircraft. This resulted in a touchdown at almost constant attitude, but without a high rate of descent.

The tail parachute was streamed satisfactorily after touchdown but required a heavy force to operate the small handle. This operation was difficult.

Mild braking was used during the landing run and did not result in judder. Steering and control on the runway were excellent.

*Summary*

The first impressions left by this flight were of a marked reduction in engine and airflow noise level in the conditions tested, and of greatly improved comfort, convenience and vision in the cockpit.

Stability and control responses were clearly recognisable as those of the standard wing P1A, and transition to supersonic speed occurred with the complete lack of buffet and little trim change characteristic of that aircraft.

Mild buffet roughness was apparent at subsonic speeds under 'g' under similar circumstances to the P1As with standard wing.

Airbrake operation was smooth and trouble-free with excellent retardation at up to ²⁄₃rds deflection. Buffeting was present above this.

Handling was therefore straightforward with the characteristics that had been expected, but made unexpectedly pleasant by the greatly reduced noise level and engine vibration level in comparison with the first prototypes.

*Defects*

None requiring action before next flight.

R. P. BEAMONT
Chief Test Pilot

The English Electric Co Ltd, Warton Aerodrome, Nr Preston, Lancs.
12 December 1958
F23/49 Summary of Flying Qualities
Mach 2.00 in the Lightning

Since the fitting of the large fin and rudder to the first prototype and some subsequent development aircraft, full handling clearance has been obtained up to design speed at 1.7 IMN/700kt IAS, and to altitudes in excess of 60,000ft at supersonic speed.

The margin of directional stability in the operational configuration of ventral tank and two Blue Jay missiles has been sufficiently satisfactory at design speed to warrant investigating further the high performance capabilities of the aircraft, and a satisfactory amount of handling, and stability and performance testing, has now been carried out in the region of 1.8-1.9IMN.

The decision to extend the range of speeds to be covered involved consideration of two other factors which had not hitherto been of significance in the Flight Test programme; the first being intake buzz, and the second temperature effects.

Wind Tunnel testing and evidence from other sources has indicated that duct instability might begin under standard conditions with engines throttled back to idling speed above M=1.80, and that this buzz might develop to very serious amplitudes at around M=2.00; and at speeds above M=1.9 excessive ram air temperatures might result in stressing problems in certain areas, and in equipment cooling difficulties. American flight experience suggested that the 'buzz' estimates might be slightly pessimistic however.

A progressive test programme was evolved calling for speed increments of 0.05 IMN from 1.7 IMN, and latterly duct pressure and ram air temperature instrumentation was added to the first prototype to record intake stability characteristics and temperature conditions.

In this series of tests air temperature limits were imposed of standard day or colder in order to maintain conditions reasonably favourable for intake stabililty, aircraft performance and structure; and at each progressive stage directional stability was checked and recorded by the control-free rudder-induced dutch roll method, while intake buzz clearance was obtained by throttling to idling at progressively higher Mach numbers, and subsequently with increased incidence under normal acceleration.

When limited handling clearance had been achieved to 1.9 IMN in the clean configuration, and 1.88 in the missile configuration, some unusual vibration conditions were experienced at 1.92 IMN which were thought to be possible intake buzz onset. After landing a single fastener on the intake bullet was found to be free and in the fully extended position, and as this could not be proved to be the result of faulty locking, it was thought for some time that it might possibly have been caused by unstable flow conditions.

Thorough investigation failed to provide a positive answer to this question but indicated that the fastener may have not been properly tensioned, and it was decided to re-investigate this flight case.

Previous flying to 1.9 IMN in both configurations had resulted in satisfactory stability and control response characteristics, and with a clearly adequate margin of Nv it was decided to continue the investigation with 'not to be exceeded under any circumstances' limits set at 2.00 IMN or 115°C indicated ram air temperature whichever was the lower, and engine speeds not to be throttled below the minimum reheat speed (96%) at speeds above 1.9 IMN.

On the first suitable occasion with the met air temperature at −75°C/44,000ft this test was completed uneventfully. After a smooth acceleration without change in noise level or increase in vibration power was reduced in reheat on passing 1.9IMN to check speed control, and on finding this positive maximum power was re-applied with immediate resumption of speed increase.

No recurrence of the previously reported vibration occurred on passing 1.92 IMN, and the acceleration continued with little apparent rate decrease. On passing 1.98 IMN power was again reduced from maximum reheat to one-quarter reheat. This was

sufficient power briefly to stabilise speed at 2.00 IMN at 42,500ft in level flight under these temperature conditions.

Flight conditions remained relatively unchanged with no increase in noise or vibration levels, and with the ram air temperature gauge indicating 94°C cabin conditions remained comfortable without reference to the temperature controller which had been pre-set at ¾ Warm.

Stability and control response remained satisfactory throughout for normal manoeuvre and flight corrections, but the expected slight reduction in damping in pitch was apparent as speed increased. Responsiveness in roll was still remarkably good, and heading holding and turn initiation presented no problems. It was interesting and significant to note that at no point during the flight was any undamped short-period oscillation apparent, other than the usual two-to-three cycles before damping following displacements in pitch or yaw at the higher Mach numbers; and that autostabilisers, which are not fitted to this prototype, were not employed: this being in marked contrast to the characteristics of the Century Series aircraft.

It soon became necessary to reduce speed for no other reason than that the aircraft had by this time run out of the available sea space and was heading in overland towards a populated area, having covered 90 nautical miles in about 3 minutes 50 seconds since leaving the North Wales coast on a northerly heading.

The throttles were moved from minimum reheat into the cold range thereby momentarily dropping RPM to 96/95% before returning the throttles to 100/100%. No adverse or unusual conditions resulted from this, and the deceleration began and continued under normal flight conditions.

On passing 1.9 IMN directional stability was checked by dutch roll in a 2g turn to starboard, and found to be perfectly satisfactory, and a throttle chop to idling was made on passing 1.8 IMN under 'g', again with satisfactory results.

At the reheat cut point the fuel remaining was approximately 1,500/1,500lb, and after a subsonic recovery to base over a range of approximately 80 nautical miles the fuel remaining in the circuit was 1,350/1,350lb. (Total prototype usable fuel 6,360lb.)

Instrumentation records confirmed that no intake duct instability had occurred throughout, and that directional stabililty had remained entirely adequate for limited handling clearance under these conditions.

While these tests cannot be taken to imply the possibility of immediate clearance to Mach 2.00, the following points have been established.

(1) There is a clear excess of thrust over drag remaining at this speed under the conditions tested, so that the optimum performance of this aircraft has yet to be established.
(2) Under certain clearly defined limiting conditions M=2.00 performance is practical with this aircraft in respect of temperature effects.
(3) Intake duct instability has not occurred in steady flight conditions up to M=2.00, or in manoeuvring flight up to M=1.9, or with engines fully throttled up to M=1.8. (The effect of the very low air temperature on the day M=2.00 was achieved being favourable as regards 'buzz'.)
(4) Stability and control has been established as adequate for flight with gentle manoeuvres up to M=2.00, without the use of autostabilisers.
(5) The cabin air conditioning system is adequate under the temperature rise conditions resulting from accelerations to the speed range of 1.8-2.00 IMN.

These results indicate that full clearance may be possible to CA Release standards for Mach numbers higher than the specification speed of M=1.7, and also that the basic aerodynamics and control systems of the aeroplane should be fully capable of further operational performance stretching to M=2.00 and beyond for future developments.

R. P. BEAMONT
Chief Test Pilot

# Lightning Prototype XA 847

XA 847 was, like many first prototype aircraft, extremely well-liked by ground staff because of its basic reaiability and also by pilots for this reason and for its straightforward and viceless flying characteristics. A logical but comprehensive development of the P1, XA 847 was the first P1B or Lightning with much increased power, new electrical and hydraulic systems, and basic provision for a complete weapons system. It flew for the first time in April 1957 without autopilot or autostabilisers as a time-saving measure. Stability and control without automatics not only proved adequate within the initial flight limits but subsequently enabled the full design flight envelope to be investigated.

The aircraft was taken to M=1.2 on its first flight and within two months and 36 flights had achieved the initial design limits of M=1.7 and had been supersonic at low level. The aerodynamic and control qualities proved to be exceptional and pilot training was carried out easily with English Electric Company pilots and Service test pilots without the dual and simulator facilities which were to come later. Conversions were generally made in two or three flights, and subsequently many pilots had their first supersonic experience in XA 847 in one straight conversion flight after Hunter or Sabre experience.

By the end of 1957 the exploratory tests had shown that speeds of the order of M=2.0 should be practical from the stability and control aspects. Some problem areas were known to exist. For instance, it was not known whether the fixed centre-body intake with a design point of M=1.7 could be taken much above this without encountering 'intake buzz'.

This was a duct pressure instability characteristic of supersonic conditions which had resulted in duct failures in other aircraft. Similarly, systems cooling which was adequate for M=1.7 might become distinctly marginal at the ram temperatures associated with M=2.0.

The limits were raised in stages and in 1958 XA 847 was taken to M=1.8, M=1.85 and M=1.9, all under conditions of excellent control and satisfactory systems performance. Pressures of official development programme prevented further immediate progress, but by late 1958 there was sufficient knowledge to indicate the conditions under which a M=2.0 run could reasonably be attempted.

A low-temperature day of ICAN −10°C at the tropopause coupled with a high tropopause was required to provide the best margins of safety. When these conditions were encountered on 25 November 1958 a snap decision was made on climb from Warton to discard the current test schedule for stability measurements in favour of the planned M=2.0 run. This intention was notified to Ulster and Warton Radars, and 847 was swung on to a northerly heading over the north coast of Wales at 38,000ft and full reheat applied.

In impressively few minutes later with the Machmeter registering 2.0, 847 was tearing across the Solway Firth under smooth and stable control conditions. The cabin was comfortably cool in spite of the 114°C ram air temperature and all systems were operating perfectly. Cancellation of reheat at this speed for the first time produced an impressive deceleration, and then 847 was put into a starboard turn which seemed to encompass most of the Lake District before we were back on heading to Warton.

Descending at what now seemed a peacefully gentle glide at 90% of the speed of sound, one reflected that this was indeed a milestone. Britain now had a M=2.0 fighter. Its existence was the direct result of the resolute determination of Teddy Petter, Freddie Page and the English Electric team to remain unimpressed by the Government edict in 1948 that manned supersonic flight was too dangerous for the British.

*Below:* 1st prototype air photography soon after it had achieved Mach 2 on 25 November 1958. *BAe*

*Right:* 1st prototype air photography soon after it had achieved Mach 2 on 25 November 1958. *Flight International*

*Below:* Flight plan for first Mach 2 test run.  *BAe*

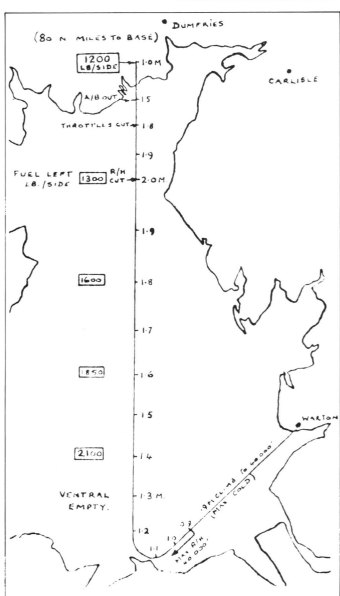

I radioed to Warton a message to the effect that Mr Page might be interested in attending the debriefing, and this proved to be a sound prediction.

The M=2.0 flight completed the technical success of the flight envelope exploratory programme. XA 847 was employed subsequently in measuring buzz boundary effects and stability in this regime as part of the progressive programme to increase the Service limits of the Lightning. It was also used in research leading to improved cruise drag for later marks.

The one adverse feature highlighted by the Mach 2.0 flight was fuel shortage. As expected, M=2.0 had been reached with barely sufficient fuel for the return cruise to base to be achieved with conventional diversionary fuel margins on arrival. It was abundantly clear that the fuel capacity sufficient for M=1.7 intercept in the specified 'narrow profile' UK defence role was insufficient for use of the aircraft in virtually any other role. I made strong recommendations that for reasonable flexibility in future varied roles, particularly overseas, no less than double the existing fuel capacity would be needed. This increase would have to be 'internal' and supersonic. It could not be met with the already planned overwing ferry tanks.

Three variations of under-fuselage tank were planned. Two of these were evaluated in mock-up form on XA 847 in association with increases in dorsal fin and ventral fin area necessary to maintain the required margins of $N_v$. As a result of this successful programme the Ministry were offered in 1959 doubled internal fuel capacity for all production Mk 3 Lightnings. This proposal was not acted on finally for four years until in 1963 the modified fuel system was ordered for retrofit to all Mk 3 Lightnings. These aircraft, in service as Mk 6s, have range and endurance capability comparable to that of most Mach 2 fighters of the 1960s, and it was this version which formed the basis for the export Lightnings for Saudi Arabia and Kuwait.

XA 847 was a key prototype in the classical tradition in all this. It was virtually always serviceable when needed, it was a delight to fly and provided an excellent example of the capacity and ability of British aviation to provide the right aeroplane at the right time in spite of irresolute procurement policies.

# Flying the Lightning

'No sweat — I was with it all the way until I let the wheel brakes off!' This comment of a fighter pilot after his first flight in a Lightning summed up one aspect of conversion to this highly supersonic fighter. Since the first Service evaluation on the P1 prototype in 1955 the speed with which pilots learnt to operate the aircraft and to like it very much indeed has been remarkable. Only the rate at which things happen has caused comment for the first few trips.

The flight development of the Lightning involved rather more than the usual progressive testing of a new type as it was carried out as part of this country's first fully supersonic research programme. This meant that the work of proving stability, controllability, systems reliability, performance, structural integrity and operational suitability, all had to be progressed in parallel with and often in the same aircraft as the basic research programme. As we have seen, this in itself involved the first British level flight at the speed of sound (in 1954) and the first British flight at twice the speed of sound three years later. The basic aerodynamics proved to be very sound. It was thus quickly possible to concentrate on developing subtle changes into the power control system to improve response and feel up to a point where on production aircraft these controls were probably the most pleasant compromise between responsiveness, effectiveness, and smoothness yet achieved on a fighter aeroplane.

Setting off for a flight in the Lightning is by no means the formidable task which it might be imagined to be. Although there are quite a number of pre-flight operations and checks to be made, these are quite easily learnt by heart. In reality it only takes a few minutes for the pilot to strap into his fully automatic low-level Martin Baker ejection seat, to set the battery isolating switch, the engine starting switches, the fuel pump switches, the inverter switch, the instrument master switch, and finally the throttle-operated high pressure cocks before pressing the starting buttons.

The engines start virtually simultaneously in a few seconds. After the ground electrical supplies are waved away or pulled out automatically on an operational take-off, only the windscreen demisting systems remain to be switched on before setting the cabin conditioning auto-control and checking hydraulic and DC and AC electrical supplies and the combined warnings system, prior to take-off. The Mk 4 BS ejection seat is adjusted for height electrically. The canopy is lowered electro-hydraulically and locked mechanically by lever with safe locking confirmed by visual check of the bolts and by two warnings lights on the canopy arch which extinguish as the mechanism goes over-centre.

Final prior-to-flight checks are carried out while taxying, or at 'readiness' (in service these checks are completed on the ORP*). After letting the brakes off and applying full unreheated power the Lightning accelerates to take-off speed, 160kt, in about 14 seconds. The nosewheel is held in contact with the runway by a light forward pressure on the stick until $V_r$ is reached. The stick is then moved firmly back and the aircraft rotated until lift-off occurs. With its very favourable power/weight ratio take-off performance is not critical and so the recommended $V_r$ has been set to give lift-off with the simplest pilot action compatible with an adequate speed margin against inadvertent tail bumper rubbing. The latter can occur if the more traditional method is employed of

*Operational Readiness Platform.

*Below:* Roll-out of first Lightning T4 trainer.  *BAe*

lifting the nosewheel at the lowest possible speed and followed by too vigorous use of the tailplane control.

Maintaining contact between the nosewheel and the runway until rotation speed also provides a greater margin of directional control in high crosswinds.

After lift-off the take-off attitude is held in visual or instrument conditions to maintain the initial climb angle while selecting undercarriage up, preferably before reaching 220kt IAS. The placard speed is 250kt but the limit for maximum rate of retraction is 220kt and this is very quickly exceeded if incidence is reduced after take-off while maintaining climb power.

With undercarriage locked away the climb attitude is reduced slightly at about 1,000ft, and as speed builds up rapidly a little nose-down trim is applied with the stick trim switch. Autostabilisers may be engaged here though not essentially, and fine trimming is completed on all axes.

At 450kt IAS the climb is resumed by a firm rotation and this speed is held until, with rapidly increasing altitude 0.9 IMN is indicated. Climb speed is controlled on the Machmeter thereafter still by tailplane and with engines at maximum 'dry' thrust. The climb angle can easily exceed 40° when the engine controls are moved into the reheat section on passing 25,000ft at only a very few minutes after 'brakes off', and Mach 1.0 is exceeded during the push-over at the tropopause. As with all aircraft of this generation reheat acceleration is made at the tropopause for either speed performance or supersonic and energy climb performance, and at maximum reheat the design limits of the aircraft are reached quickly in level flight.

In the Mach 0.9 climb the aircraft has remained virtually in trim at the original trim settings and only requires retrimming on encountering the transonic trim changes which take the following form:

At 0.95 IMN a slight nose-down trim change begins which increases to about 5lb pull force if untrimmed at 0.98 IMN.

*Left:* Preparing to fly the T4.
*BAe*

*Below left:* First flight of T4.
6 May 1959.  *BAe*

*Right:* T4 close up for the camera
on first flight.  *BAe*

*Below:* T4 landing on first
flight.  *BAe*

At this speed some slight roughness is felt and then as the shock wave passes the pitot/static holes and the ASI system 'jump' occurs from 1.00 to 1.03, the roughness ceases and the longitudinal trim returns to normal. If the nose-down trim change has been trimmed out on passing 0.95 IMN then trim becomes slightly nose-up beyond Mach 1.00. Continued acceleration from Mach 1.0 to Mach 2.0 results in the small progressive nose-down trim change characteristic of all the current generation of fighters which have slight static longitudinal instability supersonic.

Longitudinal trimming is easily taken care of with one or two blips of the trim switch, and on most Lightnings a small directional trim change which also occurs in transition to supersonic is taken out with one application of the rudder trim switch on the port console.

The supersonic acceleration in maximum reheat is smooth and fast (very fast indeed on a low temperature day), and an unwary pilot could all too easily exceed the design limits.

Having accelerated to attack speed at the tropopause one then has great flexibility in getting into an attacking position particularly against fast targets due to high speed, good manoeuvrability and remarkable zoom climb performance.

Control response is very good at all speeds and although damping of the long period oscillation is slightly reduced above Mach 1.0, stability and control are more than adequate even at Mach 2.0 without using the autostabilisers. With autostabilisation damping is virtually dead-beat on all axes throughout the flight envelope.

At Mach 2.0 with the ram air temperature exceeding 100°C and leading edges and windscreen structure becoming hot, cockpit conditions are maintained at a comfortable temperature with a fresh and even air circulation. Noise level is relatively low and altogether with the pleasantly responsive controls and ease of accurate trimming, flight at Mach 2.0 is a pleasant and undramatic experience.

Even slow and fast rolls at this speed are a simple matter of displacing the stick in the required direction, the aircraft responding accurately with little or no sideslip. As with all other aircraft of this performance aerobatic manoeuvres at the higher speeds are associated with rate of roll and 'g' limitations.

Another control feature of importance to the pilot is that the longitudinal tailplane control was developed to provide the required response characteristics throughout the whole speed range of the aircraft while at the same time achieving control-limited conditions at design speed in the normal acceleration sense. In other words, at design limiting speed the pilot has just sufficient tailplane control to achieve the design 'g' flight limits and no more.

On cutting reheat at high speed the sudden loss of thrust is very marked, the pilot being thrown quite forcibly forward against his harness and there is certainly no need for additional braking until speed is lost to the airbrake operating limit of 1.4 IMN.

In this speed area the Lightning has the unique capability of genuine supersonic performance in unreheated thrust, with stabilised level performance capability at the tropopause in the neighbourhood of Mach 1.2 depending on the temperature of the day.

It is also interesting to note that the P1 prototype WG 760 which was the first British aircraft to achieve level supersonic performance did so without reheat, and that its fighter successor was still the only operational aircraft with this capability in 1976.

Throughout the supersonic phase of the flight navigation has been by ground radar positioning cross-checked by the pilot with TACAN bearing and distance information. Continuous attention to navigation is essential at the speeds involved as these flights must be closely controlled in relation to Airways, Control Zones, avoidance of other military traffic and the effects of supersonic booming. After an interception or the completion of the test points, the recovery is carried out at Mach 0.9 cruise at the tropopause for maximum range/economy, and the ability of the aircraft, to be trimmed accurately to fly hands and feet off under these conditions as it can also at supersonic speeds, is pleasant for the pilot.

Fuel system transfer from the ventral tank and flap tanks into the main wing tanks is automatically controlled. All the pilot needs to do is to monitor the ventral tank transfer indicator against the total contents indication during the early part of the flight to ensure that transfer has been completed satisfactorily.

During the final part of the recovery air brakes are opened and power reduced to flight-idling for a steep descent at 400kt into the radar recovery pattern for GCA or ILS.

With its light and responsive controls and inherent stability the Lightning is a good instrument platform. Before the introduction of autostabilisers there was, however, noticeable

*Above and below:* Developments for the Mk3/Mk6 series. Long ventral tank, ventral fins and increased dorsal fin area.   *BAe*

*Right:* First flight-refuelling contact.   *BAe*

rolling moment due to yaw resulting from the highly swept wing which gave a quite marked dutch-rolling effect in rough air in the landing configuration. This is of course also typical of swept wing aircraft, and autostabilisation eliminates the dutch roll. The auto-ILS facility of the Elliott Autopilot is a refinement giving a most satisfactory aid in instrument weather at the end of the flight.

The aircraft is trimmed out in the landing configuration at 1,500ft and normally placed on base leg for ILS by radar control at about ten miles downwind from the instrument runway. ILS mode is selected on the autopilot and the Autopilot Engage switch on the stick selected. The aircraft immediately banks on to an intercept heading of 41-45° from the localiser beam and then rolls out wings level when this heading is stabilised. Prior to intercepting the localiser the aircraft rolls into a turn which closes the localiser beam to roll out wings level without overshoot, height being maintained at 1,500ft and speed within ± 2kt of 175kt by the servo throttle control. These conditions are maintained steadily, in fact more steadily than the pilot is normally capable of doing manually, until the appropriate glide path indication appears. Glide Path is then selected on the autopilot and the nose immediately drops with the throttle servos reducing power to take up the glide slope. Glide slope and localiser are then followed with accuracy still maintaining the constant approach speed until, operationally at 300ft but on test at heights down to as low as 150ft, the pilot flicks the disengage switch, flares and lands manually. This system gives a high degree of accuracy and relieves the pilot of much of the work load associated with flying an accurate ILS approach.

In a normal circuit under visual conditions the Lightning behaves in the approach pattern in much the same way as all the better aircraft in this performance category. If the turns on to base leg and finals are made too steeply the rapid increase in induced drag of the highly swept wing necessitates

112

*Left:* Landing the first T55 (for Saudi Arabia) at Warton on its first flight. *BAe*

*Below left:* Don Knight ejects safely over the Ribble estuary from XG 311 after undercarriage failure. *BAe*

*Bottom left:* Remains of XG 311 returned to Warton. *BAe*

*Right:* Mk53. The ultimate export Lightning which was the basis of overseas contracts worth more than £1 billion. *Ian Macdonald (Photographers) Ltd*

*Below:* Jimmy Dell encounters violent crosswind gust at Warton in a T55. *BAe*

*Above right:* Lightning T4 second prototype at Boscombe Down on 3 November 1975 makes its last flight, flown by the Commandant, Alan Merriman and RPB.
*A&AEE, Boscombe Down*

*Right:* Lightning climb! The T4 at Boscombe. *A&AEE*

*Below:* The supersonic test team at Warton in 1959. Knight, de Villiers, Hillwood, Dell, RPB. *BAe*

use of up to 90% 'dry' thrust to maintain the approach speed. On finals 79% dry thrust settles the aircraft down on to the required 3° glide slope at 175kt, and with crisp ailerons and adequately responsive tailplane the approach is easily maintained. As this approach speed is below the minimum drag speed some power adjustments are necessary during the final approach to maintain accurate speed control. Landing is then a simple matter of flaring-out at about 50ft with firm use of the tailplane control, and then throttling back to the idling stops as the main wheels settle smoothly on at 155-160kt. The tail parachute is streamed after the nosewheel has touched and with this and Maxaret wheel braking the landing run can be as low as 850yd from touchdown.

The available power is such that overshoots must be made with only a small increase in power initially to avoid overstepping the landing gear placard speed, while the single-engine overshoot case is pleasantly uncritical. Twin-engine reliability without asymmetric power trim penalties is a feature very well appreciated by all-weather pilots.

So much for the main operational features. Although a densely equipped radar fighter, the Lightning is fully aerobatic and all normal aerobatic manoeuvres can be carried out smoothly and easily. In the rolling plane particularly the crispness and power of the ailerons allows rates of roll to be achieved far in excess of the maximum normally tolerated by the pilot. In the looping plane, care has to be taken to avoid losing speed on approaching the top of the loop as the induced drag takes effect.

In spite of its considerable weight and size, the manoeuvrability of the Lightning especially at the highest altitudes came as a considerable surprise to fighter pilots. Both they and their controllers were favourably impressed by the comparison of Lightning manoeuvrability under operational conditions with that of other contemporary fighter aircraft including the best subsonic ones.

This then is the Lightning in flight; a machine of considerable complexity, designed to meet and fulfilling a vital and highly technological defence task, yet at the same time a pilot's aeroplane and a fighter pilot's aeroplane at that.

It is highly satisfying to be able to give credit where it is justly due, to the team who designed and built this remarkable aircraft.

*Above:* After the author's last Lightning test flight, a Saudi production flight on 28 March 1968; with ground staff, designers and pilots. *BAe*

*Left:* Jimmy Dell, RPB, Freddy Page. *BAe*

ENGLISH ELECTRIC AVIATION LIMITED,
AIRCRAFT DIVISION, WARTON AERODROME,
PRESTON

FLIGHT No.: 1

DATE: 5.5.59

# EXPERIMENTAL FLIGHT REPORT

AIRCRAFT TYPE ........ P11 Trainer ........ PILOT ........ Mr. R.P. Beamont

AIRCRAFT SERIAL No. ........ XL628 ........ NAVIGATOR ........

OBSERVER ........

PASSENGER ........

OBJECT OF TEST :—

Initial Flight

TAKE-OFF LOADING :—

| | | | FUEL (GALLS.) | |
|---|---|---|---|---|
| TARE WEIGHT & Equipt. | 24,379 | LB. | 506 lb Residual | ( 64 galls.) |
| FUEL | 5,577 | LB. | 2,788.5 lb Port-usable | (353 galls.) |
| MISCELLANEOUS | | LB. | 2,788.5 lb Stbd-usable | (353 galls.) |
| CREW | 208 | LB. | | |
| BOMBS, FLARES or BALLAST | 118 | LB. | 6,083 lb Total | 770 galls. |
| TOTAL | 30,282 | LB. | | |

TYRE PRESSURES :—

MAIN ... 260 ... LB/SQ. IN.  
NOSE ... 240 ... LB/SQ. IN.

OLEO PRESSURES :—

MAIN ... 425 ... LB/SQ. IN.  
NOSE ... 330 ... LB/SQ. IN.

C.G. POSITION AT TAKE-OFF ... 8.053' aft of datum 35.06% S.M.C.

TIME AT TAKE-OFF ... 11.55  
TIME AT LANDING ... 12.20  
TOTAL ... 00.25

AIRCRAFT CONDITIONS:—
See attached sheets.

---

P11 Trainer — XL 628                                   6 May, 1959

Flight No 1

Aircraft condition is as follows for Flight No 1:

(1)   No RP918 2-stage brake parachute installed (Type 7 high-speed stream). All taschengurts removed; 15ft 9in cable with clamps fitted; eye end with modified ferrule and side plate assy; shroud lines from skirt to keeper 16ft 0in. Rip cord cable spade end modified for improved locking at parachute door. No of streams — 3. Total No of streams — 3.

(2)   Oxygen regulators Mk 20, port serial No 29051/58 and stbd serial No 29038/58 installed. Aircraft altitude clearance 40,000ft with Taylor helmet, jerkin and anti-g trousers as per Dwg EB2.00.301 (Ref Design).

(3)   Engine installations, to full reheat standard, are as follows:

| No 1 | No 2 |
|---|---|
| RR Avon 210, eng Ser No 9535 | RR Avon 210, eng Ser No 9538 |
| Reheat turbo pump | Reheat turbo pump |
| Ser No B405 | Ser No B408 |
| Inter Jet Pipe Ser No JLPR4 | Inter Jet Pipe Ser No JLPR2 |
| Reheat Jet Pipe | Reheat Jet Pipe |
| Ser No MSEE102 | Ser No MSEE105 |

(4)   Martin Baker ejection seats, K.4 Port Ser No 2NS, Stbd Ser No 6 (electrically operated seat raising mechanism embodied) installed.

(5)   Alt D2 embodied, 'plain T/E flaps with additional fuel tanks'.

(6)   Alt D7 embodied, 'replacement of L/E flaps by fuel tanks'.

(7)   Alt D6 embodied, 'modified duct division and increased cold air supply'.

(8)   Alt B7 embodied, 'improved generator system for increased capacity of generator amperage output'.

(9)   Alt D15 embodied, 'increased area fin and rudder and modified feel unit'.

(10)   Alt 3275 embodied, 'alterations to tailplane trim to move trim range 2° nose down'.

(11)   Canopy power operated, the switch being incorporated in the canopy locking handle.

(12)   The operation of canopy demister lever, on port console, due to Dwg error is reversed, ie, lever in aft position the system is open, and when lever is in forward position the system is closed. Rectification action will be taken at first aircraft lay-up.

(13)   Compass swing carried out, but the error on the E2B compass was such that it could not be corrected, has been accepted for initial flying, in visual conditions only. Query T4258 refers.

(14)   Ballast (118lb) installed in rear fuselage.

(15)   A/C weighed.

(16)   American TACAN transmitter/receiver, serial No 2571, and coupler unit, Serial No 5417/58, installed.

(17)   Auto-pilot is inoperative (fixed fittings only installed). Jury struts fitted in all flying control systems in lieu of aileron, rudder and tailplane auto-stabilisers.

(18)   Further to para 16, connection link, 10HA/17585, has been fitted between TACAN T/R Aerial change-over relay cable and aerial change-over relay lower aerial cable.

(19)   An A 13 recorder and 7-off Hussenot recorder have been installed and are operative, these being the only Instrumentation Section equipment on A/C. The switch panel is situated on the port side of the Pilot's main instrument panel.

(20)   Due to fuel pressure warning snag during ground engine runs fuse No 194 was found to be blown and a replacement fuse fitted.

(21)   Ref. Pilot's snag during engine runs 'Attention getters too dim' 2 — off clear filaments type 5LX/911283 and one less dense filter, have been fitted to EB4.80.341/353 and found satisfactory.

(22)   Mk 5 PT compass glass broken, accepted for further flying.

(23)   Airframe indicator intermittent in operation, accepted for further flying.

(24)   Further to para 4, both Instructor's and pupil's seats over-run in the down position. Rectification action will be taken later.

Limitations $4\frac{1}{2}$g max and height limitation 40,000ft (for 20 flts). CG at take-off 8.053ft aft of datum.

Auto-pilot inoperative (Fixed fittings only installed).
Nos 1 and 2 VHF radios installed and operative.
IFF inoperative (Fixed fittings only fitted).
ILS inoperative (Fixed fittings only installed).
Tele-briefing inoperative. (Ref Radio Section).
A/C clean.
Instrumentation pack fitted.
AI23 inoperative. (Fixed fittings only installed).
Ventral tank not fitted.
TACAN operative.
A/C clear for night flying. (Ref WID).
Engine anti-icing operative.

For alterations prior to first flight, see attached sheets.

On entering the cockpit and strapping into the pupil's seat it was noted that the test pad on the right knee caused a further restriction in leg position leading to restriction in starboard deflection.,
    Radio checks satisfactory.
    Seat adjustment in the up sense was satisfactory, but the over-run in the down sense was excessive in comparison with the standard case.

Canopy raising, lowering and locking satisfactory.

Engine starts satisfactory. Idling 32/57.5%. At 32% No 1 fuel pressure warning indicated, and this was eliminated at 32.5%.

On one subsequent check the fuel pressure warning indicated below 32%, and re-set again above 32.5%. No further warnings occurred throughout the subsequent flight.

Fuel prior to taxying 2,500/2,500lb.

Altimeter 1,013mbs.

On releasing the brakes to taxi the aircraft did not move, and when re-checking the Instructor's brake lever it was confirmed that this was fully released. Operation of the Instructor's brake lever resulted in an initial heavy force followed by a click at which point the brakes were released and the aircrafts rolled forward. This condition occurred again on releasing the brakes for take-off, but not at any time during taxying before or after flight.

The all-round view for taxying was an improvement over the single seater, although the windscreen arch was noticeably lower in relation to the normal vision line.

Steering and asymmetric braking were rather easier than on the single seater, probably as a result of the revised rudder pedal geometry. Differential braking and brake retardation satisfactory. Brakes holding 90/90% on dry surface.

While taxying the starboard undercarriage green light could not be seen easily as it was obstructed by the lower end of the combined stores jettisoning lever.

The two fuel gauges and the accelerometer were also difficult to read owing to extreme parallax. Take-off with flap down and Hussenot Record. Fuel 2,200/2,050lb.

The undercarriage UP button was less easy to locate than on the single seater, but once located was operated without difficulty.

After lifting the nosewheel at 125kt lift-off occurred at approximately 145kt, and all three controls appeared to be lighter in the climb-out than in the single seater case. The aft CG condition contributing to the elevator sense, and the modified rudder pedals to the rudder sense. The cause of apparently lighter aileron forces was not immediately apparent, but throughout the flight the control forces on all axes seemed lighter than in the standard single seater case.

Immediately and throughout the subsequent flight, directional trimming in relation to the ball sideslip indicator mounted at the base of the servo altimeter was difficult with the indicator showing extreme over-sensitivity. Main trimming was carried out by feel and by reference to compass heading, and it was not felt that the directional trimming characteristics of the aircraft were basically different from standard, and that it was the slip indicator that was at fault.

A reduced power climb was carried out with fuel 2,000/2,000lb on passing 10,000ft. With Hussenot Record a turn to port was initiated at 350kt/15,000ft with quite light stick force per g up to 2g. From this point the sfg reduced rapidly, and at 3g the force to hold had lightened off to near zero. This confirmed the expected characteristics of the aft limit, and although there was a more than adequate margin of controllability in hand it was decided to observe a restriction in landing fuel to 1,000/1,000lb.

20,000ft/Cabin altitude 12,000ft. Cabin conditioning satisfactory with flow distribution good.

At 0.95-0.98/18,000ft very mild roughness occurred of a similar order though possibly less than the standard characteristics of the single seater in transition in clean configuration.

As speed was increased beyond 0.9 IMN, rudder trim up to 0.4 starboard was required until reversing on transition; full port rudder trim being necessary at 1.2/450kt.

In the range of 0.97-0.99 IMN directional and longitudinal trimming was less easy than outside this range, and this did not differ from the standard case.

At 28,000ft with Hussenot Record 3, power was increased to max cold at 0.99 IMN. The jump-up occurred from 1.00 to approximately 1.05 after 16 seconds at max cold, and no buffet or increase in noise level occurred.

Speed was allowed to build up to 1.08 IMN at 30,000ft before moving the throttles to max reheat for a short acceleration to 1.2 IMN. 1.2/450kt was reached quickly at 32,000ft with no further changes in flight characteristics beyond the trim reversal reported above. Stick force per g at this condition was relatively light but quite acceptable.

Power was cut at 1,100/1,400lb, and with Hussenot Record 4 a left rudder stick-free dutch roll was recorded at 0.9/450kt. Visual damping in approximately 3 cycles.

The circuit was joined at 900/1,100lb, and in the landing configuration with undercarriage, flaps and airbrakes, controllability assessed in relation to the aft CG position. Stick force per g was of course much lighter than standard but still quite acceptable at least for test purposes.

Landing runway 26, wind 270°/8kt. Fuel after shutting No 1, 800/1,000lb. Tail parachute operation satisfactory.

During the final turn the intrusion of the windscreen arch into the line of vision was more apparent than on the single seater but vision still remained quite adequate.

Final approach at 170kt with hold-off from 160kt and touchdown at 145kt with light elevator forces.

Flap times — ground check: Down 6 seconds
                                Up 4.8 seconds
Airbrakes — out 6 seconds, in 3.2 seconds.
Fuel after shutting down engines 850/950lb.

*Summary*

Within the limitations imposed for this first flight the aircraft demonstrated excellent handling qualities which were in particular cases improvements over the single seater standard.

No buffet or increase in noise level was apparent from the redesigned cockpit structure up to and including supersonic speed.

A cold thrust acceleration transonic at 30,000ft indicated little loss of performance at least up to the maximum speed checked of 1.2 IMN, as a result of the increased frontal area.

Vision properties through the forward windscreen and through the canopy were slightly improved sideways, backwards and upwards, and slightly restricted forward and upwards in relation to the single seater. The restriction caused by the windscreen arch and by the increased numbers of forward windscreen frame members was not thought to be of operational significance.

Taking into consideration the restrictions and diversions attendant on a prototype first flight, the layout of controls and vital instruments in the cockpit proved satisfactory for operation from the pupil's seat only. Some difficulty is experienced in operating the engine starting panel from this seat, and it is necessary not to tighten the top harness strap before completing the starting operation. Otherwise no discomfort or difficulty was experienced throughout the flight in operating the necessary controls and in viewing the main instruments and systems indicators.

An important exception was the fuel gauges which are viewed with excessive parallax from the pupil's position. These and the accelerometer require angling inwards as far as practicable to improve vision from the pupil's seat.

The revised rudder pedal system results in reduced feel forces both for taxying and in flight, and this factor coupled with the reduced sfg in this aft limit CG configuration resulted in an overall impression of reduced feel forces under all flight conditions. This is pleasant, and with a normally operating directional trim indicator this aircraft may well demonstrate a general improvement in overall flight characteristics over the single seater standard.

Engine handling satisfactory in the conditions tested.

R. P. BEAMONT
Chief Test Pilot

# Lockheed F-104 Starfighter

In June 1958 I was privileged to visit California for the purpose of evaluating some of the 'Century' series supersonic fighters. The quid pro quo for this arrangement being that our new Lightning fighter would be offered for assessment by the USAF in due course. At the time of the visit we had just completed the handling clearance of the Lightning to the flight envelope required for initial release to the RAF. It was thus a suitable moment to compare its capabilities with those of the best of the new generation of American aircraft in this category. On the agreed programme were F-100, F-101, F-102 and F-104, and all these were to be covered in a ten-day visit. The F-100 would be perhaps a waste of valuable time relative to the others as it was already four years old and no faster than our P1A of the same vintage. But there was one aeroplane not listed which was clearly of considerable interest and probably the most nearly comparable in terms of mission requirement to the Lightning, and this was the F-106. Accordingly I had asked for it through the official channels before leaving UK, but on reaching Los Angeles and making contact with Edwards Air Force Base I learnt that nothing had apparently filtered through on this. I telephoned the British Joint Services Mission in Washington and also got in touch with Dick Johnston, Chief Test Pilot of Convair, project pilot on the 106 and an old friend since my Wright Field visit in 1948. The former sounded doubtful and the latter said he would see what could be done. Meanwhile I elected to waive the F-100 and started in on an intensive programme at Palmdale beginning with the F-102.

With admirable discretion the USAF insisted that although I was to do the full conversion course on each single-seater, my first flight would be on an F-102B two-seater under the supervision of my escorting USAF captain. This was a comparatively tame aeroplane with operational performance limited to subsonic speed for practical purposes. It provided, however, a useful introduction to the severe effects of induced drag that resulted from a pure delta configuration. It seemed virtually to stop dead under 'g' without benefit of airbrakes under the combined influence of lift-loss due to up-elevon and the induced drag of the wing, and the high-profile drag of the blunt side-by-side two-seater windscreen and cockpit. But it was a gentle, likeable aeroplane in the handling sense, and with the approbation of my escort 'you've been there before Bee!' I was cleared for a single-seater 'A' version. This was very similar to the 'B' but had a better cockpit layout. It showed a genuine supersonic capability at altitude where about 1.14 Mach was a practical level maximum, but this was soon lost to subsonic in any degree of combat manoeuvre. With light, well-harmonised controls and marked ground effect from the low delta wing, landing was pleasant and precise. In all the F-102 left the impression of a nice aeroplane with performance only a little better than the

Javelin, and one which depended considerably on auto-stabilisation. It also provided a useful introduction to flying over the Mojave desert in the rather complicated traffic patterns of the Palmdale and Edwards control and test route complexes.

For the next evaluation I moved over from the vast Convair production factory at Palmdale to the Lockheed centre on the south side, and there began briefing on the F-104 Starfighter.

This was a very interesting project. After showing remarkable performance in prototype form on the power of one dry thrust Armstrong Siddeley (British) Sapphire engine, it had during the past year with a reheated J79 engine become the first fighter aircraft to acheive Mach 2. It did not have a good reputation at the time following a number of fatal accidents involving experienced test pilots. It was apparent that the 104's wafer-thin and highly-loaded supersonic wing and — at the time — very unreliable engine, were proving to be an unhealthy combination. There were also other serious disadvantages in the design.

Sqn Ldr Stan Hubbard from the Royal Aircraft Establishment Aero Flight had recently flown it, and it appeared that I was the first civilian test pilot from this country to do so. In particular we were interested to find out at first hand how far its high wing loading, critical high tail stall characteristics and general design optimisation for high speed, were compatible with operational flexibility.

After a systems briefing on a training mockup at Lockheed which was not lengthy because of the simplicity of the design, thorough briefings were given in various aspects of handling by specialist test pilots. All of them emphasised the need to understand fully the recommended though somewhat exotic engine-out recovery technique. The reason for this was the prevalent high rate of engine failure coupled with an unfortunate design feature in the escape system which was a Lockheed design. It ejected the pilot downwards through the bottom of the fuselage. Whatever the curious thinking behind its philosophy, in practice the system had failed to save the lives of 21 pilots already in the relatively short trials life of the aeroplane. In particular it was stressed that in the event of a bale-out being necessary in any circumstances below 2,000ft it was essential to roll inverted first so as to eject upwards through the belly of the aircraft. This was despite the fact that Ivan Kincheloe, a leading USAF test pilot, had only recently lost his life attempting to do this following a flame-out after take-off.

All this was quite impressive and I was easily persuaded to pay close attention to the engine-out recovery drill which seemed to be regarded as preferable to using the escape system. But the 104 with its minimal wing area loaded in excess of 100psf gave little impression of being a glider, and

*Above:* F-104 Starfighter.

so the recommended engine-out landing drill was, not unexpectedly, spectacular. In the event of engine failure at altitude I was briefed to keep ASI above 250kt and arrive back over the Edwards runway on the runway heading at not less than 17,000ft (High Key). From this point a 360° turn would be made at 1.5g holding 250kt at the end of which the Starfighter should be 4 miles short of the runway threshold at 5,000ft. If at this point it was pointing at the runway, we should continue to 1,500ft, start to flare and lower the undercarriage and touch down at 185-160kt. But if it was pointing short of or beyond the runway at the 5,000ft point, there was no recourse but to abandon!

This performance had been developed for use at the dry lake emergency landing area of Edwards AFB where it had saved a number of 104s including, I was told, another one while we had been briefing. It was considered worth trying at the much shorter but still over 4,000yd runway at Palmdale. Nevertheless I was briefed to go for Edwards under these circumstances if at all possible.

Following this impressive discussion I was then delivered to the experimental project office for a briefing on the high tail pitch-up characteristics at the stall and its effects on spinning and spin recovery. When the propensity of this configuration for stalling the tailplane in down-wash from the wing at high incidence had been explained, the brief from spinning project pilot Dave Holloman amounted to 'don't do it'. Holloman then went out to fly and I was returned to the Production office to kit up. When this process had been completed and I was about to go out for cockpit briefing under the blazing Californian sun, a stir was apparent. A column of black smoke over the desert marked the end of Holloman's flight when engine failure had occured on finals and too low for a safe ejection.

In this rather discouraging atmosphere it was perhaps unkind of the fates to arrange for zero engine oil pressure indication to occur immediately after take-off on my first 104 sortie.

In the final take-off checks and up to lighting the afterburner, oil pressure had been normal. The pressure loss had been therefore sudden. While automatically reacting to the possibility of immediate power loss by starting a right turn back towards the base, I decided hopefully that it could

possibly be only an electrical failure. This was all happening too quickly for comfort at just after unstick when first impressions of handling were being absorbed. In commencing an emergency turn downwind at 220kt with the undercarriage retracted, necessarily maintaining maximum power, heavy buffet followed by the stick-shaker demonstrated that about 0.5g incremental was about the limit of manoeuvrability in this configuration.

Calling the Tower resulted in the following dialogue:

'Air Force 762 to Lockheed Test — I have an emergency — do you read?'

'Lockheed to Air Force 762 — state your emergency.'

'Air Force 762 — I have zero repeat zero oil pressure.'

'Lockheed to Air Force 762 — understand you have zero oil pressure — what are your intentions?'

By then downwind and lowering the undercarriage I could not resist replying —

'Air Force 762 to Lockheed — what do you suggest?'

This caused a distinct pause and then the instruction —

'We suggest return for immediate reland. You are clear right-handed number 1 for landing runway 25.'

The undercarriage locked down and flaps and power were set to the briefing speeds — plus 15kt added for the high fuel weight — With the engine still sounding healthy despite the indicated lack of oil pressure, it was apparent that this was a heavy-feeling aircraft for such a small one, with in this condition at least, a very small usable 'g' margin. This meant a comparatively large minimum radius of turn and led to some difficulty in lining up with the Palmdale runway because of the frequent phases of stick-jerker. Engine power seemed unaffected, however, and on reaching the runway threshold the 104 responded precisely to elevator and was flared out for a gentle landing at about 165kt.

With throttle closed, tail parachute streamed and nosewheel steering engaged through an awkward-to-depress button on the stick, all was well and on looking at the oil pressure gauge it was seen to be indicating back in the 'green' quadrant! Subsequent investigation confirmed a loose electrical connection.

In two satisfactory flights on the next day the first impressions were confirmed. The F-104 was a small, rough-engined aeroplane with good basic longitudinal characteristics, neutral lateral static stability with inadequate directional damping characteristics which gave a persistent low-amplitude short-period oscillation with rudder autostabiliser engaged that became divergent with autostabiliser off at high Mach number.

The 104's most unsatisfactory feature was the severe effect of its minimal area, highly loaded and very thin supersonic wing on turning manoeuvrability. When attempting to manoeuvre Lightning-style at any speed below 500kt, the 104 was extremely limited by buffet and stick-jerker. It was clear beyond doubt that the manoeuvrability of this aircraft was far less than the standard expected of a conventional fighter.

Nonetheless, on the third flight it was exhilarating to accelerate out to Mach 2, albeit with delicate throttle handling to guard against the briefed sensitivity to surge and flame out. There was also heavy aerodynamic vibration and noise as the ASI approached 700kt and with a large green 'SLOW' light flashing on the central warning panel to indicate that limiting recovery temperature (120°C) was not far away.

From these flights it was obvious that although the Starfighter was an intriguing design and a successful attempt at achieving Mach 2 performance with the power of one readily available series production engine, it had a number of serious drawbacks to operational capability. I felt that it had one of the best examples of fighter cockpit design that I had come across. Apart from that and the excellent vision through windscreen and canopy and its high performance, it had little to commend it as a modern fighter interceptor. Still less was it suitable for its future role as a tactical strike aeroplane. It was already apparent that the USAF were preparing to cut back on their own initial order severely. Later at Edwards I was told that the Air Force no longer contemplated large scale purchase and would have no all-weather role for the aircraft. It would now equip only two wings.

Against this background I added a warning note in my subsequent report to the Ministry. With an unplanned excess production capability at Lockheed following the USAF cancellations, I said, a powerful effort could be expected to export this aircraft to the Air Forces of the western world. Many were already becoming interested in replacements for their postwar first generation jets in the late 1950s. Back home I suggested that the F-104 would prove to be of very limited value in all but the most sophisticated air forces and that it would be likely to suffer a high accident rate, I was soon afterwards asked to present my report to a selected audience at the Air Ministry. There it was received by some members with a certain scepticism based it seemed on the assumption that anything I had to say against the 104 must be part of a pro-Lightning lobby!

Subsequent events in the 1960s amply justified the prediction however when the Starfighter became notorious for its high accident rate, especially in the German Air Force.

The following extracts from the flight reports illustrate both the characteristics of the aircraft and its lack of suitability for the role in which it was eventually sold in remarkably large numbers — though not of course to the USAF.

What *Der Spiegel* said of the aircraft in 1966 is also not without interest.

---

FLIGHT REPORT No 6

Aircraft: F-104A No 762      Engine: J79-7
Date: 27 June 1958
Lockheed Production/Palmdale
Weight: 18,886lb
Fuel (Usable): 5,889lb
Limitations: M=2 or CIT 100°C. 575kt EAS below 30,000ft
Flight Time: 35 minutes

After a third 104 sortie had been aborted on the runway due to UHF radio failure, a final sortie was successful.

As before entry into the cockpit, seat adjustment, accessibility, readability and layout of all controls and instrument was appreciated.

Engine start satisfactory. Systems and warnings normal.
Engine idling 68%, 420°C, nozzle $\frac{3}{4}$.

The view on taxying was again noticeably improved over the Convair fighters, but holding in of the nosewheel steering button on the stick was inconvenient especially on the long taxying involved between the Lockheed plant and the threshold of the runway in use (25, approximately $1\frac{1}{2}$ miles from start-up point). Fuel 5,400lb.

With power at 95%, 590°C, reheat was lit by simple rotation of the throttle outboard, and after the initial roughness had steadied power was increased to max reheat with brakes off.

Acceleration was of a similar order to P1B at max cold, and during initial acceleration short periods of stick jerker vibration occurred.

Rotation was initiated at the briefed speed of 165kt, and as the aircraft flew off smoothly periods of stick shaker vibration occurred on passing through rough air. This condition continued until the angle of climb was reduced very slightly, when the climb-away was continued smoothly during undercarriage retraction, and landing flap retraction at 260kt IAS.

While initiating the required traffic pattern turn to starboard at this speed the stick shaker was again in evidence, but at upwards of 300kt IAS normal course changing manoeuvres could be executed without coming on to this condition.

(Alt 29.9)

| | | | |
|---|---|---|---|
| 16,000ft AMSL | .85 | Zero+2 | Max reheat climb continued. |
| 36,000ft AMSL | .86 | Zero+3 | |

A 1.5g turn to port was initiated at max reheat, 91%/595°C, fuel 3,850lb. The ASI system jump-up occurred during this turn which was held through 210° prior to levelling and continuing the acceleration.

| | | | |
|---|---|---|---|
| 36,000ft AMSL | 1.2 | Zero+5.30 | |
| 36,000ft AMSL | 1.5 | Zero+6.30 | |
| Fuel 3,000lb | | | |
| 36,000ft AMSL | 1.8/500 | Zero+7.10 | |
| | | (Compressor inlet temperature 80°C) | |
| 37,000ft AMSL | 2.0/700 | Zero+8 | |
| | | Noise level and roughness increase from 1.84. Compressor inlet temperature 90°+ and SLOW light indicator flashing. | |
| Fuel 2,500lb | | | |

From subsonic and throughout this acceleration a small amplitude one cps directional oscillation had been present, and this was disturbing to the point of being nearly unacceptable for normal flying purposes. It would presumably be quite unacceptable for gun platform conditions.

The yaw damper was disengaged before decelerating, and the directional oscillation was immediately trebled in amplitude although it did not become divergent.

Pitch damping stabilisers IN at this point was satisfactory, and the aircraft could be pulled into a turn and levelled out without over-correction in pitch or in roll. Aileron response was noticeably more sluggish than at lower speeds, but was still adequate although the lumpy break-out force was not liked.

Engine roughness at Mach 2 was considerable, and owing to the critical nature of the engine installation in these flight conditions care was taken in following the briefing as closely as possible to avoid flame-out. Reheat was cut to max cold, and the resultant deceleration was sharp and associated with 1-2 cycles of oscillation in pitch.

At Zero+12 the descent was begun with indicated fuel now at 2,900lb, 90%/400°C, nozzle $\frac{1}{4}$, oil pressure 42psi, hydraulics 3,000psi.

The next four minutes were devoted to navigation as the high speed run had taken the aircraft out of sight of Muroc on an easterly heading (these flights are not conducted under radar or UHF/DF control), and during this phase the excellent layout of the cockpit, coupled with its simplicity, and the good forward and sideways view was again noted.

Zero+18. Descent continued at 10,000ft, 300kt/88%, fuel 2,250lb; entering recovery pattern from Mojave to Rosamond Lake.

Zero+25, 5,000ft. Rolls to right and left were carried out at 550kt in mild turbulence, and although the ailerons were responsive and powerful the lumpy break-out force resulted in over-correction and a tendency to become slightly out-of-phase with the high rates developed.

On rejoining circuit with 1,900lb fuel airframe buffet was experienced when reducing below 240kt in the clean configuration. This was eliminated with use of landing flap, but after lowering the undercarriage with speed steady at 220kt downwind the stick shaker continued to make itself felt during passage through rough air. On pulling the turn from base leg to final at 190kt the stick shaker came in at approximately 1.3g, and the turn was completed with this continuing.

Directional control in turbulence during the final approach was quite satisfactory with an occasional tendency to lurch sideways, and providing that the correct approach speed of 180kt was maintained at 88% no difficulty was experienced in maintaining the approach to the correct hold-off point, although the aircraft felt critical at all times and aileron lumpiness was again disliked when correcting for rolling moment due to yaw in turbulence.

The hold-off and touchdown were straightforward providing that power was not altered from the 88% set, as to do this would reduce flap blowing and cause a high rate of descent. The soft Dowty liquid spring system undercarriage eliminated all landing shock and assured a smooth touchdown.

After lowering the nosewheel the tail parachute handle was operated, but the parachute was not felt and it was reported by the Tower that it had developed and self jettisoned. Use of the pedal operated wheel brakes was smooth and decelerated the aeroplane reasonably rapidly with moderately heavy use to normal taxying speed in well under 2,000yd.

It was again pleasant to be able to lift open the sideways opening canopy for taxying in under the hot desert sun.

## Conclusions

The relatively poor standard of development of this aircraft in respect of stability and control was unexpected.

Inadequate directional damping even with auto-stabilisers, coupled with excessive break-out forces giving poor feel in the aileron sense, when associated with the critical low speed characteristics of the very thin and highly loaded wing, result in subsonic handling qualities which are at no point pleasant, and which in the take-off and landing configuration are critical and not compatible with bad weather operation.

At supersonic speeds stability and control are adequate for normal operational manoeuvre although again aileron break-out forces are at all times excessive, but at least on the aircraft flown the

auto-stabilisers did not damp the persistent directional oscillation which remained of unpleasant amplitude and was almost certainly in excess of gun platform tolerance.

Normal take-off and climb is dependent on reheat, and the acceleration rates experienced were similar to those of a P1B in cold thrust under more temperate conditions. Overall climb and level acceleration were again similar to the values normally experienced with the P1B, but here allowance must be made for the lower temperatures prevailing over California than the UK average.

Layout and engineering of the cockpit and reduction to the minimum of pilot operations in connection with the emergency and standby systems were of the highest quality experienced to date by this pilot. Conversion to this aircraft could be achieved in half the time and with far less effort than on any other known aircraft of supersonic performance; and in flight vision and accessibility of all essential items coupled with excellent all round external vision resulted in an unusual degree of immediate confidence in these aspects, and allowed full attention to be applied from the start to the required tests. Cabin conditioning was satisfactory also, and during the final flight involving a max reheat climb and acceleration to M=2, only one adjustment of the auto-controller was needed to maintain comfortable cabin conditions. Slight pulsing was experienced during the subsequent descent below 20,000ft.

As in all the aircraft flown the clearly and simply presented combined Warning system was much appreciated.

From this limited experience it seemed most unlikely that without considerable further development this aircraft could be used operationally under other than favourable weather conditions. This was confirmed at Edwards where it was stated that no all-weather role was anticipated for this aircraft. It was not possible to obtain positive comment on the residual short period directional oscillation still present at supersonic speeds.

Further to its inability to operate in bad weather, it is felt that the critical low speed handling characteristics allied to the gross under-development and unreliability of the engine installation will continue to result in a high loss rate on this aircraft independent of the screening standard maintained for pilot selection.

Any suggestion that this aircraft is suitable for introduction to NATO Air Forces as an all-weather fighter would be dangerously misleading, and this seems to be a matter of considerable importance at the present time.

*Below:* After flying the F-104 at Palmdale, California, in 1958. *Lockheed Corporation*

# STARFIGHTER

Translation of article in German magazine *Der Spiegel*, No 5
24 January 1966

The fire spitting, 20,000hp jet engine behind him, Lt Peter Kmonitzek raced across the evening sky in his Starfighter bomber F-104G. It was a training flight. Altitude: 9,000m.

Suddenly, exactly 11 minutes after take-off, the Lieutenant felt a sick and choking sensation. His arms and legs began to shake.

Hastily Kmonitsek, one of the best qualified Starfighter pilots in the Air Force, reached to the right for the oxygen control switch and increased the supply from 60 to 100%. But sickness and shaking of his arms and legs still did not stop.

Kmonitzek pushed the control stick forward and allowed the aircraft to throttle back. His left hand held the catapult lever of the ejection seat.

At 5,000m altitude Lt Kmonitzek pulled the oxygen mask off his face. He looked into the mirror: his lips were white.

Kmonitzek abandoned the flight. After landing the Squadron Safety Officer said: 'It could have been his death'. The Lieutenant was sent for medical treatment to the Air Medical Institute at Fürstenfeldbruck.

Eight days prior to this, on 6 December 1965, at 17.09hrs, the 33-year-old Starfighter pilot and Squadron Commander, Major Klaus Keinrich Lehnert, had started from Nörvenich for a training flight. Eleven minutes later Lehnert reported for the last time over Dortmund, giving the registration of his aircraft: 'Delta Alpha 254 ...'. Then, in the middle of the sentence, the radio contact broke off with Major Lehnert hanging, leaning forward, in his pilot seat, the atomic bomber raced northwards without control at 9,000m altitude and at almost the speed of sound. Two hours and 33 minutes after take-off the tanks were empty. The aircraft hit a rock near Ankones, 7km south of Narvik, Norway.

One of the possible causes of the Lehnert crash: traces of poisonous gases in the air flow of the oxygen supply system. Reason for the premature landing of Starfighter pilot Kmonitzek: fear of poison in the oxygen.

The fatal crash of Major Lehnert and the emergency landing by Kmonitzek accentuated the obscurity of the reasons for accidents in the 10th year of the history of the Air Force.

It was to have been a year of achievement for the flying forces in Germany. Five years previously, when on the occasion of the aviation exhibition in Hannover a Starfighter was demonstrated for the first time, the Air Force Chief (at that time), General Josef Kammhuber, had predicted that by end 1965 the German Starfighter fleet would be complete and ready for combat. The new German flying force would then 'belong to the best equipped Air Forces in the World'.

Now, however, it became a year of doubts and criticisms of this weapons system. The Starfighter's usefulness and safety were questioned more than ever.

Like Lenhert, altogether 15 Starfighter pilots were killed during 1965 during training and manoeuvre flying. They crashed immediately after take-off during climb, like Capt Dieter Thormeyer, who crashed near Memmingen seconds after the start from an altitude of 250m.

They crashed to death during a landing approach like Capt Wolfgang Willam, whose aircraft dropped 1km from the runway at the airfield of Upjever, 6km from a house; Willam ejected and smashed with his ejection seat against an earth mound.

Flt Sgt Günter Walzak dropped from the sky in the middle of a flight, due to engine defect. He was recovered dead from the Bay of Jade (=Jacebusen). Naval pilot, Lts Com Helmuth Groh, lost his life during Starfighter training in Arizona, when the air stream pulled the canopy away.

Two days before Christmas, the 29-year old Capt Josef Weiher of Fighter Bomber Squadron 32 (Lechfeld) crashed. During a dive he lost control over the aircraft, presumably because his sense of balance was disturbed (Vertigo effect). He dived vertically downwards.

During the past year alone 26 German Starfighters were lost in smoke and ruins — price each: approximately DM 6m. And the chain of accidents did not terminate in the New Year either. On Thursday of last week a Starfighter crashed near Wittmund in Ostfriesland due to engine defect. The pilot, Flt Sgt Klaus Dieter Tuleweit, lost his life.

Since the introduction of the new aircraft, the Air Force lost altogether 45 Starfighters — more than a war size combat squadron plus reserves; in value of money as much as 2,000 World War II fighters of the Me 109 type.

In actual fact, according to estimates by experts the loss is very much higher when repair of twisted undercarriages, radar noses and dented fuselages following fail starts or emergency landings, and failures caused by ground personnel (which is often unavoidable due to lack of mechanics) are added.

Already the squadron commanders are worried about their pilots' attitude and readiness to fly the Starfighter. Uneasiness is growing steadily in the officers' mess and club rooms on the German Air Force stations. Excited debates occurred in Nörvenich, where the Starfighter parade squadron *Boelcke* is stationed, and where Major Lehnert and Lt Kmonitzek were stationed.

The Weapons Officer at Nörvenich, Capt Siegfried Heltzel, tactical adviser to the commander and holder of the highest Nato Secrets licence ('Cosmic'), gave a talk to the pilots on the shortcomings of the aircraft. Squadron Commander Obleser said to Heltzel, who once saved his own life by ejecting from a crashing Starfighter: 'You have poisoned the mood in the Squadron. You have caused a crisis of confidence'.

The disastrous news from Germany's Starfighter fleet made headlines and filled opinion columns. Angry words appeared in large print like 'Widow maker', 'Flying coffin' and 'Beautiful death' (as US airmen had named the Starfighter years ago). The Hamburg newspaper *Welt* called it at the end of December the Starfighter Tragedy, and added 'The accident series has become a public matter. It is a matter for Parliament'.

# Convair XF-106

Following the F-104 experiences at Palmdale a welcome message was received from the Pentagon that I would be permitted 'one flight only' on an F-106 and should report to the General Dynamics base at Edwards.

I flew in the next day in the prototype Eland Convair with Mike Randrup who was carrying out the certification trials for Napiers from Santa Monica at the time. Mike insisted on my driving the Convair into the landing. At Convair speeds the early morning white desert floor seemed endless and the runway reluctant to grow from a speck in the distance; but we reached it eventually.

After meeting escorting officer Bob Rushworth (who later became a qualified astronaut on the X-15 programme) we drove round the western perimeter towards the General Dynamics hangars. As we entered the security gate, for me the clock seemed to turn back ten years. Against the glare of white concrete, white salt lake beyond and white and grey buildings, stood the sleek delta shape of the 3rd prototype XF-106 serial No 6453. The only difference over the decade that had passed being that the site then had been North American and the aeroplane the second prototype F-86 Sabre.

On this occasion Dick Johnston had me well briefed on this advanced aeroplane in the space of the remainder of the morning, and after a quick lunch at a nearby desert 'diner' we were ready to fly.

At that time in (1958) the delta configuration had just come through a difficult seven-year development period in which most of the early experimental deltas in USA and Europe had experienced stability and control problems in varying degrees of severity. Some of the prototypes had been lost with their pilots, and most of the test pilots involved had had interesting experiences. Dick Johnston himself had spent some time in hospital following a hasty and unplanned arrival in the open desert in one of the F-102's predecessors.

By the 106 period American experience of deltas had become comprehensive and they were confident that the earlier problems had been solved. We at English Electric on the other hand had concentrated on the low tail configuration for supersonic flight and were enthusiastic about the

*Below:* F-102 over the Mojave desert. 1958.  *General Dynamics*

effectiveness of this arrangement on the P1 and P1B. So it was with particular interest that I approached the F-106.

The briefing had stressed performance limitations due to an engine/intake mismatch existing at that time, but I was permitted to go to Mach 1.5. Mach 1.6 was not to be exceeded under any circumstances. In addition I was warned of a surge-line problem at about Mach 1.1 at the tropopause, and not to throttle back sharply through the range Mach 1.2-0.95 for this reason. In the event I forgot the latter with salutary though only transient results.

The 106 cockpit was spacious by Lightning standards and easy to settle and strap into. As usual at Edwards heat and glare were problems to this lilywhite Englishman among the modern redskins. Otherwise with well-geared nosewheel steering — a facility consistently and remarkably absent from British fighters until the late '60s — and with the canopy open for the cooling draught, taxying was simplicity itself. Lining up on the runway gave cause for thought as it did not seem decent to have no flap to set for take-off. Then with take-off checks complete, 'ready to roll' from Bob Rushworth in his 'chase' F-100 behind me, and 'Airforce 256 you're clear all the way' from Edwards Tower, simple outboard rotation of the single throttle lit the afterburner and the

106 was away at something less than the exhilarating reheat acceleration of a Lightning. Nevertheless the aeroplane felt comfortably similar to a Lightning and not at all strange (as had the 104) with the initial take-off run easily controlled with the nosewheel steering. The only bad feature was the split vee windscreen through which I kept on experiencing blind spots on one side or other of the centre line. This much-discussed characteristic is generally held to be acceptable with practice, but it remains clearly preferable not to have one!

$V_r$ was reached after the prescribed number of seconds with engine conditions within limits and with the briefed light stick force rotation into the climb was smooth, well damped and slightly more responsive than the Lightning. I felt at home at once in this fine fighter. I flew the rest of the sortie profile over the by now familiar Californian desert and mountains as planned except for a brief period of loss of communication while radio channel changing. When it occurred, Rushworth appeared smartly from behind to provide assistance.

It was subsequent to this that in a descending turn towards the Edwards recovery pattern I completely forgot the briefed engine handling limitation and throttled into surge when just

72453

AIR FORCE

supersonic at about 35,000ft to the accompaniment of several very loud bangs. As I mentioned subsequently in debriefing we were not accustomed to such sensitive behaviour with our Rolls-Royce engines!

In the circuit and approach, light control forces with good auto-damping and little apparent tendency to dutch roll or adverse yaw (rudder turn-co-ordinating mode selected) made for singularly pleasant and relaxed flying. I enjoyed an over-shoot and another circuit before a final, easily-judged and smooth landing during which the only point of criticism was once again losing sight momentarily of an aircraft (the prototype Lockheed Jetstar) that had landed ahead and on the right hand side of the runway.

As the following report suggests I felt that the F-106 was in many ways potentially as good as the P1B/Lightning, but not quite in terms of acceleration and sustained manoeuvre capability especially at altitude. But it was superior in range/endurance owing to significantly greater fuel capacity — a limitation of the Lightning which I have already discussed.

*Below:* XF-106 over the Mojave desert. 1958. *General Dynamics*

FLIGHT REPORT No 7

Aircraft: F-106A No 6453          Engine: J75-9 'Unmodified'
Date: 30 June 1958
Convair Experimental/Edwards AFB California
Weight: 31,000lb
CG: 28% MAC
Fuel: 8,000lb (7,800lb indicated)
Special limitations: 1.5 IMN with intake slotted ramps de-activated.
Flight Time: 45 minutes

Cockpit layout, dimensions and drill were almost identical with those of the F102A with the exception that electrical controls have been re-grouped and slightly simplified.

A canopy locking warning light was fitted to the main panel, and on the first and second attempts at locking this light remained on. It was finally extinguished by operating the manual locking handle with greater vigour.

Engine checks prior to taxying:

57%          310°C          Oil pressure 43psi

All systems normal, all warning lights out.

Taxying control was improved over the 102 with less coarse nosewheel steering gearing, and on the extended taxying to runway 04 in the intense heat at Edwards it was pleasant to be able to lock the canopy in the half open position with the locking switch provided immediately forward of the manual raising handle.

After checking ratiometer setting with Convair radio the short pre take-off check list was completed, maximum cold power set against the brakes, and reheat nozzle position checked.

With stop watch Zero brakes were released, and reheat was lit with only a small delay after simple rotation of the throttle outboard. With reheat functioning smoothly the throttle was advanced to max power, and the resulting acceleration rate was felt to be rather less than that of a P1B in cold thrust at similar weight (but UK temperatures).

Directional control of the initial take-off run was good using nosewheel steering, and on rotating into nosewheel lift at the briefed 120kt, the relative lightness of the elevon was unexpected, and the unstick occurred quickly though quite smoothly. Immediately after becoming airborne lightness of the controls in pitch and roll was apparent but not as over-sensitivity.

The undercarriage was selected UP at approximately 170kt and was fully retracted by 200kt. As with the F-102 it was found necessary to grope around the outer side of the throttle to reach and operate the undercarriage selector lever which was easily visible at all times.

After a short check for acceleration a shallow climb away was initiated which was steepened on reaching 500kt IAS.

Total fuel indicated at take-off 6,850lb. Engine speed 98%.

| (Alt 29.8) | | |
|---|---|---|
| 20,000ft AMSL | .88 | Zero+2.20 |
| 30,000ft AMSL | .9 | Zero+2.55 |
| 40,000ft AMSL | .89 | Zero+3.42 |

Control of the climb was smooth and accurate with response in pitch and roll nicely harmonised, and little or no adverse yaw in aileron turns. At no time did the climb angle approach that experienced at max power on the P1B.

Cabin conditioning had been set as briefed in the Auto range, and no re-adjustments were required during this climb as the cockpit temperature was maintained at a comfortable level throughout.

With max reheat maintained a turn to port was initiated at 41,000ft at approximately 1.6g and held through 210° before straightening out. During this turn the ASI system jump-up occurred at 40,000ft. A level acceleration was recorded while maintaining max power at 98.2%/595°C.

| 39,000ft AMSL | 1.1 | Zero+5.30 | Total fuel 4,000lb |
|---|---|---|---|
| 39,000ft AMSL | 1.23 | Zero+6 | |
| 39,500ft AMSL | 1.31 | Zero+6.30 | |
| 40,000ft AMSL | 1.4 | Zero+7 | Total fuel 3,400lb |

At 1.43 with the acceleration continuing at the same rate 2g was pulled and maintained in a climbing turn to port. On passing through 45,000ft speed had dropped to 1.2 IMN after turning through approximately 90°. Total indicated fuel 3,200lb.

Power was cut from max reheat to max cold and this occurred with a slight thump and fluctuation of the engine gauges. The wrist movement throttle action for this operation was well liked.

A left rudder induced stick-free dutch roll at 1.08 IMN/1g was visually damped in 2½ cycles, and again at 1.02 damping occurred in approximately 2 cycles. These tests were carried out with all dampers in and turn co-ordinator, and this damping rate was therefore a slight deterioration over that experienced at a similar flight condition with the F-102A which had damping in ½ cycle transonicly with dampers in.

As in the original transition at 40,000ft after the climb, control response and trim changes in transition between 1.00-0.9 IMN were exceptionally good with very little trim reversal or variation being detectable in 1g flight, and only small changes under 1.5g conditions. (Trim co-ordinator inoperative.)

In this speed range the elevon trim actuator operated jerkily in the longitudinal sense, and it was not easy to trim out precisely at the transition point of approximately 0.98 IMN. Owing to briefed engine handling restrictions max cold power had to be maintained while speed was being reduced; however while passing through 27,000ft in a 2.5g turn to port at about 0.85 power had been reached smoothly though accidentally to 75%, and at this point a muffled explosive condition occurred which gave a pressure pulse through the cabin conditioning system. A check with Convair radio confirmed that this was a compressor stall which was to be expected in this flight condition, but as no flame-out or other disturbance resulted no further attention was given to this condition, beyond the required increase in engine speed while at altitude.

At Zero+15, 20,000ft, total fuel indication was 3,000lb, and after checks of all services and warning systems which were normal, handling checks were continued at subsonic speed.

At approximately 20,000ft/400kt IAS the buffet threshold was found at 2.5g, and in manoeuvre below .9 IMN in the range .9-.85 control response and damping on all axes was excellent, with forces light and harmony very good; the longitudinal control being just sufficiently heavier than the lateral sense to give good harmony.

Some radio difficulty with a sticking channel selector was experienced at this stage, and so a precautionary return to circuit was made slightly earlier than intended.

The circuit was joined with 2,300lb total fuel, and control under circuit conditions from 300-350kt IAS was entirely straightforward.

On lowering undercarriage downwind at 250kt little trim change occurred, and the undercarriage lowering was associated with two small jolts. Locking down occurred in approximately 8 seconds.

The pattern was carried out at the briefed speeds without difficulty and with little adverse yaw in rough air, the final turn being made at 88% cold power and at approximately 200kt without any feeling of approaching the buffet boundary.

While following the next aircraft ahead (a Lockheed Jetstar) the initial final was made rather too high, and in correction of this the approach speed was slightly higher than briefing at about 190kt reducing to 180kt using 88%. Control of the glide path in pitch and directionally was good and no difficulty was experienced in correcting the original error.

With power set at approximately 85% the round-out was begun over the runway threshold at 168kt, and this resulted in an easy flare-out and short float before touching down gently at around 140kt IAS.

The tail parachute was streamed after nosewheel on, and the resulting landing run controlled comfortably with the pleasantly geared nosewheel steering.

During the final stages of the approach when it had become necessary to land on the starboard side of the runway owing to the presence ahead of the Jetstar on the port side, some difficulty was experienced with the central reflection screen in the V windshield. When looking through the port panel the Jetstar was in sight throughout, but the starboard side of the runway could not be seen easily. On shifting vision over to the starboard panel in order to maintain full vision of the starboard side of the runway, vision of the aircraft ahead was then lost at touchdown point owing to cut-off by the dividing screen. During the latter part of the landing roll when the head was centred vision on both sides of the dividing screen was regained, and although this is the correct drill for use of this windscreen geometry, it was not immediately straightforward in use by this pilot.

As before taxying off and return to the tarmac was easily controlled with nosewheel steering, and it was again pleasant to be able to unlock the canopy, raise it to approximately one-third open for cooling draught purposes, and lock it in that position with the locking switch provided.

Fuel at landing 2,100lb total. Landing distance to normal taxying, with tail parachute and moderate use of the pleasantly smooth operating wheel brakes, approximately 1,500yd.

The tail parachute is jettisoned simply by pushing in the tail parachute handle which is pulled out for deployment.

*Conclusions*

The basic characteristics of the 106 are similar to those of the 102 as are also the systems and cockpit layout, and it was possible to make some attempt at measuring performance from the start on this one flight.

From this limited experience it was clear that the 106 contained many control features which were developments from and improvements of the 102 production standard; in particular transition trim changes had been reduced (stabilisers IN) to insignificant proportions, and the turn co-ordinator clearly takes care of the adverse yaw characteristics which are still quite apparent on the 102.

The result is a pleasantly balanced aircraft which is easy to control and pleasant to fly throughout the limited conditions experienced.

The performance, which during the climb phase promises well, is disappointing at altitude, and as measured does not approach the standard at present achieved with the P1B series.

The high rate of fuel consumption rather off-sets the 7,800lb indicated fuel on start-up, and with total production fuel it seems that the P1B is likely to be quite as well off in this respect.

In the cockpit seat-comfort and control layout were good, but forward vision through the Convair V windscreen was found to be very restricting.

It can be said therefore that at the present time on the F-106 a high standard of artificial stability and control has been achieved, and that in its present form as a flying machine the aircraft is likely to be suitable for all-weather operation up to and including supersonic speeds.

No information was available on the present time scale of the ultimate weapons system, but it was clear that much work remains to be done on the intake/engine installation to design performance, before a production configuration with specification performance can be achieved.

# Vickers VC-10

In 1963, quite soon after the formation of BAC, the prototype Vickers VC-10 was undergoing its initial flight tests at Wisley. Although these had been going very well this new airliner was the centre of a storm of political and press criticism, much of it ill-informed or misled. The VC-10 had been originally ordered by BOAC for the 'Empire' routes which at the time had included many short and hot-and-high airfields demanding exceptional take-off and landing performance. By the time the aircraft was ready for its entry into airline service most of the countries on these routes had developed Boeing-sized runways at their international airports. This primary design advantage of the VC-10, short field operation, had become irrelevant.

At this crucial time the Chairman of BOAC was making public statements to the effect that the VC-10 order would have to be cut back owing to basic inefficiency of the design in comparison with the Boeing 707. Further fuel being added to this particular fire by drag problems which were encountered initially on the prototype.

Despite all this criticism, Chief Test Pilot Jock Bryce and his team at Wisley and the Weybridge design office were all confident that the VC-10 was a break-through in airliner technology. It offered greater simplicity of operation and ease of handling, superior engine-out performance and safety, and new standards in cabin quietness and passenger comfort. There was also confidence that the drag problems could be overcome and range performance guarantees met or approached so closely as to allow any shortfall to be more than offset by the greatly increased passenger appeal of the aircraft.

As the Corporation's deputy chief test pilot I took the first opportunity to fly the prototype and see for myself. This proved a remarkable experience. As a military and mainly fighter pilot I was inexperienced in big aeroplanes. I had checked out many years previously on the Lincoln which was thought at the time to be an effective bomber but in my view bore very little resemblance to an aeroplane. The VC-10 thus seemed an enormous device as I walked up the staircase from the tarmac half expecting to find a chandelier at the top as I turned into the palatial room at the front known as the 'Flight Deck'. There the comparison ended once I was seated at the controls. The instrument and systems controls layout was logically organised and from the Captain's seat there was no impression of great size and only one of efficiency coupled with good vision and comfort.

In flight the VC-10 was a delightful experience reminiscent in many ways of Canberra ease of control and noticeably faster, M=0.85 being a practical high cruise figure with maximum level speed in excess of M=0.9. It was fascinating to be able to get the 'feel' of this big aeroplane so quickly.

There is no doubt that the VC-10 set new standards of controllability for big jets and once in service with the airlines it proved to have greater passenger appeal than all the other long range jet airliners of the 1960s. It was still carrying greater load factors than the competition well into the 1970s and turning BOAC's publicly expressed fears into a highly profitable fact. But of course the harm had been done by apparent official British lack of enthusiasm for their own product in the early critical days, and the world's airlines quite reasonably had been reluctant to order VC-10s in face of the apparent hostility of our national carrier.

My brief experience of this fine aeroplane, on which I subsequently travelled round the world as a passenger by preference on all possible occasions for the next decade, is summarised in the following memorandum distributed at the time within BAC.

*Above right:* VC-10 prototype on first flight out of Brooklands in the hands of Jock Bryce. 1961. *BAe*

*Right:* VC-10 prototype on test at Wisley. Winter 1962. *BAe*

Memorandum from: R. B. BEAMONT          Date: 9 May 1963.

### VC-10 Flight Characteristics

The following brief notes of points observed during a $2\frac{1}{4}$ hours' flight (30 minutes as 1st pilot) in VC-10 No G-ARVB from Wisley on the 6 May may be of interest.

The flight was for PE runs with the Boscombe calibrated Javelin at 40,000ft and 32,000ft, and for constant C1 fuel consumption cruises at 10,000ft.

The PE's were carried out up to 0.88 IMN (0.86 TMN)/40,000ft, and were free of any detectable buffet vibration.

The aircraft was flown manually throughout these tests and the test points were maintained to $\pm 50$ft overall with the altimeter '1,000s' counter showing a steady 40,000ft for impressively long periods. The pilot said that damping of the long period oscillation was less than desirable at altitude (though satisfactory at low altitude) and that constant anticipation was necessary to avoid phugoid conditions; this was not apparent from watching him. Subsequently when the writer flew the aircraft up to 310kt IAS the absence of this tendency at low level was confirmed.

Engine order noise level was impressively low in this trimmed, but not furnished aeroplane; and at all stations, except at the rear of the main cabin adjacent to the engines, the air conditioning noise level predominated in cruising flight at engine speeds in the range of 80-90%rpm. It was felt that this noise source was probably greater than that in the 707, but that full furnishing and compartmenting would probably reduce this to a very comfortable level. This was stated to be the case in a more fully furnished aircraft in which Mr Amery* was flown on the same day from Wisley.

Airbrake operation at 0.8 IMN/40,000ft was accompanied by a buffet level which would probably require some explanation to the travelling public, as would the quite powerful deceleration resulting. This permitted a satisfactory rate of descent to be established quickly.

After three 10 minute attempts at the 10,000ft cruise points the schedule was abandoned due to major variations in ambient temperature resulting in ASI drop-off of as much as 9kt from the stabilised condition in 1-2 minutes. After returning to base and landing the writer took over the left seat and was checked out for 30 minutes in take-off, circuit and landing drill including a brief run in the clean configuration to 310kt IAS/2,000ft.

Maximum power at 100%×4 was held against the brakes, and initiating the take-off run was a simple matter of releasing the smoothly operating pedal brakes and steering with nosewheel steering.

The gearing of the latter appears to be just about right for the job and first-time steering of the runway centre line was achieved without over-correction. Nosewheel feel force appeared to be higher than desirable both for low speed taxying and for controlling the take-off run.

$V_r$ at this condition was 135kt, and steering control was transferred easily and naturally from nosewheel steering to rudder in the neighbourhood of 110kt.

Rotation was straightforward with a firm and relatively long rearward movement of the stick, and the rapid increase in cockpit height to achieve lift-off $C_L$ was very noticeable to the pilot. In this aircraft the leading edge slats were fixed in and modified in geometry as part of the performance programme, and this resulted in higher than standard critical speeds.

Lift-off occurred imperceptibly owing to the very soft damping action of the undercarriage, and the climb-out angle to maintain the recommended 165kt at maximum power with take-off flap would have been rather steep for a first experience, and a more comfortable climb-out was established at 185kt before reducing power at 2,000ft.

In this phase the elevator response and feel force seemed just about right, but the pilot becomes conscious of relatively low roll response and high feel force which initially leads to some under-estimating of roll correction in the event of wing dropping when encountering rolling moment due to yaw under cross-wind conditions.

This slightly 'out of phase' feeling disappears at IAS above approximately 200kt, and the longitudinal trim changes with gear selection and flap selection are pleasantly innocuous as are trim changes due to normal power alterations in establishing speed changes in the range 180-300kt IAS at 2,000ft. No checks were made of longitudinal trim changes in maximum range power alterations.

At 300kt/2,000ft control harmony was excellent and pitch and roll response and forces were considered most suitable for an aircraft of this size and type of operation.

Use of more than half aileron wheel throw in higher rate rolls resulted in distinct spoiler buffet and what appeared at first experience to be a flattening of the roll rate curve.

Selection of gear, and stage selection of take-off flap, approach flap and landing flap were accompanied by relatively small longitudinal trim changes which could be held easily on the stick and only required trimming out for fine adjustment; and although an extended pattern was flown on the writer's first landing it was found that the aircraft could be positioned and lined up with impressive ease for an aircraft of this size.

During the final approach for a calculated threshold speed of 137kt (high due to fixed slats), speed was rather too high initially at 150-145kt. This was due to an unfamiliarity with the relatively large throttle lever range from maximum power to idle. Before short finals the measure of this was obtained however, and 137kt was achieved at the threshold at the right height.

Response in pitch in the flare-out was precise and very satisfactory, and with power cut during this phase the aircraft was held quite easily on the centre line with a 10° cross-wind although a slight tendency to become out-of-phase in roll control was again encountered.

The touchdown was unexpectedly gentle on the very forgiving undercarriage, and as the writer had been briefed to place the nosewheel firmly on with forward stick movement before applying brakes and thrust reversers, this action was taken perhaps a little too firmly and the result of the nosewheel connection with the runway was somewhat noisy, though not exceptionally so apparently.

With the nosewheel on, steering was taken over on nosewheel steering and light wheel brake application made with an immediately noticeable effect. Gentle braking was continued as thrust reversal was applied by the second pilot and the landing run was exceptionally short with slow taxying speed reached in little more than 1,400 yards without trying.

Subsequent taxying and marshalling in a confined space was very easy and straightforward with nosewheel steering and occasional light touches of the pedal brakes.

These brief first impressions were enhanced by the spaciousness and relative quiet of the flight deck with its excellent air conditioning and first class lay-out, and the writer was left with the feeling that subject to improvements in aileron response and feel, and if the current performance problems can be sorted out to meet specification then the VC-10 must, inevitably, become very popular with the pilots.

R. P. BEAMONT
Manager: Flight Operations

*Minister for Defence.

# BAC 1-11

In 1960 came certain responsibilities outside those at Preston with the merger of English Electric with Vickers. Although I was not directly involved in the commercial aviation activity at Weybridge of the new British Aircraft Corporation, I was expected to co-ordinate flight test administration with Jock Bryce, the Chief Test Pilot. Nothing had been spelt out on the question of direct deputising, mainly because of the rapidly increasing gap in techniques and performance developing at that time between military and civil aircraft. Nevertheless it was understood that we would each gain experience of the other's primary activity, and by 1962 I had flown the VC-10 prototype while Bryce had done some Lightning flying at Warton.

In 1963 the BAC 1-11 prototype programme had begun and had got into stability and control difficulties which led to the tragic loss of the lead pilot Mike Lithgow and his crew in a deep-stall accident in the autumn of that year. This compromised the development flying programme severely and was shortly followed by another set-back when Jock Bryce was taken off flying for medical reasons, leaving the 1-11 test team critically short of experience and continuity.

Meanwhile flying was continuing on the second aircraft, often with a training crew on airline-captain familiarisation flights as part of the critical customer relations campaign. The 1-11 had been in the best possible position up to that time to strike a bonanza as the first 'bus-stop' jet for the world's short-sector and domestic routes, and early success and a good reputation were vital to this end. At about this time I made it my business to watch some take-offs and landings at Wisley, some in the hands of Company pilots and some by senior captains from foreign airlines — and I was surprised at what I saw.

Frequently the aircraft seemed to snap up at $V_r$ into over-rotation and had to be corrected nose-down to obtain the appropriate initial climb attitude. Further although the landing approaches looked normal down to the last 50ft, behaviour from that point was generally erratic in pitch suggesting difficulty in achieving accurate flare-out. On more than one occasion what looked like an overflare was followed by an over-correction nose-down and a heavy arrival followed by por-poising and swerving down the runway in a very odd manner.

In Bryce's absence it was obvious that something needed to be done about this, so after sounding out the Weybridge management to make sure of no objection I arranged to take part in the next suitable flight. Although mainly concerned with supersonics at the time I was still in practice on Canberras, and as the 1-11 was a Canberra-sized aeroplane with rather less performance I did not anticipate difficulty in getting the feel of it.

On 6 March 1964 at Wisley I took the left seat of G-ASJD with Brian Trubshaw, who was also new to the programme and had only just been brought in from VC-10 testing to take charge, in the right seat. The take-off roll was reasonable until pulling smoothly back on the wheel at $V_r$ when there was a momentary sensation that nothing was going to happen at all. Then it all happened at once and the aircraft over-responded in pitch, leaped off the ground and continued to increase the climb angle while I instinctively applied forward stick to correct. Response to this action was also slow but as speed increased the elevator began to bite leaving a clear impression that conditions had been very close to PIO* at take-off. This confirmed my suspicions and turning straight downwind I prepared to look at the approach case.

At speeds above 140kt stability and control were conventional. It was not until groping round the final turn in the existing mist and light rain that I began to notice difficulty with speed trimming due either to poor basic speed stability or to unsuitable engine response/throttle gearing characteristics — I was not sure which first time round. With plenty of time in hand at $V_{appr}$ 128kt, acquisition of the final approach slope at stable speed should have been easy but in the event was not. Then when initiating the flare-out there was an uncomfortable lag in response countered by an instinctive increase in demand and finally an over-response in pitch which resulted in slight 'ballooning'. Subsequent attempts to sort this into a gentle touchdown failed in this sense and a relatively hard arrival resulted after an unpleasant moment of feeling out of phase in pitch and liable to touch down nosewheel first, with equally unpleasant implications on this short-coupled undercarriage.

Immediately after the firm though not particularly heavy touchdown a series of violent swerves occurred due, I was told later by the engineering department, to my 'coarse' braking. This also seemed odd as I was not exactly out of practice in steering aeroplanes at the time. A further circuit and landing confirmed all these conditions as fundamental and it was clear that all was far from well with this aeroplane, particularly in relation to its design role as a simple-to-operate 'bus-stop' jet for world-wide use into unsophisticated airfields.

My subsequent report featured urgent recommendations for immediate actions to avoid what I felt sure was the strong likelihood of another accident. In fact this occurred at Wisley only four days after circulation of the report when the first prototype on a training exercise with experienced pilots was over-flared, pitched on to the nosewheel, bounced enormously, and ended up flat on its belly surrounded by pieces of undercarriage.

When fully developed the 1-11 went on to become one of the most effective light twin jet airliners of the late 1960s and early 1970s. Instead of capturing the world market, however, its reputation in its bad period of 1963-64 held it back for some years and enabled its only rival the Douglas DC-9 to go clear ahead in the sales race after being well behind at the start.

In the business of aviation serious faults in the early flight stages are seldom ignored by the potential market.

*Pilot-induced oscillation.

Memorandum from: R. P. Beamont     To: Mr M. Crisp,
                                       Chief Flight Test
                                       Engineer, Wisley.
Ref: 7.3                               10 March 1964

BAC 1-11 No G-ASJD. Handling in landing configuration
Wisley, 6 March 1964

*Above:* First prototype BAC 1-11 on test. 1964.  *BAe*

The aircraft was flown from the left-hand seat for 40min in one
overshoot, one roller, and two full-stop landings; with gear down
throughout, auto-stabilisers in, flap 18° for take-off, 26° base leg,
45° (Full) for landing.
  Moderate crosswind from port.
  Visibility reduced in smoke haze and snow showers.

*Taxying*
Straightforward with pedal-operated differential braking. Nosewheel
steering coarse resulting in over-correction. Restricted range of
movement of small ¼ wheel does not help this case. High residual
thrust from engines results in need for frequent use of brakes.

*Take-off*
Maximum thrust held by brakes. Initial roll with nosewheel steering
showed strong tendency to over-correction which was still present
on third take-off.
  Rudder effectiveness satisfactory from about 80kt.

*Lift-off*
Though briefed to avoid over-rotation, the elevator was felt to be
initially insensitive with the result that pitch demand was held in
until response was sensed, by which time rate was already too great
and immediate correction was again subject to a distinct lag. Thus
over-rotation and subsequent over-correction resulted on the first
take-off, and although this was improved by anticipation on
subsequent take-offs this was clearly some way from being an
adequately precise elevator control. As speed built up in climb-out
this characteristic became less noticeable.
  Lateral control (aileron and spoilers) was precise and responsive
but undesirably heavy under all conditions experienced.
  Lateral and directional trimmers were set at zero for take-off and
did not require readjustment during climb, circuit and landing.

*Approach*
Increase in flap angle from 18°-26° caused little trim change, and
26°-45° resulted in a small nose-down change easily held on the
stick.
  The increase in drag expected from these long span flaps at the
maximum flap position was not apparent, and did not necessitate a
marked increase in power to maintain the 3° approach; but

accurate speed control in this phase was difficult, and after four
approaches difficulty was still experienced in setting up and holding
$V_{appr}$ to better than ±10kt.
  It was also noticed on the approach at 145-125kt that variations
more than 10kt required re-trimming longitudinally.
  Part of the difficulty in fine speed control was the throttle
movement/engine speed relationship, which required large lever
movements for the small power variations in the 80-85% range
necessary to control the approach.
  Line-up and maintenance of the centre-line presented no problem
in the crosswind prevailing (14-15kt component).

*Landing*
Again following the briefing, with a light touch on the wheel, in itself
not very practical due to the firm hold necessary for making lateral
corrections, the flare-out at the right place and height felt imprecise
with a tendency towards over-shooting the pitch demand and to two
or three subsequent over-corrections which left the aircraft in
landing attitude at a few feet, but without a feeling of precise control
of the longitudinal situation.
  If power was bled off while holding this attitude as accurately as
possible a reasonably gentle touchdown would occur, generally on
one main wheel followed by a pitch forward on to the nosewheel
before the other main wheel touched.
  The aircraft would then roll-out reasonably straight with use of
rudder and differential braking, and reverse thrust caused no
directional problem.
  On the second landing nosewheel steering was used at the reverse
thrust stage and, apparently due to over-correction following the
nosewheel lifting and losing contact momentarily, a series of
unpleasant swerves developed which required coarse use of rudder
and differential brake to correct.
  In sum this short experience left the following impressions:-
(1)  In the landing configuration, pitch and speed control leave
much to be desired by any standards, especially for an aircraft of
moderate performance for specific 'bus-stop' activity where precise
ease of control near the ground is a basic essential.
(2)  Areas where improvement should be effective:-
a  Reduce initial lag in elevator response and possibly decrease
   subsequent rate by non-linear gearing.
b  Reduce lateral stick forces while retaining existing rate/
   effectiveness.
c  Alter throttle gearing to reduce by half throttle movement in
   80-85% range.
d  Gearing of nosewheel steering requires modification to reduce
   over-sensitivity.

                                              R. P. BEAMONT

# Handley Page HP 115

In striking contrast to the highly loaded high-performance characteristics of the Lightning series, the HP 115 provided an intriguing low-performance experience. As part of a working-up programme to gain further practical knowledge of delta and highly swept wing leading edge characteristics in the development of the large Mach 2 aircraft of the future, this aircraft was flown at Bedford in 1963.

Weighing around 5,000lb with a 1,850lb thrust Viper 9 engine and a wing loading of 28lb/sq ft it was virtually in the light plane class. Although I sat seriously through a lengthy briefing with Jack Henderson who was its project pilot and chief pilot of Aero Flight at the time, it was difficult to believe that there was so little to do once in the cockpit.

Fuel on, HP and LP cocks, throttle, basic engine instruments and flying panel checked and trimmer set, and with a fixed undercarriage and no flaps that was it. After the prolonged ground roll expected of an underpowered aircraft 'rotation' was simple with early response to elevon, and the briefed incidence of about 13° the take-off was smooth and entirely normal. Rate of climb was poor and the expected effects of induced drag were quickly apparent in the suddenness with which this rate reduced to zero with a relatively small increase in incidence. This characteristic, typical to a degree varying with thrust/weight ratio and leading edge sweep angle of all swept wing designs, became very marked under increased normal acceleration and in a limit 'g' level turn pulled from 200kt the aeroplane seemed to be about to stop dead.

Rolling moment due to yaw was no more than anticipated, though it did become noticeable in turbulence.

Apart from these expected characteristics the 115 flew quite conventionally in the climb and indeed subsequently in all normal flight manoeuvres, and it was only in extreme corners of its flight envelope that unusual things occurred. As Henderson and the project pilots had established, the aeroplane had proved to have classic flying classroom attributes for demonstration of the effects on stability and control of the spread of the leading edge vortex of a highly swept wing at increasing incidence. To investigate this I set up level flight at 5,000ft at 90kt and then slowly reduced power until the minimum-drag speed was established at about 80kt.

Leaving power set at this point while maintaining height resulted of course in further drop in speed, and it was apparent that control on all three axes remained responsive though becoming sluggish at 75kt. Flight was otherwise non-oscillatory in the prevailing calm air at this height. Then, quite suddenly at 70kt and about 15° incidence, a lateral oscillation began at about ½cps and ± 10° of bank. This was instantly stabilised by reduction of incidence with forward stick, or reduced but not stopped by lateral control input.

Increasing to about 20° incidence brought the speed off to 63kt before it could be balanced with full power in a slight descent, and here the lateral oscillation had developed in amplitude to ± 30° but was still stable.

A further increase in incidence to 21° with speed dropping off to below 63kt produced sudden classic divergence of the oscillation to ± 45° of bank and increasing, and forward movement of the stick to reduce incidence resulted in immediate response and damping of the oscillation to zero as IAS increased past 65kt. In this configuration a high rate of descent had developed and this was checked by diving out to climb speed and re-climbing for a repeat of the slowdown which gave identical results.

In conventional flight the 115 was a pleasantly harmonised and responsive aircraft. Once the lack of flaps and undercarriage selection had become familiar and due power compensation made for the high induced drag in the approach pattern, the final approach and landing were pleasant and straightforward with the aircraft obligingly assisting in the final flare for touchdown by responding suitably to ground effect.

As a flying demonstration of classic delta manners and vortex effects without hazardous characteristics the 115 was a notable success, and it was also very enjoyable to fly.

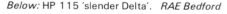

*Below:* HP 115 'slender Delta'.   *RAE Bedford*

## Some Brief Experience of the Handling Qualities of the HP115 Slender Delta
### Bedford — 19 August 1963

After a comprehensive briefing by Sqn Ldr J. R. Henderson, OC Aero Flight and Project Pilot on the aircraft, two flights were made of 25 and 35 minutes duration.

*Brief Description*
Weight: 5.071lb
Span: 20ft
Wing area: 430sq ft
T/C Ratio: 6%
LE Sweep: 74°

*Elevons*
With aerodynamic balance and spring tabs, plus geared tabs operating in the anti-balance sense. The elevons constitute approximately 1/8th of the total wing area.

*Rudder*
Straight manual with geared tab locked and biased for trim. Control circuits are cable, and circuit lag improves the lateral damping.

*Engine*
Viper 9 with 1,850lb installed static thrust and sensitive throttle control relative to JPT limits. Recommended maximum for take-off and climb, 98%.

*Fuel*
140 gallons, giving approximately 30 minutes flight time under normal circumstances.

*Electrical System*
Battery operated with 2×24 volts Varley batteries (no engine services).

*Brakes*
Pneumatic accumulator with pedal and hand motors.

*Airbrakes*
Pneumatic accumulator (pressure 3,300lb).

*Briefing Speeds*
Rotate: 90kt
Unstick: 120kt
Climb: 140kt
$V_d$: 250kt
Approach: 120-110kt
Touchdown: Minimum 90kt (ground angle)
Slowdown: Minimum 60kt above 5,000ft

*FLIGHT 1*

Pre take-off checks:   rpm 40%, JPT 460°C.
                                  OP 26½psi
                                  25 volts
                                  Airbrakes 2,500psi
                                  Fuel 138gall
Runway 27.   Wind 240°/11kt

During initial take-off run the undercarriage was harsh on Bedford's relatively rough runway.

The stick was pulled firmly back on passing 90kt but the nosewheel was reluctant to lift, and rotation did not commence until passing 100kt. Unstick occurred at approx 125kt, and on breaking ground a few cycles of small amplitude pilot induced lateral oscillation occurred largely due to the relatively heavy up-elevon stick force needed in relation to the very light lateral forces in the prevailing mild turbulence and slight crosswind.

It seemed necessary to ease the stick forward slightly after breaking ground to hold the required climb-out attitude, but this might as easily have been the result of rotation continuing immediately following unstick as of clearing ground effect.

In climb to 3,000ft dutch roll was apparent in passing through turbulence at 140-150kt although not present in calm conditions, and it was noted that in all conditions subsequently roll acceleration predominated in the dutch roll.

Whenever dutch roll was excited by passage through turbulent air it could be damped by lateral control input, but if left stick-free it built up quite quickly to ±10-15° with low damping.

Stick-free left rudder dutch rolls from 3,000-1,500ft.

110kt   3½ cycles to visual damping.

100kt   4 cycles to visual damping.

 88kt   8 cycles to visual damping.

150kt   3½ cycles to visual damping.

Fuel at last point, 100gall gauge/103.5gall flowmeter.
Downwind at 90gall, 1,000ft/100kt, cockpit checks:

| 97% | 560°C | 25 volts | OP 28psi |
|---|---|---|---|

In the circuit, control co-ordination and harmony was quite pleasant with the exception of the dutch roll tendency in passage through turbulence, and the aircraft felt quite stiff directionally.

In bank reversals at approximately 100kt, slip ball displacements of up to half-ball width each way indicated adverse yaw but not to an unpleasant or embarrassing extent.

In an approach at 100kt with 80gall gauge/82.5gall flowmeter, the aircraft could be placed on the approach and glide path with ease and would maintain the approach condition virtually stick-free with little attention from the pilot. An overshoot was carried out from 20ft and the final approach was set up with 65gall gauge/65gall flowmeter at 100kt on to Runway 27 with wind 240°/10kt, moderate turbulence.

The slow final approach, flare and touchdown were extremely straightforward once the need to maintain a high proportion of power to counterbalance the induced drag had been appreciated. In a gentle touchdown the undercarriage was harsh, but with up-elevon there was little or no tendency to pitch forward on to the nosewheel and the nose up attitude was easily maintained in using aerodynamic drag to slow down without tail parachute.

The aircraft ran true on the landing roll with little need for correction.

*FLIGHT 2*

Engine checks before take-off: 98%, JPT 740°C.
OP 23psi
25 volts
140gall

Rotation at 100kt and unstick at 122 kt with no lateral oscillation.

On climb to 5,000ft two 90° heading changes had to be made to clear turbulent cloud, and in these the drop-off in rate of climb was immediately apparent.

| 5,000ft | 98.5% | 730°C | 30psi | 105gall gauge/110gall flowmeter |
|---|---|---|---|---|

Slowdown and dutch rolls, 5,000-4,000ft

100kt  Left rudder stick-free dutch roll, visual
       damping in 4 cycles.

88kt   Left rudder stick-free dutch roll, visual
       damping in 6 cycles.                        100/106gall

72kt   Left rudder stick-free dutch roll undamped at
       ± approx 10° of roll.                        90/107gall

67kt   Left rudder stick-free dutch roll undamped at
       ± approx 20° of roll.                        80/ 89gall

Speed trimmed back to 63kt on the longitudinal trimmer, and dutch roll immediately became divergent. No buffet present.

The roll amplitude was reduced by about half by port roll control input, and then stopped completely by reduction of incidence with forward stick.

In this slowdown lateral damping appeared to become neutral in the region of 70kt, and the dutch roll oscillation was of a 2-4sec period.

As the dutch roll diverged below 65kt the rolling displacement developed to approx ±25-30°, and recovery action was initiated to avoid further build-up which the briefing had indicated could develop to ±40° at 60kt. (According to briefing the wing incidence at 65kt/80gall/4,000ft is 21.5° and $C_L$ 0.65: PEC+2kt approximately.)

The effect of adverse yaw in bank reversals was further investigated from 80-130kt at 3,000ft, and this confirmed that with bank application there was the usual initial short hesitance before rolling moment and yaw became apparent, and that the maximum slip ball displacement in normal rate reversals was approx half-ball width. In general the adverse yaw and dutch roll characteristics were reminiscent of the P1 in the undercarriage only configuration and therefore quite flyable without auto-stability, although the predominance of rolling acceleration particularly in turbulence would not be compatible with operational needs.

Approaches and overshoots were carried out at 70 and 60gall, again with precise and steady acquisition of the approach centre-line and glide path, with rolling oscillation in turbulence the only adverse feature. At one point at 115kt/1,000ft, poorly damped roll oscillation of ±20° was encountered when passing through turbulence stick-free.

Landing at 55gall gauge/52gall flowmeter, runway 27, wind 270°/8-10kt. Touchdown 92kt, nosewheel held high until 70kt.

*Summary*

Two short flights were sufficient to establish the following impressions.

(1)   Although dutch roll damping is low the yaw/roll ratio is also low, and crispness of response to roll control coupled with adequate response to pitch control add up to quite acceptable control characteristics in calm air.

In turbulent air the predominance of rolling acceleration in the dutch roll is disturbing if the pilot needs to divert his attention from damping the roll, although this is a more acceptable condition than is a poorly damped dutch roll with a high yaw/roll ratio.

It is felt that this low level of roll damping would be an embarrassment in instrument recovery without benefit of auto-stability, in turbulent conditions.

(2)   The coupling of yaw with lateral control was thought to be no worse than the adverse yaw characteristics of the first P1 configuration with undercarriage down, and therefore quite adequate for experimental purposes and for emergency recovery of an operational aircraft with auto-stabiliser failure.

(3)   Rudder inputs were not found necessary for turn entry and turn co-ordination at speeds above 100kt, and below this speed there was a progressive though not critical need for rudder co-ordination.

No use of rudder was required for damping transient oscillations in the conditions tested, as all the roll oscillations could be reduced in amplitude or stopped entirely by lateral control inputs.

(4)   A tendency towards pilot induced lateral oscillations was noted at unstick when unfamiliar with the aircraft, but this improved with experience. It was thought that the predominant rolling acceleration characteristics were made more acceptable by the light and responsive lateral control, and that adverse control-circuit characteristics such as friction, backlash, etc, would, if present, seriously affect the handling qualities in this respect.

(5)   There was no time for detailed assessment of rolling power in tight turns, but no serious loss was apparent in this respect when rolling out of a 2g turn at 150kt. In normal circuit manoeuvring no loss of rolling power was noted in turns.

(6)   It was not possible to assess the technique necessary for crosswind landings in these two short flights, but according to the briefing the wings level technique followed by a rudder kick-off of drift angle has proved to be a reasonable manoeuvre up to 17kt component at least.

(7)   Engine/Fuel system limitations prevented assessment of the effect of zero g on dutch roll damping, as push-overs were not permitted.

(8)   The aircraft could be stabilised at a given speed and height with surprising ease even down to low speeds, but at 21.5° incidence a rate of descent of about 400fpm was present at maximum power (98%)/4,000ft.

No buffet or trim change was noticeable in turns up to $2\frac{1}{2}$g in the speed range 175-120kt.

In all a pleasantly responsive aircraft with adequate longitudinal and directional characteristics in the range of flight conditions checked. Adverse yaw was no more obtrusive than on the P1, and low dutch roll damping coupled with predominant rolling acceleration was the main adverse aerodynamic feature.

R. P. BEAMONT

# TSR 2

The year 1960 brought momentous changes in the Aircraft Industry. At Warton during the previous two years English Electric had been working on a project as a logical follow-on to the Lightning called the P17. This was for a supersonic bomber replacement of the Canberra embodying our latest state-of-the-art knowledge of Mach 2 engineering and aerodynamics, and approached with the confidence of the by now famous Canberra programme and the successful entry into service of the Mach 2+ Lightning.

Official policy had been reticent to the point of negativeness in the period following the infamous Defence White Paper of 1957. This had stated the remarkable conclusion that there would be no requirement for supersonic aircraft in the RAF after the Lightning. That evaluation of the needs of UK defence must stand as one of the most inept and damaging government decisions of the period. Perhaps it was the most damaging single decision of all time in British military aviation for it arrested the continuous process of evolution and development in this primary defence field, lost our technical lead to the competition and ushered in for the first time an era in which foreign purchase of fighter aircraft became inevtiable when the penny subsequently dropped in high places. But in the early 1960s there was to be a short respite.

After much debate the Air Staff and the politicians found a formula for changing their position and issued a requirement for a tactical strike and reconnaissance aircraft which would supersede the V-bombers and some of the roles of the ageing Canberra from the end of the 1960s. Hawkers and Vickers tendered for this as did English Electric with a proposal based on their P17 concept; but then a new factor emerged. It was clear from experience with the Lightning and other similar programmes in Europe and America that Mach 2 performance cost money. The TSR specification called for this performance with range and load capabilities which would result in an aircraft in the 100,000lb class and be very costly by the then current standards. Accordingly the Government instructed the Industry that it would not place an order for this and similar new aircraft in Britain unless the major companies merged to produce more economic units whose combined resources could provide, in the Government's estimation, a more viable basis for these undertakings.

Questionable at the time and even more so in retrospect was whether this would be more effective than selecting the best firm for the work and letting them get on with managing it, subcontracting in areas where their own resources were insufficient to meet the needs of the task. Nevertheless in the outcome Vickers and English Electric worked together successfully to rationalise their two design proposals to meet the Air Ministry specification. They finally announced a merger to include the Bristol Aeroplane Company with hold-ings of Vickers 40%, English Electric 40% and Bristol 20%. The new company which was to manage all the aircraft programmes of the parent companies to be named the British Aircraft Corporation.

It began really to look as if the TSR 2 as it was nominated was a going concern. A massive and generally successful effort was set up in the management and integration of the two design and engineering organisations mainly concerned, Vickers at Weybridge and English Electric at Preston.

Prior to the announcement the necessary formal arrangements were made in a rush under Government pressure to get the programme started. I had no idea what my part would be in the new venture but assumed that our 15 years of continuous experience in this field would be called upon. Subsequently it became apparent that some strong views were held at Weybridge to the effect that their experience of V-bombers with the Valiant should entitle Weybridge to lead the whole TSR 2 design and flight development.

Late one evening I received a telephone call from Viscount Caldecote, Managing Director of the Aircraft Division of English Electric, who said that as part of the newly formed Corporation's proposal to the Ministry it would be recommended that I should lead the flight testing which would be centred at Warton. I would do this as deputy to Jock Bryce who would be Chief Test Pilot of the new Corporation. I was asked to accept this immediately or at the latest on the following day as the proposal had to go in by then. My natural inclination was to accept this interesting job at once for its own sake and in the interest of the Preston Division, but on reflection it seemed that there ought to be some further explanation of the relative posts.

Robin Caldecote and Freddie Page, however, both said that the decision had been based on the expected predominance of civil aircraft (Bryce's specialist field) in the new Corporation's activities, and suggested that my acceptance of the situation would be of benefit to the Corporation, and so I got on with it.

Much has been written of the TSR 2 design and of its successful initial flying programme and of its political cancellation. Much was also learned in the course of its evolution. On the test flying side it served to disprove a fallacy which gained ground at the time with enthusiastic promotion by the news media. This was to the effect that the days of traditional test flying were past. As the pilot could (in their judgement) no longer cope with the complexities of testing modern high performance aircraft he would be relegated in the system to the status of driver-airframe with the sole duties of conducting the take-off and landing and operating the test instrumentation and on-board computers. The Press were not alone in this thinking. It had to some extent been encouraged by engineers and scientists at the

*Above:* TSR 2. Preparation for first flight. Boscombe Down. September 1964. *BAe*

Establishments and in Industry who had allowed themselves to become carried away by the prospects of complex airborne instrumentation and computerised systems and data processing. In our own Corporation there were young and inexperienced engineers for whom TSR 2 was their first hardware project who jumped with enthusiasm on the bandwagon of 'bigger and better instrumentation' for this biggest military aircraft programme the UK had ever seen. In the outcome events in the flying programme demanded more accurate and discerning qualitative evaluation by the pilot than ever before. So much was at stake that time and again decisions on whether or not to continue flying in the face of potentially serious system defects or problems affecting control and operation were made, not solely on computerised evidence but on the balanced judgement of the pilot co-ordinated with the engineering specialists. The instrumented evidence seldom revealed the whole picture and more often only provided partial though valuable supporting data. Nevertheless it was the extent and accuracy of this evidence that enabled the maximum momentum to be maintained in decision making and an exceptional rate of progress to be achieved up to the point of political cancellation in 1965.

135

# Flying the TSR 2

The pilot's approach to conversion on to this aircraft did not require to be significantly different from that for other supersonic aircraft. With a wing loading at training weights approaching 120psf in association with a 60° swept delta wing, the effects of induced drag were expected to be — and were — considerable. This had to be recognised in relation to low speed handling. But speed stability proved to be unexpectedly good so that less concentration on throttle adjustment was necessary when at or below the minimum drag speed than is required on many swept wing aircraft. It compensated to a degree for the disadvantages of high induced drag. TSR 2 was in fact as easy to fly as the best Mach 2 fighters.

Systems briefing was a programme of similar magnitude to those of the V-bombers but once learnt the systems were straightforward and not complicated in normal operation. Some of the emergency cases called for quite elaborate progressive drills and here a thorough knowledge of the

systems was required to ensure correct interpretation and quick action. Comprehensive check lists for normal and emergency drills were carried in stowages in both cockpits and the standard drill for a systems emergency was for the navigator to read off the appropriate sequence of checks for action by the pilot.

Cockpit layout was designed for maximum convenience and accessibility with successful results. In association with the unusually high level of comfort provided by the Martin Baker Mk8 rocket-powered ejection seat, the general design provided the most comfortable and convenient military cockpit in the writer's experience of military aircraft from 1939 to 1968.

On completion of engine and systems pre-flight checks which included CG control by fuel balancing, maximum dry power was set against the brakes which would not hold reheat thrust. Brakes were then released and maximum reheat engaged. Nosewheel steering by rudder pedals in fine (8°/in pedal movement) and coarse (40°/in) gearings was straightforward, but slight oversensitivity due either to circuit friction or phase-lag was noticeable and would have been corrected in development. During fighter-rate acceleration the take-off roll was true, even in crosswinds, with pleasantly positive nosewheel steering control.

At $V_r$ the nosewheel was lifted with exactly matched stick movement/pitch response with no tendency to over or under-controlling, and rotation was continued until reaching $V_{LO}$. The latter was set in relation to minimising the single-engine risk with the critical derated engine power necessary due to the induced drag of the highly loaded delta wing at high angles of attack. The rough-field-operation undercarriage was

*Above left:* Eric Allwright, chief systems designer TSR 2 (left). *BAe*

*Left:* Ready for Flight 1. Boscombe Down, 27 September 1964. *BAe*

*Above:* Crew aboard. *BAe*

*Right:* Cockpit drill. RPB and Don Bowen. *BAe*

*Below right:* Start drill. *BAe*

soft in action and tended to mask the unstick point, but then mild airframe buffet present in the gear/flaps 20° configuration gave physical confirmation of take-off. Undercarriage retraction was virtually symmetrical and free of trim change and the units went into lock with reassuring thumps.

Reheat was cancelled to maximum 'dry' during this process and even so an initial climb angle of about 30° was developed in keeping below the undercarriage and flap placard speeds. Flap 20° was then retracted and the last vestiges of buffet vibration died away as speed was increased for the 0.85/400kt climb.

From take-off pitch and yaw damping were deadbeat (basic aircraft characteristics without stability augmentation), and roll damping was not quite deadbeat and was subject to the effects of intertia, as predicted, at some points in the flight envelope if sharp stick inputs were made. As speed was increased longitudinal and directional stiffness were further increased and lateral response became more sensitive in the range 450-500kt where some increase of damping (to be provided later by auto-stabilisation) was desirable though not essential. However as speed was increased above 500kt, Mach number effect resulted in reduction of this roll over-sensitivity until at the high IAS/low level design case three-axis control harmony was already ideal for the task without modification of airframe controls.

This precise, responsive but well-damped standard of controllability rapidly encouraged confidence in the aircraft. Pilots were soon able to contour-fly manually at 0.9IMN over hill country under relaxed conditions in which even flying in-trim stick-free at very low level became quite practical for short periods. Contributing to this ease of control was the remarkable trim symmetry of the aircraft which enabled it to be flown through whole sorties from take-off to landing without a single trim adjustment on any axis.

The trim changes that did occur were in the normal sense ie nose-up with speed increase confirming positive longitudinal static stability, and directionally in the sense corresponding to any marked engine power asymmetry. In fact trim changes with all configuration or speed changes were of such low values that they resulted in only small fin or tailplane corrections to trim and therefore in very light out-of-

trim feel force to hold if untrimmed. On the climb to altitude the trim speed was held without need for power adjustment, and it was in this phase that the unusually good heading-holding characteristics became very apparent.

The aircraft stayed on heading without any tendency to wander off at both high and low altitude at the 0.9IMN cruise condition. At the supersonic regime control characteristics were again exceptionally good.

The basic handling characteristics (without autostability) in transition to supersonic flight were as follows at 30,000ft:

IMN = 0.9. Vibration free. Control harmony satisfactory for continuous cruising without autostabilisation. Lateral response perhaps a little too sensitive relative to the effects of inertia.

IMN = 0.94. Onset of very slight buffet vibration. No trim change.

IMN = 0.98. Cessation of any buffet vibration. No trim change. Lateral control sensitivity reducing.

IMN = 1.0-1.02. No vibration. No trim change. PE* jump as shock wave passed static holes.

IMN = 1.1+. No vibration or buffet. No trim change. Lateral control response in exact harmony with pitch and yaw axes, and virtually ideal for the flight condition.

The control characteristics at the maximum design speed of Mach 2.25 will now never be known but there was every indication that all would be well in this area too.

In manoeuvring flight at transonic speed the low tailplane position was highly effective in maintaining longitudinal stability. Transition from supersonic speed occurred even in turns without sign of the pitch-up normally encountered in other supersonic aircraft of the period. Trim changes due to airbrake operation were negligible up to 0.95IMN and were not checked above this as supersonic drag made their use of academic interest only. Airbrake drag was effective and approximately of the order predicted and some buffet was

*Position Error.

138

Far left, top: TSR 2 Flight 1.  BAe

Above: First turn, 3,000ft.  BAe

Left: New shape in the sky.  BAe

Below left: TSR 2 approaching the runway for its first landing. Support party in background. BAe

Bottom left: First landing. Photographic Canberra in background.  BAe

*Above left:* Satisfied driver.   *BAe*

*Above:* Satisfied navigator.   *BAe*

*Left:* Political occasion. Freddy Page, Julian Amery, Henry Gardner and RPB after first flight.   *BAe*

*Top right:* Flight 3. Left undercarriage trouble.   *BAe*

*Above right:* Trouble on Flight 4. Right undercarriage fails to retract.   *BAe*

*Right:* Flight 5. Both sides fail to retract and then fail to derotate for landing.   *BAe*

*Below right:* Flight 5. The landing has to be *very* precise.   *A&AEE*

experienced over the last few degrees of deflection; this might have needed further development.

During preliminary handling the PE jump point (transition from 1.0-1.02 IMN) was encountered unexpectedly at 62% of specified maximum thrust at ISA temperature. The first deliberate acceleration through the transonic drag-rise was carried out to 1.12IMN quickly and easily with one engine in max reheat/Intermediate and one at max dry/Intermediate. This gave immediate confirmation that total drag in this regime was certainly no greater than prediction. Control of the Olympus 22R engines was satisfactory in all conditions tested within the existing severe engine limitations, and throughout the trial reheat ignition was never faulted. Instrument recovery characteristics were straightforward and very pleasant due to high directional and longitudinal stiffness with deadbeat damping, and to excellent three-axis control response and harmony in association with an unusually high degree of speed-stability which simplified the setting up of trimmed power.

Descent was normally set up at 0.9IMN reducing to 400kt with airbrakes at 40° deflection. Under test conditions the recovery with offset computer TACAN, radar-monitored, was then a precise and secure operation with the comfort and convenient lay-out of the cockpit contributing to this feeling of confidence. Some minor changes to the relationships of some of the 'head-down' instruments were thought desirable and were planned for introduction from the 10th aircraft.

The circuit pattern was entered and flown like any other supersonic aircraft in that speed was not lost easily in level flight, but use of the high induced drag in turns was an effective way of quickly reducing to undercarriage placard speed. The highly loaded delta wing did not permit a dramatic level of manoeuvrability in the clean configuration below 300kt where the buffet boundary was about 0.75 g increment, or in the landing configuration where turning radii greater than with say a Lightning and similar to an F-104 were the order at base leg and finals. Again in the landing configuration longitudinal and directional stiffness and control harmony resulted in immediate feelings of security and confidence. A 2° approach slope was flown with unusual ease owing to the unexpectedly high speed stability which called for no throttle juggling even when well below the minimum drag speed at around 165kt IAS. Landings with 20°, 35°, and 50° flap settings with flap blowing were straightforward, and with more than adequate pitch control available rotation to 14-15° incidence resulted in positive flare and gentle touchdown. In 13 of the 30 touchdowns made final rates of descent of 3fps or less were recorded and the TSR 2 was one of the easiest landing supersonic aircraft yet devised.

Incidence was not critical at tail parachute development and this could be streamed either immediately on touchdown nose-high, or at any stage until after the nosewheel touched; and there was remarkable lack of tendency to weather-cock with tail parachute under crosswind conditions. The rough-field long stroke undercarriage with low pressure (85psi) tyres and heavy capacity brakes together with a 26ft diameter parachute resulted soon in landing roll-outs of as little as 850 yards without attempting to optimise either approach speed, parachute or braking techniques, and the specified short field capability was assured.

The TSR 2 thus turned out to be a brilliantly successful pilots' aeroplane which had, at the time of cancellation, already demonstrated successful accomplishment of its most significant aerodynamic and engineering features. In parallel

it had reached a similar point of success in the development and testing of its advanced navigation/attack and reconnaissance electronic systems.

Potentially one of the most effective military aircraft of all time the TSR 2 was specified by, designed, built and flight tested for the Royal Air Force. That it would have achieved all that was expected of it is beyond serious doubt, to the lasting credit of the team that designed and built it. It would have provided for the Royal Air Force a unique combination of striking power and reconnaissance capability for the 1970s and 80s, but this possibility disappeared with its cancellation in April 1965.

*Left:* TSR 2 arriving at Warton with Jimmy Dell's 'chase' Lightning. *BAe*

*Below:* Taxying in to a great reception. *BAe*

*Right:* Navigator Peter Moneypenny and RPB. *BAe*

*Below right:* TSR 2 test crews, Jimmy Dell, Don Knight, RPB and Don Bowen. *BAe*

BRITISH AIRCRAFT CORPORATION (OPERATING) LIMITED
PRESTON DIVISION

Total Flight Time: 00.14      Flight No.: 1

Take-off: 15.28    Landing: 15.42    Date: 27th September, 1964.

# EXPERIMENTAL FLIGHT REPORT

Aircraft Type: TSR2      Pilot: Mr. R.P. Beamont

Serial No.: XR.219      Navigator: Mr. D.J. Bowen

OBJECT OF TEST:

     Initial flight, at Boscombe Down.      Schedule No.: 1

TEST CONFIGURATION:

     Undercarriage extended.
     Auxiliary Air Intake Doors locked open.
     Intake cones "fixed".

TAKE-OFF LOADING:

Fuel: Indicated contents:     Tare Weight and Equipment..58098 lbs.
    Forward group   9050 lbs.
    No. 2 tank     3000 lbs.   Crew   ...   ...   ...   340 lbs.
    Aft group     6550 lbs.   Stores ...   ...   ...    lbs.
    No. 4 tank     2000 lbs.   Water ...   ...   ...    lbs.
    Total ind. fuel   15600 lbs.   LOX ..   ..   ..   .   24
    Usable fuel    16151 lbs.   Fuel   ...   ...   ..17838 lbs.
    Unusable fuel   1687 lbs.

Total Fuel   ...   ...   17838 lbs.   Total Weight ...   ...76300 lbs.

C.G. POSITION AT TAKE-OFF: 21.6ins.A.O.D. (39.8% S.M.C.) U/C DOWN

ENGINES: Type: Olympus 320X      Ser. No.: 1. 22218

OTHER RELEVANT AIRCRAFT CONDITIONS      2. 22221

XR 219                           27 September 1964

## FLIGHT NO 1

Alterations since Taxy Test 11:
(1) Turn round inspection carried out.
(2) Aircraft refuelled to Load Sheet 219/3, Case C.
(3) Ref Pilot's query: 'Stbd forward brake indicating 2,000psi'
This has been accepted for first flight.

Cockpit checks completed to Flight Reference Cards, Issue 3 amended.

Fuel on entry: F.9,200/A.6,400lb

CG 39.0% (G) 39.2% (F)

Undercarriage indicator: Three Greens, Nosewheel Red

Brake accumulators: 3,200/3,000psi

Parking brakes: 1,500/1,600psi
                1,500/1,600psi

HDD Attitude Indicator, 2° port bank error

Main Altimeter set 1,013.2 mbs

Oxygen: Full/95psi

Air Data Test: 1. 6,450ft
               2. 45,100ft

*Engine starts*

No 1   33%/400°C   35.0 seconds
       58.2%/310°C    1min 15 sec

No 2   No cycle.
       After discussion with Flight Test Van it was decided to recycle, and this second attempt was satisfactory.

       56.2%/294°C.

Brake accumulators: 4,200/4,000psi

143

Hydraulic services:

| No 1 controls 3,500psi | No 1 services 3,600psi |
|---|---|
| No 2 controls 3,500psi | No 2 services 3,700psi |

Cabin Air selected from Manual to Full Auto Cool, and high flow conditions occurred at 70/70% which persisted for 2-3 minutes before reducing to normal.

During the high flow condition the use of the shut-off cock was investigated, and it was confirmed that this cut off airflow into the cabin after approximately 30 seconds. The cock was returned to normal and power increased to above 70% $N_H$ where flow conditions were found to have returned to normal with a comfortable cabin temperature.

It was decided to continue the sortie on the basis that if unacceptably high flow rate was encountered in flight, it could be eliminated by use of the shut-off cock.

### Reheat checks

No 1  99%/680°C, 1st gutter light-up, satisfactory.
No 2  99%/685°C, 1st gutter light-up, satisfactory.

Loud crackling background and distorted reception were experienced on UHF Channel 3 with ground stations and the chase aircraft, and this was isolated to the upper aerial. Radio conditions on lower aerial were satisfactory.

### Take-off

The aircraft was lined up on Runway 24 with all systems serviceable.

Wind: 290°/11kt

Ground level ambient temperature: +18.2°C
Altimeter 1,013.2mbs

After burning off and balancing, fuel was adjusted to 13,300lb, differential 8,000/5,300lb for take-off.

Brake temperatures: 50/50°C.

Max dry intermediate: 98.5%/690°C, 97.5%/698°C.

Flaps 35°, blow in mid 35° segment.

Reset to flaps 20°, blow in mid 20° segment.

Nosewheel steering, FINE gear.

Reheat lights to 3rd gutter, satisfactory.

Runway acceleration normal.

Initial rotation at 125kt and nosewheel checked at 1-2ft.

Rotation continued at 170kt with lift-off occurring with buffet vibration at approximately 180kt (CSI).

In slight crosswind conditions a small lateral correction was required and achieved.

Acceleration in the initial climb-out was slow, and attitude was corrected at about 500ft in order to establish 200kt before resuming the climb incidence necessary to hold 200kt at max reheat.

From 1,000ft speed was increased gradually to 240kt, and reheat cancelled at approximately 3,000ft with unevenness through the gutters.

Buffet was present throughout this phase, of moderate amplitude and predominantly 4-5 cycles lateral at the cockpit.

On climb:  5,000ft  220kt  97.7/97.2%  696/698°C

During the initial climb-out phase the attitude developed was such that forward vision was lost, and the seat was raised to establish forward view. The seat raising switch was conveniently placed and easy to use in this situation.

### Normal Flight

Level flight was established at 6,500ft and a rate $\frac{1}{2}$ port turn set up beginning at 93/93% and increasing to 96/96% to sustain.

On levelling out, 35° flap was selected and produced a nose-down trim change of 3-4lb stick force. As the incidence changed with flap the buffet level was reduced but not eliminated.

Response in roll and pitch was assessed at 200kt in this configuration, and pitch damping was dead-beat; roll damping was low and subject to the effects of inertia. It was established that control in pitch and roll was adequate for gentle manoeuvres.

Control inputs in yaw and co-ordinated control movements resulted in relatively low response rates but otherwise normal response, with some adverse yaw from the roll inputs, and speed was reduced as scheduled to 180kt in the landing configuration (35° flap).

Buffet continued down to 180kt where it increased in amplitude slightly, and the chase Lightning reported 172kt.

This was accepted as evidence of possible adverse position error, and adjustments were made to the minimum speeds selected for the remainder of the sortie.

180kt CSI was sustained in level flight in the landing configuration at 35° flap (and blow) at 7,000ft with 94/94% $N_H$.

Up to this point re-trimming had not been required on any axis.

A gentle descent was set up at 80/80% achieving 250kt passing 5,000ft, and buffet amplitude remained as before. It was confirmed that the predominant characteristic was a 4-5 cycle lateral mode with some higher frequency background.

At the planned point in the first circuit review of the state of fuel and general systems serviceability confirmed that the second scheduled circuit was practical, and this intention was confirmed by radio.

The base leg turn was completed at 3,000ft, 210kt, and it was a simple matter to line up and establish the approach path, though a slight tendency to chase the glide slope was noticed due to low pitch response rate and light feel force.

Overshoot was initiated from 1,700ft at max dry intermediate, and an adequate though small climb rate established before retracting flap to 20°.

On levelling out for the downwind leg a left rudder stick-free dutch roll was carried out at 240kt, flaps 20°, developing approximately 45° port bank with damping to half amplitude in approximately 2 cycles and 2 seconds.

A stick jerk in similar conditions produced low rate but adequate response in pitch, with damping dead-beat in one cycle.

Flaps 35° selected for a PE check at 2,000ft CSI 201kt — Lightning 199kt.

### Landing

The aircraft was turned on to base leg at Thruxton as planned ($5\frac{1}{2}$ miles from 24 threshold), and lined up easily at 1,500ft/190kt CSI: and the centre-line and glide slope were maintained relatively easily, though with inertia affecting positive precision in roll and a very slight tendency to over-controlling in pitch, again due to low response rate and light feel force.

Final adjustments to landing attitude at short finals including a check in flare response were satisfactory. The threshold was crossed at 190kt CSI/100ft and power reduced very slightly during positive flare initiation at approximately 180kt. Control of dry engine power was adequate for approach speed adjustment in the prevailing favourable conditions.

As predicted the change in attitude was positive but the effect on the glide slope small, though sufficient to reduce the rate of descent at contact to a low value.

The rear main wheels were felt to touch smoothly at 500-600yd from the threshold as planned, wings level and without detectable drift; and immediately after contact 2-3 cycles of heavy amplitude undercarriage/structural vibration was felt (wind 290°/15kt). Power was reduced to idle/idle, and the undercarriage vibration was eliminated apparently as the forward main wheels touched; and the nose was allowed to descend gently into contact with the runway with little forward movement of the stick.

At nosewheel contact the speed was down to approximately 155kt, and the tail parachute handle operated. After a relatively lengthy pause development was felt, and subsequent de-reefing produced a powerful, smooth deceleration.

The landing was made with nosewheel steer engaged and no sharp steering effects were noted. It should however be practical to delay nosewheel steer to low speeds in future.

As landing roll conditions were entirely smooth and satisfactory use of wheel braking was delayed to approximately 100kt, and this resulted in brake temperatures registering only 80/80°C at standstill. Accumulator pressures 4,000/4,000psi.

The tail parachute was jettisoned normally at approximately 20kt. Fuel 5,100/2,900lb. Wind 280°/13-15kt.

The navigator reported that the starboard undercarriage bogie rotation may not have been fully complete at the touchdown point, which could have led to the vibration condition experienced.

Cockpit temperatures high throughout the sortie with Auto Full Cold selected.

After taxying back, shut-down checks:

58.5%/314°C     57%/294°C

Brake temperatures: 180/300°C

Brake accumulators: 4,100/4,200psi

*Summary*
Due to virtually complete serviceability this first sortie was carried out in full accordance with Flight Test Schedule No 1.

Stability and response to controls was found to be adequate and safe for flight under the conditions tested, and to conform closely to predicted and simulated values.

Noticeably high induced drag was experienced after take-off, due possibly to adverse position error resulting in too early lift-off.

Moderate amplitude buffet was experienced at all speeds tested, and this was found to vary in amplitude with incidence.

Control of the approach and landing was especially excellent having regard to the current absence of auto-stabilisation.

Engine control and behaviour was adequate at all points in the flight, except in disengagement of reheat during the climb-out where the usual difficulty was experienced in throttle-box disengagement of minimum reheat.

Engine speed adjustment of the approach was not faulted, but is should be noted that the prevailing weather conditions on the approach were non-turbulent.

All supporting systems functioned perfectly with the exception of the temperature and flow control of cabin conditioning, which tended to pulse throughout the sortie and was too warm.

The warning system functioned satisfactorily, and no spurious warnings occurred.

Fuel balancing was not required during flight, and fuel system performance was not faulted.

Cockpit layout was satisfactory with some detail exceptions described at Addendum I.

The forward windscreen and instrument shroud layout were particularly excellent and virtually no significant reflections were seen in the glasses in spite of the intense sun-glare during approach and landing.

The canopy transparencies were of very low vision quality as reported previously.

In general the performance, stability and reponse to controls conformed closely to the briefed values and especially to the simulator studies.

Virtually all scheduled test points were achieved on this flight and this, coupled with the high standard of systems serviceability and the adequate level of un-auto-stabilised control and stability in this high drag, low-speed configuration, reflects a very high standard of design, preparation and inspection.

In this 1st flight configuration and under the conditions tested, this aircraft could be flown safely by any moderately experienced pilot qualified on Lightning or similar aircraft, and the flight development programme can therefore be said to be off to a good start.

With present engine ratings the aircraft is, however, clearly critically short of thrust, and this situation is likely to dictate the rate of flight development.

R. P. BEAMONT
Manager: Flight Operations

*Defects*
(1)   Canopy conditioning temperature and flow control unstable.
(2)   Canopy jettison handle safety pin on floor of Navigator's cockpit (in console).
(3)   Upper UHF aerial unserviceable.
(4)   2° bank error on pilot's HDD Attitude Indicator.

*Below:* Turning Finals . . . 'we've got it made!'. *BAe*

# TSR 2 Retrospect

A unique combination of flying characteristics from bomber-style inertia with fighter-style control responsiveness, power margins approaching Lightning performance, symmetrical trimming characteristics over much of the flight envelope and only small trim changes at extreme configurations, to stability and control in supersonic transition like the best of supersonic fighters with response to gusts and turbulence of so low an order as to create an entirely new piloting experience — this was the TSR 2 in flight. The low-lift-slope wing in combination with a wing loading in excess of 120psf had been designed especially to provide acceptable ride characteristics at high penetration speeds at very low level. The successful result gave the pilot, seated in a comfortable, well-laid-out cockpit, an altogether new and almost unreal experience. The aircraft did not give the usual indications of change of flight condition by 'talking to the pilot' through changes in noise and vibration levels with variations in speed and height or air turbulence. In the early stages more continuous attention than usual had to be paid to flight instrumentation to avoid overshooting the limits set for each flight. It was quite reminiscent in fact of flying the fixed-base simulator, the aeroplane doing precisely what was required of it but with hardly any 'seat of the pants' indications to the pilot!

All this was not achieved without problems of course, and while aerodynamically the TSR 2 behaved in an exemplary manner, a number of engineering problems were encountered as was only to be expected in the early prototype phase. The most serious and delaying feature apart from engine defects, was the undercarriage which malfunctioned in a number of ways and resulted in failure to achieve the undercarriage 'up' configuration for the first nine flights. A major difficulty was insufficient rotational force at the tandem wheel bogey beam to rotate it against air loads into the 'up-lock' position. When this was finally overcome and the undercarriage fully retracted on flight 10, such was the confidence of the test team that the flight envelope was extended in that flight from the previous highest speed of 275kt (with the undercarriage down) right out to 500kt, and within five more flights to 600kt and to M=1.1.

Another aspect of the undercarriage which gave trouble was more predictable, namely a coupling between the undercarriage natural frequency and that of the main fuselage mode. But this resulted in a surprise for the crew during what looked like a very smooth first landing when, as the rear wheels touched allowing the bogey beam to rotate and the front wheels to touch down, all hell broke loose in the cockpit with instrumentation-measured values of $\pm1.8$g lateral and $\pm1.5$g vertical at 5.6cps. This level of oscillation was not only disturbing but for some seconds it blurred pilot vision at the critical point in the landing where drag 'chute operation, pitch attitude correction and steering all needed close attention. Luckily the aircraft proved so docile that it looked after the latter two operations virtually by itself until vision returned to the pilot. This problem remained for a number of flights but was soon understood and damper strut modifications were ready for fitting by early 1965. Then at the abrupt political ending of the flying programme it could be seen that there were no major problems to resolve in aerodynamics, stability and performance.

Trouble areas at cancellation still included engine development which was behind airframe progress and also the undercarriage vibration and associated fuselage modes. But these problems were well on the way to solution and the aircraft was close to evaluation by Service pilots as a first stage towards acceptance by the RAF when it was cancelled on 5 April 1965.

In later years hindsight did not reveal anything to suggest that our appreciation of this aircraft was wrong at the time. A long-range, very low-level strike and reconnaissance capability by TSR 2 would in 1970-80 have ensured a unique role for the RAF at a period when the widespread abdication of British influence had dramatic effects on the balance of power in many of the world's unstable areas.

None of the three pilots who flew the TSR 2 in the fateful months of early 1965 will ever doubt the quality of the aircraft. Those of us who experienced skimming through the Pennines down to treetop height on low-level high-speed tests in rock-steady security while the Lightning 'chase' pilot had often to pull away up to higher, smoother air saying that he couldn't stay down with us owing to the extreme turbulence, knew that in TSR 2 we had in our grasp one of the most remarkable designs in aviation history. But our grip on it was forced and the consequent loss in potential power and flexibility of the RAF became a significant factor in our national affairs in the latter half of the century.

*Below:* TSR 2 on test from Warton in March 1965 before programme cancellation. *BAe*

# No Glory

An odd facet of the 1970s was a widespread attitude of critical and even in some areas derisory disbelief of the traditional accounts of the major battles in the 1939-45 air war. This stemmed perhaps inevitably from the over-glamorised excesses of the film media in the postwar period in such epics as *Angels One Five* and *Battle of Britain*. None of them captured the essential feel of the times and events portrayed and all of them suggested in varying degree false heroics. These were seized upon by a new generation of authors, the majority of whom were not alive in the times they claimed to portray, to raise doubts about the value of these operations and of the recorded results. *Who did really win the Battle of Britain?* was a question repeatedly raised in public in the middle 1970s, but surviving German bomber pilots were in absolutely no doubt that they were in no state to continue the fight in daylight over England after September 1940. Their opinion, however, was apparently not often sought by the historians of the period.

In similar vein the media attacked the RAF 'bomber offensive' in general and 'Bomber' Harris their greatly respected leader in particular. Inhuman actions were implied which, it was widely claimed, were wasted effort involving criminally high losses with no significant impact on the final outcome of the war. Many of these voices echoed a common theme — the attempted discrediting and destruction of the 'establishment' attitude to defence and of the 'relevance' of being prepared mentally and materially to fight for the country. In this process the anti-war faction was vociferous in the media in sneering attacks, branding patriots as 'war lovers' and all the other dreary platforms of militant and mindless pacifism. But they all failed to recognise or acknowledge the vital fallacy in their argument.

There is no glory in killing. There is no glory in causing destruction, mass injury and death, and none in fighting any form of war for its own sake; but in self-defence, defence of others and defence of country there must be honour or, in default of these paramount duties, dishonour. It has become fashionable in some quarters to deride both these beliefs and the morality of preparing and maintaining our armed forces to an adequate level for the defence of these Islands. The pacifists, permissives and appeasers have much to answer for in the reduction of this country to the state of puzzled incapacity in which it found itself at the turn of the 1960s. But no pilot of a Spitfire or Hurricane climbing out over the sun-washed South Coast in 1940 with his small group of friends forward-leaning in their narrow cockpits with straining eyes and listening to the RDF* controller's calm voice advising of '100 plus coming your way straight ahead', was ever in any doubt of his place in the scheme of things or what he ought to be doing about it. In the fleeting moments before the 'Tally ho, enemy in sight' he will have experienced elation, cold fear and instant counter-reaction of duty, followed by seconds of supreme concentration in the confusion of battle. Then as the sky miraculously cleared the drained sensation as the adrenalin ran out. Alternatively there was perhaps a new crisis of a battle damaged, faltering aircraft, the anxiety of a forced, crash-landing or an escape by parachute; and the ultimate contrast of flying home to the unreal atmosphere of the disciplined, orderly RAF station with the mandatory combat report interview with the Intelligence Officer, and finally the clean-up positively required before that drink in the Mess.

In all this there was an impelling amalgam of training, conditioning, duty and responsibility to the ideas of service to country, fears of the day, of injury and death though not of the enemy, pride of service to country, to one's unit and of one's own very small part in the team, and perhaps desperate concern about possible personal failure to meet these demanding and demanded standards. But the fears were not dwelt on and were kept in their proper place.

There was total unquestioning acceptance that this was the job they had been trained for and were better at than anyone anywhere. Confidence increased with the daily successes reported in the whole of the fighting area. This and the underlying note of humour and refusal to appear to take it all too seriously covering total dedication were the essence of the fighter pilot's morale.

They were young and lost no sleep at night despite the traumas of the day, and their battles were fought with extraordinary determination, elan and gaiety. It was a job which had to be done each and every day until it was over and one for which they were well trained, prepared and equipped, and it was done without self-congratulation and with pride — but no glory.

*Radio direction finding, later called RADAR.

*Above:* Hurricane squadron. 1940. *IWM*

# The End of the Test Pilot - a fallacy of the 1960s

In the testing of aeroplanes three main requirements emerge, first controllability, second reliability and third systems and equipment suitability. The final outcome cannot be acceptable if any one of these features remains unsatisfactory.

Over the period covered by this book emphasis has changed very considerably. Beginning with the simple biplanes and early monoplanes of the 1930s it extended to the complex, highly automated and densely equipped machines of the 1970s with computer-based stability-augmentation and control systems which tend to isolate the pilot from direct control of the aeroplane. Yet while he is still required to command the aircraft, the end-product of whatever control system is employed, be it manual through cable or control rod direct to the control surfaces or by dynamic hand-controller input to a fully-computerised electronic control and stability-augmentation system, must be aircraft response matched to the human range of response capabilities. In other words it has to 'handle'. In the three decades of aviation since World War II an intensive effort has been made to quantify 'handling' criteria so as to be able to express in numbers the design qualities needed for pilot-acceptability in new designs. Somewhat surprisingly in a technological age this effort has been only partially successful. While much is now known of the limits of control forces and response and damping rates acceptable to pilots, the translation of this knowledge into engineering fact seldom achieves first-off conditions of control harmony in a new type which are completely acceptable to pilots as a good standard. Hence one of the basic needs for 'flight development'.

In pilots' terms good handling qualities can ensure the best operational capability in a military aeroplane or the most efficient and safest conditions in a transport. When these conditions are achieved to an exceptionally high degree the result is known as a 'pilot's aeroplane'. Few that have achieved this accolade on test have subsequently turned out to be failures and it remains one of the earliest targets for prototype testing after establishing that the flying qualities are safe, to see that they give confidence to the pilots.

It is possible of course to manage a basically unstable aeroplane by complete dependence on artificial stability and control. Safety, however, demands that so much back-up duplication is necessary, sometimes even quadruplication, as to result in heavy penalties in cost. This not being a very practical concept, it has been normal to provide a back-up emergency hydro-mechanical control system giving minimal handling qualities sufficient only for safe recovery. But with the total and successful dependence on fly-by-wire control systems in manned spacecraft and in reliable experience of the advanced avionics of aircraft such as the Tornado it is likely that direct mechanical connection between the pilot's stick and the flight controls will soon become a thing of the past. Nevertheless each new aircraft demonstrates that we have not yet reached the point when aircraft response can be exactly matched at the design stage in the 'black boxes' to pilot demand throughout the whole of a complex performance and loads flight envelope. So it remains essential for the test pilot to be able to identify areas of shortfall and assess for example where the avionics are wrong. He has to

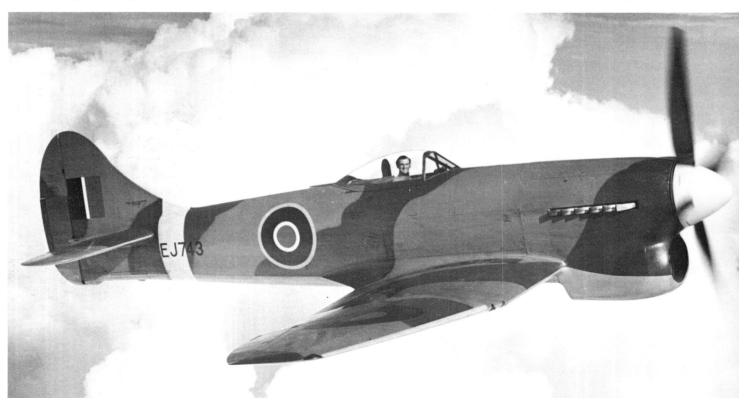

suggest, too, what is required to improve the situation, and this aspect underlines an anomaly in the present system for test pilot training.

With the immense cost of development of supersonic aircraft conflicts of interest occur inevitably in the planning stages. The advent of computer-based flight testing has brought heavy pressures on the test pilot to fly every valuable minute of every test flight from take-off to landing in precise and systematic accordance with an immensely detailed flight test schedule. This in itself is the product of many hours of intensive work and cross-referencing by a team of flight test engineers and design specialists. This practice, extended over the months and years of a test programme, can result in inhibition of the test pilot's initiative. It can stultify his ability to give a consistent and progressive appraisal of the progress of the aircraft towards the goal of into-service.

The days are long past when the sole information available to engineers on the characteristics of a new type came from the test pilot's note pad and his 'feel' for the aircraft. Total reliance on pre-planned testing followed by dependence solely on computerised data for decisions on progress and modification, however, can lead to serious pitfalls. One example of this was a high performance aircraft when delivered to Boscombe Down after what had been thought to be a comprehensive three-year period of flight testing. It was found by the Boscombe test pilots to have inadequate lateral control in combat conditions at high speed, and it was subsequently revealed that in planning the tests to maximum design speed only 'flutter' clearance and longitudinal control assessment had been scheduled. Because they had not been briefed formally (and it was not in the test schedules) the company pilots had not thought of assessing the lateral control beyond gentle manoeuvring at these speeds. This led to costly redesign late in the programme — it could also have caused an accident.

Technology is constantly advancing and not least in the field of data gathering, but in 1979 the awesome weight of computer-based design technology still fails on occasion to get an aircraft control system right first time. Nor can it positively identify where it is not adequate for full pilot confidence. There is still much vital qualitative work for the test pilot, now and in the years ahead.

*Left:* Tempest testing. Langley 1944. Pilot Humble. *BAe*

*Above:* Jaguar testing. Warton 1970, with John Cockburn. *BAe*

*Right:* Tornado testing 1975. *BAe*

# The Enthusiasts

One day in 1968 when walking through the Canberra overhaul shops at the BAC Samlesbury factory I noticed a small white aeroplane parked in a corner under a Canberra's wing. A closer look proved very interesting. Of wood and fabric construction it was a side-by-side cabin aeroplane with partial dual controls, and it seemed remarkably well-finished both inside and out with a Rolls-Royce Continental 90hp flat-four piston engine and a laminated wood propeller. This was intriguing on two grounds, firstly because as the director responsible for operations at both of our airfields I thought that I should have known about the presence of a strange aeroplane, and secondly because although not particularly familiar with little aeroplanes, I very much liked the look of this one.

Enquiries soon confirmed that the owner was one Stan Jackson, superintendent of the Company's plating and processing department at Preston, and that he had obtained the General Manager's permission to hangar it at Samlesbury. Then my informant said — 'and he built it himself!' This was even more intriguing and I decided to find out more about the project.

It transpired that Jackson had indeed built the aeroplane over a period of four years in his bedroom and garage. His long-suffering wife had not only to put up with this without complaint but had taught herself aircraft fabric work and completed the covering of wings, fuselage and control surfaces for him.

Word of this venture had got round of course and Jackson soon had very able advice from the relevant specialist departments culminating in Inspection and Airworthiness. It was at this point that I became involved.

In the process of four years of dedication to building the aeroplane Jackson's piloting currency had been lost. Although he held a private pilot's licence he felt he needed some professional help when it came to the test flying. One day while in one-sided conversation with this supreme enthusiast the subject gradually turned to flight trials and went something like this:

| | | |
|---|---|---|
| SJ | — | She should be ready for taxying trials quite soon. |
| RPB | — | Oh, good. |
| SJ | — | Inspection have agreed to sign up for prior-to-flight inspection for the authorities (Popular Flying Association) to issue the Flight Certificate but there's one problem. |
| RPB | — | What's that? |
| SJ | — | I need to find a test pilot for the flight trials. |
| RPB | — | You'll need to be quick then. |
| SJ | — | Well, I was wondering whether you might . . . ? |
| RPB | — | Funny you should say that as I was just going to suggest it! |

During the period that followed Jackson must at times have wondered about his decision because I had to make a few enquiries. Here was an aeroplane waiting to be tested, built not by an approved factory but by one man and his wife, and about the design or previous history of which I had no knowledge whatsoever. So I set a few targets for cross-checking information and finally held some meetings with the enthusiastic co-operation of the many relevant company specialists involved. A suitable level of technical assurance was achieved and plans were set for a test programme.

This began on 24 May 1969. With the owner in the right seat we established the ground handling characteristics and subsequently the basic take-off and landing characteristics in short straight hops to 5-10ft at up to 65kt along the main runway at Samlesbury. Apart from a slow tick-over which stalled the engine on one run, and rather nasty little heel-pedal-operated wheel brakes which took some getting used to, the aeroplane felt neat and tidy and pleasantly responsive

*Left:* Owner and builder Stan Jackson starting up the Minicab for first flight. Samlesbury 1969. *BAe*

*Above:* Success! *BAe*

*Right:* First flight. *BAe*

*Above left:* First flight for the owner. *BAe*

*Above:* The Minicab meets the Press. *Daily Express*

*Left:* Over its home airfield, Samlesbury. *Daily Express*

*Below left:* 'We'll have to do something about those fasteners.' *Daily Express*

*Top right:* Preparing for first flight of Sprite. Warton February 1979. *BAe*

*Centre right:* First flight of Sprite. *BAe*

*Bottom right:* With builders of Sprite, Barry Parkinson and Roy Tasker. *BAe*

to elevator and aileron but, I suspected, a little overlight in the rudder.

It was agreed that fuel and engine oil filter checks should be done and then we would fly on the first day of suitable weather. I wanted no more than 15kt wind within ± 5° of the runway, cloud base above 2,000ft and good visibility. This happened on 21 June 1969 and with a brisk 14kt wind from the south Echo Papa was eased off the Samlesbury north/south runway after about 200 yards' roll with flaps at 30°. Any doubts about use of the short runway for first flight were soon dispelled as with full throttle giving 2,450rpm, a 65kt climb showed 500ft by the boundary and 1,000ft above the hill to the south of the airfield.

In moderate turbulence the Minicab felt light and very responsive, but stick-free checks showed excellent damping and stability on all axes. The pitch and roll controls were responsive and deadbeat, and only the rudder seemed a little too light and sensitive. The first flight report emphasised the confidence which this little aeroplane produced so quickly. In the ten years which followed it continued to give enormous pleasure to its owner and to this grateful author.

With the sensitivity of an ultra-light coupled with a short fuselage, high ground angle and a tailwheel undercarriage, landing required the delicate touch of a Spitfire pilot. In fact the overall control harmony is not dissimilar to that classic aeroplane although at under 1,200lb with fuel and two crew the inertia characteristics are rather different and the Minicab responds energetically to turbulence.

Perhaps the most pleasant feature is the lightness and precision of pitch and roll control. This is coupled with good static stability which provides stick-free trimmed flight at cruise. It also permits a continuous curve approach to land to be set up and flown almost without guidance from the pilot. The flare and final judgement of touchdown is less easy due to some areas of distortion at the foot of the windscreen coupled with sensitivity to turbulence or to crosswind in ground effect. Once the pilot has become accustomed to judging whether to go for a three-point landing or a 'wheeler', however, landing is no problem but it is always interesting!

With exceptional visibility from the cockpit and the ability to fly at light load at speeds down to 40kt some interesting situations are possible. For example approaching and landing at around 25kt relative ground speed in a 20kt wind will permit (and necessitate) landing diagonally across a large runway if it is not into wind, or on a suitably into-wind perimeter track if the runway crosswind is too strong. These performance characteristics together with very precise controllability have enabled me many times to fly alongside birds going about their lawful business. On one fascinating occasion I was able to join formation with a skein of about 40 pink-foot geese at 1,000ft over the Ribble estuary and stay closely on their right wing for some minutes as they veered nervously to the left while maintaining only slightly disturbed formation and eventually ended up heading 180° away from their original course. While admiring their beautiful and effortless flight I suddenly became aware of the comical impression made by 40 pairs of goose eyes nervously focused over their owners' right shoulders as they flew on not looking where they were going!

These experiences together with first and subsequent test flights in 1979 of Sprite and Petrel light aircraft at Warton, the former an all-metal tricycle undercarriage two-seater beautifully home-built by Warton engineers Barry Parkinson and Roy Tasker, and the latter a similar category light air-

153

craft to a different design well-built by British Aerospace Preston apprentices under the expert guidance of Sumner Miller, all added a different dimension to the experiences of a fascinating lifetime in aviation. (Hopefully there is more to come.) These aircraft confirmed for me that all aeroplanes, large and small, fast and slow, have their own interesting characteristics, and that most of them need in their early days the attention of an understanding pilot to make them safe and efficient.

The purpose of most of the aircraft I have tested has been necessarily deadly. Some of them more recently have been purely for pleasure. All have been satisfying experiences in themselves — taking the author with gratitude out of the turmoil of ground-borne activity into the clean, untroubled spaces of the skies.

*Above right:* Preparations for first flight of Petrel. June 1979 at Warton.  *BAe*

*Right:* First flight.  *BAe*

*Below left:* After the first flight.  *BAe*

*Below right:* Flying the Petrel over Warton on Flight 6.  *BAe*

# Tornado Multi-Role Combat Aircraft

At the beginning of the 1970s a major international programme was commenced to develop the first strike aircraft for the NATO air forces of Italy, West Germany and Britain with realistic all-weather day and night capability. This was to be a complicated operation involving the major national aircraft firms of Fiat in Italy, Messerschmitt in Germany and the British Aircraft Corporation at Warton. It involved the setting up in Munich of central management organisations to represent the customers and to manage the contractors. The customer organisation, Namma, was headed by a seconded Luftwaffe senior officer, General Kruger, and the industry organisation was managed by Professor Gero Madelung who was seconded from Messerschmitt.

In the formation of the necessary management structure it was then decided that specialist areas would be needed to monitor and co-ordinate the quality and efficiency of this widespread and massive operation. In this activity I was invited by Freddie Page to take on the co-ordination of the flight testing programme in all three countries of this major military aircraft which was now to be called the Multi-Role Combat Aircraft. I was told that this arrangement had been endorsed by the national authorities concerned. It seemed something of a tall order because as was well-known in the industry the co-ordination of the views of test pilots with those of the engineers was an area which often ran into difficulties even in a one-country programme. When exposed to trinational bureaucracies, local parochialism, inconsistencies in management structures and nationally independent attitudes, it was likely that complications would arise.

Subsequent events amply justified these doubts. Although one of my early stipulations of the need to start with a strong team was supported by the release to me by BAC of their Chief Flight Test Engineer, Dicky Dickinson and their recently retired Chief Test Pilot, Jimmy Dell, less support was received from the other national companies in providing high-grade personnel. The next few years often seemed to be less preoccupied with building an aeroplane than with damping down emotional brush fires and providing 'visibility' of company flight test activities to the customer, to each of

*Below:* The first production Tornado.　*BAe*

*Above:* All-weather, day and night weapons system for NATO. *BAe*

the companies, and to almost anybody who had some complaint to express about the progress or otherwise of the flight development programme.

This was all part of the process of building an effective European organisation to produce an advanced aeroplane for four air forces and three Nations.

Flight tests were not alone in this experience which was also the pattern for most other specialist departments in the programme but as the flight testing phase comes last it inevitably coincided with the greatest pressures to meet contract dates. In the process the Tornado, as it was now named, began to emerge as an altogether remarkable aircraft. After first flight in 1974 crewed by Paul Millett and Nils Meister it had by 1979 achieved 2,500 test hours and had in the process been proved to more than 90% of its ambitious design targets. In this development period it came in, of course, for its expected share of hammering by the news media and politicians. When compared to the early difficulties of other comparable military aircraft test programmes during the supersonic era such as the F-104 with 22 aircraft lost on test, the Mirage with five aircraft lost on test, and the Phantom, Lightning and the F-14 each of which suffered prototype losses in their test programmes, the Tornado record in its first four years was seen to be exceptional. It was also exceptional to fly and with variable wing sweep and advanced avionics flight control and automatic flight systems an entirely new level of precision high-speed flight was achieved.

In the main I had to judge the aircraft from the test reports and verbal accounts of the international team of test pilots who achieved excellent results in the face of some years of frustrating and at times hazardous engine development problems. There is, however, no substitute for personal experience and in August 1975 the back seat of dual control Tornado prototype P03 was sufficient to give me a lasting impression of the dedicated suitability of this major military aircraft for service in NATO through to the end of this century.

At the beginning of World War II the fighter aircraft had been seen only as a bomber destroyer. Subsequent events had seen the development of its valuable additional role in accurate pin-point tactical ground attack for the interdiction of airfields and communications and for the close support of armies in the battle zone. By 1944 these roles had been well developed and heavy dependence was placed on them in the African desert, Italian and European campaigns, but they were at all times subject to one major disadvantage. Fighter ground attack was vitally dependent on good visibility both for accurate navigation into the target area and for sighting and attacking the targets. For all practical purposes therefore fair weather was essential for success. Although much courageous activity was undertaken in bad weather the results in terms of damage to the enemy were seldom cost-effective in poor visibility or at night.

For the next three decades this problem remained unresolved. Even the first generation of dedicated jet strike-fighters such as the Jaguar and the F-7 Corsair, although achieving higher than ever standards of low-level performance and navigation with their highly loaded swept wings and inertial navigation systems, could still not claim full bad weather day and night capability. Thus a dangerous gap was left in the NATO defences facing the opposing night-manoeuvrable Eastern bloc tank forces.

With the roll-out of the first series production aircraft in June 1979, all was set for the major breakthrough. NATO air forces will receive with their Tornados for the first time ever in aviation true tactical pin-point attack capability in defence against all-weather day or night action by aggressor ground forces.

# Epilogue

In 1968 the author was privileged to join the group of pilots selected by Allen Wheeler to fly the treasured relics of the Shuttleworth Trust at Old Warden. These aircraft were for the most part actual originals with authentically antique engines and controls. They were fascinating examples of the beginnings of aviation and unique in being in most cases the only surviving flying specimens of their type. Ranging from examples of the first aeroplanes such as Bleriot and Deperdussin, through the classic Avro 504 trainer of 1914 and the Sopwith Pup of 1915, one of the first true single-seat fighter 'scouts', to the quite substantial Bristol Fighter and LVG (German) of 1917 and the classic British fighter of the time the SE5A, they included as well representatives of the golden biplane era of 1920-1935 such as the DH Moth, Avro Tutor and Gloster Gladiator. All these aircraft were maintained with dedicated skill and care by the Old Warden engineers and were resplendant in the correct paintwork and markings of their time. These activities were supported by a continuous and mammoth exercise in searching out long-forgotten spare parts and relics from museums, private collections, barns and backyards from all over the country and outside. As a result suffecient genuine spares were obtained or in many instances replacements made to original drawings, to enable these unique aeroplanes to be flown publicly two or three times each year.

Comparison of flying techniques between the aeroplane of the 1970s and these early biplanes is fascinating not so much for its differences as for its similarities. Basically since the Wright brothers the applied philosophy of aerodynamic stability and control has not changed fundamentally but only become better understood. While the response to elevator of the Bristol Fighter and Pup at take-off and landing are very like those of a modern light aeroplane, control in roll of these aeroplanes is vastly less effective than in current small aeroplanes and requires assistance with rudder-co-ordination to a degree which would be regarded as unacceptable today.

Nevertheless after some brief conversion on a Tiger Moth biplane, a modern pilot can safely fly the 1917 vintage Bristol Fighter from take-off to landing using the techniques and skills he has learnt on postwar aircraft. These need be modified only in relation to lifting the tail with forward stick initially on take-off, countering propeller torque swing on take-off with rudder, co-ordinating aileron-banked turns with rudder and sideslipping height and speed off on the approach to land in the absence of flaps or other high-lift devices. The landing is also entirely straightforward with responsive elevator control so long as one takes a positive decision in good time on whether to hold off for a classic 'three point' stalled landing or to 'wheeler' it. Either way a few knots of crosswind will have it away in an embarrassing and uncontrollable ground loop — quite unlike the insensitive characteristics of the tricycle undercarriages of today. Take-off and landing must therefore be strictly into wind.

*Right:* Checking out on the Vickers Gunbus on 7 June 1968 at Wisley with 'Dizzy' Addicote. This aircraft is now at the RAF Museum, Hendon. *BAe*

157

*Left and below:* Checking out on the Vickers Gunbus on 7 June 1968 at Wisley with 'Dizzy' Addicote. This aircraft is now at the RAF Museum, Hendon. *BAe*

*Bottom:* Demonstrating the SE5a at Old Warden 1977. *Shuttleworth Collection*

*Right:* Leading a unique formation of Sopwith Pups with the Bristol Fighter at Old Warden on 30 June 1974. *Air Portraits*

*Below right:* The Bristol Fighter at Old Warden. *Air Portraits*

The SE5A is another case of extreme sensitivity to crosswinds or bumps on the airfield. Apart from this it is perhaps the best of the World War I aircraft to handle and is often described as 'better than a Tiger Moth and with 200hp'.*

Crouched down behind the minuscule windscreen which does little to reduce the icy slipstream blast that tears at the pilot's goggles, and squinting through the Aldis sight alongside the big Vickers gun on the port cowling and with the Lewis gun in reach above on the centre section of the top wing, it is easy to understand why McCudden and other SE5 aces felt that this aeroplane was the finest fighter of its time — it is still great to fly today.

So, what types stand out in one man's experience of 40 years of aeroplanes?

Certainly the SE5A and the Bristol Fighter for their gentle, viceless (except for ground looping!) fresh-air flying with the wind singing in the wires. But also the Hawker Hart, one of the last of the military biplanes and an unforgettable experience for an 18-year-old training in Scotland under imminent threat of war.

Then the reality of war in the Hurricane with its solid characteristics of stable, uncritical yet powerful control and ruggedness in combat which undoubtedly saved his life a few times in 1940.

The Spitfire with its inspiring beauty, delicate landing characteristics and 'fighter boy' charisma.

The Tempest V, a Typhoon with the bugs sorted out, faster than the 190 and supreme for the medium and low-level war from D-Day onwards. And so to the postwar the F-86 Sabre, truly transonic and such an honest fighter.

The Canberra was his first personal Prototype First Flight and memorable on that score but also on so many others. It was so easily capable of out-flying the fighters of the time and had outstanding range and altitude performance — all with an ease and lack of complication that still makes it unique in many ways in Service today 30 years later.

The TSR 2 on First Flight with its burst-prone engines encased in fuel tanks with capabilities unmatched today

*The Tiger Moth has a 140hp engine.

14 years after its cancellation and with the flying qualities of a good simulator.

The VC10 with the ambience of a flying mansion with butler in attendance, yet a real pilot's aeroplane from the cockpit.

The Jaguar, unique as the first specialised daylight low-level attack aircraft weapons system in Europe, and its fully all-weather day and night replacement the Tornado.

Not forgetting the Minicab, surely one of the most delicate and delightful of all very light aircraft.

But above all these a mile high stands the Lightning, supreme in performance and controllability. An incomparable experience on every flight for the pilot who flew it first and who together with the brilliant English Electric team at Warton had some small part in making it so.

Still with aviation in the late 1970s and concerned with the international European Multi-role Combat Aircraft, the author sat frequently in the stuffy confines of the company 125 executive jet between Warton and Munich. Poring over technical papers along with other members of the BAC design and engineering team, all of us had in common a love of (and some would say obsession with) aeroplanes coupled with a conviction that air defence remains essential to our national security. Sometimes when glancing out of the window at 30,000ft it was to leave this association behind with a momentary cold chill on seeing the Dutch Islands stretching out mistily below into the North in the soft light of a summer evening with broken cumulus clouds etched golden in the setting sun. The yellow beaches below curving in sharp contrast against the milky blue of the shallow North Sea were so reminiscent of the days with the Tempest Wing in 1944. Instinctively one felt ready once again to dive away in the lead of those 20-year old Tempest pilots from many countries. Conscious of the flashing streaks of tracer and the dark brown clumps of 88mm flak coming up at us from the Dutch Islands, not too bothered by them — we had been there too often for that — we dived in to attack the 88mm anti-aircraft gun emplacement on the improbably (but we thought appropriately) named island of Overflakkee. Then a voice from one of the other passengers would perhaps say 'can we manage a 4g limit for Farnborough, Bee?' and the moment would be gone.

But the continuity is still there. Our parents' generation created and operated the first practical aeroplanes. We ourselves developed and flew a generation of aeroplanes that contributed to winning World War II. Since then we have worked on some of the best jet aircraft the world has seen and supplied them to air forces throughout the world. Now inbound from Munich to Warton in the 125, a British product of our colleagues at Hatfield and one of the best of its class in the world, at the end of another 14-hour working day the task is together with Italian and German colleagues, a European aircraft to become a mainstay of NATO defence in the next decades.

There are many today who say that all this endeavour and the theme of defence itself are irrelevant to the times we live in, but are they? Is not the real irrelevance in 1979 the widespread propaganda proclaiming that to survive in a computerised world and a virtually nationalised country, individual effort and endeavour are no longer necessary and the state or the union will do it all?

In this century Britain has faced threats to its very existence in the two world wars and has survived because of many unique qualities including determination in adversity, exceptional technical and scientific capability, and the will to work. In the 1980s the nation faces even greater self-inflicted danger stemming from a 30-year run-down in self-confidence coupled with loss of recognition of the essential need for unity and a sense of purpose.

The record of British Aviation can stand as just one example of the ability of this country to achieve greatness by team effort and daring. With a resurgence of these natural abilities which must surely be in only temporary danger of eclipse, and with a return to the national spirit which beat the enemy in the air in 1940, which successfully pioneered the jet bomber, the jet airliner, the Mach 2 fighter, the supersonic airliner and jet vertical take-off, Britain will inevitably come through to greatness once again.

The air is one of the regimes in which we can confidently show that ability.

*Below:* TSR 2 on test from Boscombe. *BAe*